"Rotabi and Bromfield deliver a much needed book, compelling, hard to put down and hard to ignore. The chronicling of intercountry adoptions – in the North and South Americas, Asia, Europe, Africa and Oceania – and the beginnings of the surrogacy boom brings together the leading research of our time. Hard facts are not compromised by sentimentality and important questions are posed. A human rights and global perspective tells a story that is complex and multifaceted. Rotabi and Bromfield are not ideologically driven. They are genuine in encapsulating the research and respectful of all perspectives. There is much that is new in this book, particularly the story of Guatemalan adoptions. The lived experiences of those families whose human rights were trampled upon are vivid and the cases of child stealing, abduction, fraud and trafficking are chilling and frightening. Everyone involved in intercountry adoptions and surrogacy should read this book if only to prepare for the questions from the children at the heart of these practices when they inevitably discover the debates about their lives and families. This book is long overdue and should be on every book shelf."

– *Patricia Fronek, Griffith University, Australia*

"Rotabi and Bromfield introduce readers not only to the history and politics of inter-country adoption but also its parallels with the controversial inter-country gestational surrogacy industry. This book makes a refreshingly clear, meticulous and important contribution to critical analyses of the politics of intercountry adoption and the booming fertility industry."

– *Amrita Pande, University of Cape Town, South Africa*

FROM INTERCOUNTRY ADOPTION TO GLOBAL SURROGACY

Intercountry adoption has undergone a radical decline since 2004 when it reached a peak of approximately 45,000 children adopted globally. Its practice had been linked to conflict, poverty, gender inequality, and claims of human trafficking, ultimately leading to the establishment of the Hague Convention on Intercountry Adoption (HCIA). This international private law along with the Convention on the Rights of the Child affirm the best interests of the child as paramount in making decisions on behalf of children and families with obligations specifically oriented to safeguards in adoption practices. In 2004, as intercountry adoption peaked and then began a dramatic decline, commercial global surrogacy contracts began to take off in India. Global surrogacy gained in popularity owing, in part, to improved assisted reproductive technology methods, the ease with which people can make global surrogacy arrangements, and same-sex couples seeking the option to have their own genetically-related children. Yet regulation remains an issue, so much so that the Hague Conference on Private International Law has undertaken research and assessed the many dilemmas as an expert group considers drafting a new law, with some similarities to the HCIA and a strong emphasis on parentage. This ground-breaking book presents a detailed history and applies policy and human rights issues with an emphasis on the best interests of the child within intercountry adoption and the new conceptions of protection necessary in global surrogacy. To meet this end, voices of surrogate mothers in the US and India ground discourse as authors consider the human rights concerns and policy implications. For both intercountry adoption and global surrogacy, the complexity of the social context anchors the discourse inclusive of the intersections of poverty and privilege. This examination of the inevitable problems is presented at a time in which the pathways to global surrogacy appear to be shifting as the Supreme Court of India weighs in on the future of the industry there while Thailand and other countries have banned the practice all together. Countries like Cambodia and potentially others in Africa appear poised to pick up the multi-million dollar industry as the demand for healthy infants continues on.

Karen Smith Rotabi is Associate Professor of Social Work at the United Arab Emirates University. Her work combines historical, sociological, and ethical dimensions in a policy analysis framework, especially considering the human rights of vulnerable populations. She has published extensively on intercountry adoption and relevant laws, particularly focused on the USA and its powerful interface with impoverished countries such as Guatemala where she has worked in a variety of initiatives to include rural health promotion programming for children. Her research agenda is focused on global social work practice, child protection, and family support, to include families impacted by war. She has consulted on child-protection initiatives in a number of countries including Belize, India, and Malawi and co-edited the 2012 book *Intercountry Adoption: Policies, Practices, and Outcomes*, which was awarded a Choice Outstanding Academic Title in 2013. Rotabi was involved in the early stages of USA implementation of the Hague Convention on Intercountry Adoption as she assisted in the accreditation process from 2008-2012, evaluating dozens of US-based adoption agencies to ensure that they were effectively practicing within international standards. More recently, she has turned her attention to commercial global surrogacy as a replacement for intercountry adoption. Today, Rotabi's service work in this area includes joining an expert group on child rights and global surrogacy, convening under the leadership of International Social Services in Geneva, Switzerland.

Nicole F. Bromfield is Associate Professor and Associate Dean for Academic Affairs in the Graduate College of Social Work at the University of Houston. Her research interests are on women and children's health and social wellbeing, with most projects being driven by community needs with the desired outcome being social policy change. She has a PhD in public policy with a specialization in social and health policy and holds an MSW with a community organization concentration. Bromfield's dissertation research was on the development of federal human-trafficking legislation in the USA, where she interviewed over 20 key policy players involved in its making. She has published on issues relating to human trafficking and has more recently taken an interest in global surrogacy arrangements, as well as social issues occurring in the Arabian Gulf nations.

FROM INTERCOUNTRY ADOPTION TO GLOBAL SURROGACY

A Human Rights History and
New Fertility Frontiers

Karen Smith Rotabi and Nicole F. Bromfield

Routledge
Taylor & Francis Group

LONDON AND NEW YORK

First published 2017
by Routledge
2 Park Square, Milton Park, Abingdon, Oxon OX14 4RN

and by Routledge
711 Third Avenue, New York, NY 10017

Routledge is an imprint of the Taylor & Francis Group, an informa business

British Library Cataloguing in Publication Data
A catalogue record for this book is available from the British Library

Library of Congress Cataloguing in Publication Data
A catalog record for this book has been requested

ISBN: 978-1-4724-4885-9 (hbk)
ISBN: 978-1-138-24263-0 (pbk)
ISBN: 978-1-315-58338-9 (ebk)

Typeset in Bembo
by Out of House Publishing

For my mother, Irma Smith, who suffered infertility and sought medical support for my conception—I always knew that I was a much wanted child! For my father, Michael Howard Smith, who has always believed in me and encouraged an academic life of exploration and science. For my husband, Paul Martin, who is my ultimate support and it is he who encouraged me to simply ask the Indian surrogate mothers for their viewpoint. I love you all and I do not underestimate the power of our family life in my success! And, finally, for Marie O. Weil, who taught me to look closely, listen to the voices, and always consider gender and human rights in my research.

KSR

For my grandmothers, Clara (Clarissa) Moses and Emma Mallow.

NFB

CONTENTS

List of figures   xi
List of tables   xii
Notes on the authors   xiii
Preface   xv

1   Rescue, refugees, orphans, and restitution   1

2   The politics of adoption from Romania to Russia and what we know
    about children languishing in residential care facilities   36

3   Poverty, birth families, legal, and social protection   52

4   Guatemala: violence against women and force, fraud, and coercion,
    including child abduction into adoption and a new system emerging   64

5   Child-protection systems of care to ensure child rights in family
    support and adoption: India and the United States   89

6   "Sins of the saviors": Africa as the final frontier   103

7   From intercountry adoption to commercial global surrogacy   121

8   Voices of US surrogates: a content analysis of blogs by US gestational
    surrogates   132

9 Perspectives of Indian women who have completed a global surrogacy
contract
With Lopamudra Goswami 142

10 The future of intercountry adoption, global surrogacy, and new frontiers 155

Index 174

FIGURES

1.1   Child in a residential care institution   1
1.2   Total number of intercountry adoptions to the United States
      compared to flow of children from China (fiscal years 1990–2014)   16
2.1   Children play at a residential care institution fence   36
3.1   Mother and baby embrace in Guatemala   52
4.1   Indigenous mother and her baby in Guatemala   64
4.2   Total number of intercountry adoptions from Guatemala to the
      US, 1990–2014   65
5.1   United States outgoing adoptions overall with more than 50 percent
      of all cases being processed by Florida adoption agencies   95
6.1   Children line up in a residential childcare institution   103
9.1   Women working in fields in India   142
10.1 Women walking in India   155

TABLES

1.1   Countries of origin for children sent to Spain as international
       adoptees (2000–2014)   26
2.1   Total Romanian adoptions by US citizens 1990–2013 with age
       of child   39
3.1   Convention on the Rights of the Child: Articles most directly
       related to intercountry adoption   60
4.1   Chinese, Guatemalan, and Russian adoptions to United States in 2006   65
4.2   The old Guatemala system of ICA versus the reformed system   82
5.1   The old US system of ICA versus the reformed system   97

NOTES ON THE AUTHORS

Karen Smith Rotabi is a social worker with over 25 years of practice and academic research experience in family support and child protection. As an adoption social worker, she has completed countless home studies, supporting prospective individuals and couples as they build a family through adoption. Also, Rotabi has been involved in the implementation of the Hague Convention on Intercountry Adoption in the United States, specifically evaluating numerous US-based adoption agencies for accreditation. While she was working on a rural child health-promotion project in Guatemala in the year 2000, the Millennium adoption boom was taking off and Rotabi became concerned about human rights abuses. Undertaking research into the problems and ultimately compelled to see that adoption system reformed, Rotabi began collaborating with a number of Guatemalan human rights defenders as a US-based advocate. In addition to Guatemala, she has also worked in a number of countries on broad child-protection initiatives to include Belize, Malawi, India, and the United Kingdom. In Belize, Rotabi helped establish the Belize National Organization for the Prevention of Child Abuse and Neglect as she was that agency's first national program coordinator. From a research perspective, for over a decade Rotabi has been committed to scholarship on intercountry adoption and more recently commercial global surrogacy. Rotabi co-edited *Intercountry Adoption: Policies, Practices, and Outcomes* (Ashgate Press, 2012). In 2014 she was a co-chair of the *International Forum on Intercountry Adoption and Global Surrogacy* held in The Hague, Netherlands. As an intercountry adoption expert, Rotabi has appeared on National Public Radio as well as being interviewed by other international media to include the Wall Street Journal, the BBC's Live at Five, and Voice of America-Moscow. Rotabi received her PhD from the University of North Carolina at Chapel Hill and her masters in social work and public health from the University of South Carolina. Rotabi is currently Associate Professor of Social Work at the United Arab Emirates University.

Nicole F. Bromfield is Associate Professor and Associate Dean for Academic Affairs in the Graduate College of Social Work at the University of Houston. Bromfield's research interests are on women and children's health and social wellbeing, with most projects being driven by community needs with the desired outcome being social policy change. Bromfield started studying human trafficking over a decade ago while working on her dissertation, in which she interviewed 22 federal policy players involved in the making of US human-trafficking legislation. Bromfield became interested in global surrogacy arrangements after the number of surrogacy arrangements increased exponentially, while at the same time critics likened surrogacy to human trafficking. As Bromfield had been following online surrogacy bulletin boards and blogs for some time, she did not believe that to be the case, at least among US surrogates. Bromfield has studied or written about human trafficking and sex trafficking, surrogates and surrogacy arrangements, divorce from arranged marriages in the United Arab Emirates, and vulnerable road users in several Arabian Gulf nations, among other inquiries. Most research projects have been qualitative in which the voices of participants are honored and emphasized.

Lopamudra Goswami is the co-author of Chapter 9. Goswami is Assistant Professor for Montfort College, Bangalore, India. She was a critical research assistant in Gujarat, India as she took the lead in carrying out interviews with gestational surrogates. Goswami holds both a master of science and a master of philosophy in psychology.

PREFACE

This book has been an undertaking that began well over ten years ago when I first began exploring the practices and problems of Guatemalan adoptions. The research undertaken, in the years since, seemed to have endless pathways for discussion when considering rights, responsibilities, and regulation. What began as a conversation about intercountry adoption and commercial global surrogacy turned into our co-author partnership and ultimately this book, bridging from what is known about intercountry adoption to commercial global surrogacy.

That which we have focused on here is expansive while being mindful of the need to tell the story clearly while integrating policy and human rights. Drawing upon historical documentation, we lay out a timeline of the practice of intercountry adoption and then move onwards to contemporary events as we look at countries like Russia and India. We have drawn upon academic research as well as news reports, as necessary. When considering intercountry adoption and commercial global surrogacy, we found it essential to include media stories as these sources are often the earliest of documentation of emerging issues and problems. Ultimately, media portrayal of the dynamics is a part of the story, often shedding light on *how* we talk and think about intercountry adoption and commercial global surrogacy in the greater society.

As we undertook this project, we were committed to empirical evidence throughout our narrative. This is most evident in our efforts to present new and original research in Chapters 8 and 9 where we investigate perspectives of gestational surrogates in the United States and India. We were committed to their voices and we've chosen to lay out Chapters 8 and 9 in a manner that illustrates their perspectives, including similarities and differences of gestational surrogates in each country. Also, while we do not present a detailed analysis of human rights instruments and international private law as related to the topic at hand, we do weave the critical elements throughout the book. We took this strategy as a way to make the narrative useful for all readers with practical application of human rights conceptions to known abuses, keeping the ideas manageable while considering complex phenomena and human right approaches.

Encouragement from friends and colleagues, most especially Jini Roby and Kelley Bunkers, is so very appreciated. We would also like to acknowledge a number of other adoption researchers who also provided feedback on this book, often reading a chapter and suggesting additions, to include Bert Ballard, Hollee McGinnis, Carmen Mónico, Sarah Richards, Beatriz San Román, and Peter Selman. Also, Lucy Armistead, an adoption agency director, has given periodic feedback and offered her professional insight. Specifically checking in with an adoption agency director, for her practice perspective, created times in which we found moments of respectful disagreement about some points while being in complete agreement about the importance of ethical intercountry adoptions. In regards to commercial global surrogacy, Lopamudra Goswami was an invaluable research assistant on the ground in India. Her contributions to the research are noted as we include her as a co-author of that particular chapter. We also would like to thank the US women who blog about their gestational surrogacy experiences, as well as the Indian surrogates who agreed to share their stories with us. Finally, the capable and conscientious assistance of Maya Porter, who provided editing support throughout, was important in reaching the finish line.

Karen Smith Rotabi, June 2, 2016

1

RESCUE, REFUGEES, ORPHANS, AND RESTITUTION

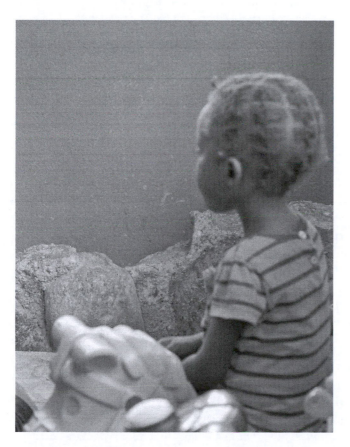

FIGURE 1.1   Child in a residential care institution
Source: Photo courtesy of Tony Bradley

Just over 1 million children have been adopted internationally since the mid-1950s, at least half of them adopted by US citizens, while other countries such as Australia, Canada, Spain, France, Italy, Sweden, and other Western European countries have also been integrally involved in adoptions (Selman, 2013, 2015). Today, the practice has declined by more than 65 percent since the peak of 2004 when 45,000 children were adopted globally (Selman, 2012a, 2012b, 2015). This decline has led some to ask if we are now seeing the beginning of the end of intercountry child adoption as we know it (Selman, 2010, 2012a, 2012b).

It is impossible to tell the history of intercountry adoption (ICA) or even predict the future of the practice of ICA without linking the phenomena to conflict, poverty, and global inequality (Ballard, Goodno, Cochran, & Milbrandt, 2015; Gibbons & Rotabi, 2012; Briggs & Marre, 2009). Included in the history is our notion of family building, and in the case of ICA, ideas about child rescue and the construction of an intentional family illustrate our most basic human instincts: the need to coexist in family life and our human impulse to protect the young—or even "save" or rescue an orphaned or vulnerable child.

Telling the story of the complex ICA phenomena has its challenges. Although there is no definitive research on the motivation to adopt internationally, most people who seek to adopt frequently have multiple reasons (Young, 2012a). Some say that they have always wanted to adopt—as a lifelong commitment. Others say that they both wanted and needed to adopt and intercountry adoption seemed to be the easiest solution to their need; the simplicity of such a position is often rooted in infertility and the term *need* should not be underestimated. This motivation is particularly true for women who delayed marriage in their childbearing years, often because of educational and career opportunities, and then, when they were childless in their late 30s and early 40s and found conception difficult, intercountry adoption was one viable option to build a family. An international adoption is most commonly completed by middle- and upper-class families, most often by prospective parents who are predominantly White and have completed a university education. This social dynamic is partly driven by the fact that the cost for intercountry adoption in recent years typically ranges from US$25,000 and upwards (US Government Accountability Office, 2005).

Many people will talk of doing something good in the process of building their family through ICA. Making a difference in a child's life is a religious calling for some—caring for the orphan is a virtuous act (Joyce, 2013) or fulfills a spiritual mission (Moore, 2009). Regardless of the motivation and specific characteristics of each case, intercountry adoption is anything but simple. The practice has brought together wants and needs of individuals and couples building their family life for well over 50 years.

"Saving" a child is a common theme in the ICA discourse; the practice began quite legitimately as a humanitarian intervention (Cheney, 2014, in press; Herrmann, 2010; Lovelock, 2000; McGinnis, 2006; Young, 2012b). Marketing of the service by adoption agencies today often capitalizes on the child rescue or "giving a child a better life" message (Cheney, 2014). The messaging is oriented around children needing homes, sometimes including compelling photographs of children living in extreme poverty and suffering from the effects of neglect. Sometimes the agency's marketing photos include children languishing in impersonal institutional care usually called "orphanages"[1] as well as stories of hope in a social entrepreneurial approach to communicating their mission (Cartwright, 2003; O'Connor & Rotabi, 2012).

As a result, the idea of a win-win scenario is frequently promoted by those who encourage intercountry adoption. In fact, a triple win-win-win scenario is often suggested. That is, an impoverished family of origin is relieved to have their child placed into the hands of an individual or a couple with a warm and nurturing home life, and the child "wins" as she grows up in a middle- to upper-class family with all of the benefits, like financial and sense of permanency, afforded such a child their family of origin otherwise could not provide. This notion includes the reality of that child's new rights to citizenship in a high-resource country. This second country, and family, is often viewed as superior to the impoverished country of birth and family of origin. The three parties in this triple-win conception are frequently referred to as the "adoption triad" of the child, biological mother/family, and the adoptive family (Baden, Gibbons, Wilson, & McGinnis, 2013).

Without argument, bringing a child to the safety of family life is one of the most profound ways in which an individual or family can intervene in a child's life when the child is legitimately without parental and family care and living in an institution or other dire circumstances (Ballard et al., 2015; Gibbons & Rotabi, 2012; Pertman, 2001). Children adopted from such environments in their early years often have positive health and child-development outcomes. In fact, many children make a remarkable emotional and cognitive recovery in the context of family life (Dalen, 2012; Juffer & Van IJzendoorn, 2012; Miller, 2012; Nelson et al., 2007). These facts demonstrate positive outcomes of ICA, and they give a compelling reason not only to adopt children, but also to adopt them young when there is the greatest potential for recovery from trauma and developmental delays (Bakermans-Kranenburg, Van IJzendoorn, & Juffer, 2008).

However, when one takes a closer look, that view of life *after* adoption is far too simplistic, and it is disingenuous to ignore the ethical dilemmas and history of illicit adoption practices (Ballard et al., 2015; Gibbons & Rotabi, 2012). Lack of support for adoptive families, challenges with identity, lack of records and knowledge of an adoptee's origin, lack of connection to birth culture and family of origin, experiences of racism, guilt over relinquishing their child to be adopted, and lack of feeling connected to a cultural community are just a few of the challenges experienced by members of the adoption triad *after* placement (Ballard et al., 2015; Gibbons & Rotabi, 2012). This is coupled with that which is often overlooked—the child's life *before* intercountry adoption. How did the child come to be deemed adoptable and what was their family life like prior to their adoption? The answer is often complex, and it challenges the notion of "orphan," as the vast majority of children are not truly orphans.[2] Today, studies from different regions around the world have consistently demonstrated that 80–90 percent of children in residential care institutions have at least one living parent (Williamson & Greenberg, 2010). This fact raises some troubling questions about the origins of children and the real *need* for intercountry adoption rather than seeking interventions which support the biological family to care for their child. In this book, we take a closer look at these dynamics and the practice of intercountry adoption, including the ethical quandaries, while considering human rights within a historical context. We begin with the history, offering narrative of how we arrived at the complexities of intercountry adoption today while highlighting some of the important human rights dilemmas and changes in policy and practice.

Early beginnings of intercountry adoption: missionaries and war

Intercountry adoption, as it is known today, dates largely back to World War II,[3] and while this conflict was a critically important turning point in adoption history (Herman, 2008), the practice actually began on a small scale much earlier. That history is typically overlooked. The lesser told part of the intercountry adoption story dates back to at least the 1920s when Christian missionaries began to bring children back home from their overseas missions, thereby creating a de facto adoption without the paperwork that characterizes the process today.[4] One such early adoption of a Chinese girl by Pearl Buck became a source of inspiration for the writer who went on to win a Pulitzer and Nobel Prize for literature (Beimers, 2006). Then, as the World War II adoptions were beginning to truly emerge, Buck (1955) wrote passionately as an adoption advocate promoting the practice, saying "thousands of children waiting… These are the citizens of my new world, the children without parents and the parents without children, pressing eagerly toward each other" (p. 130).

Race and transracial adoptions: controversies and change

Buck went on to coin the term "Amerasian" as a racial descriptive for children born to an Asian mother and US serviceman who were brought together by the circumstances of war (Beimers, 2006). In addition to the child from China, Buck later also adopted a child born to a German mother and an African American serviceman as well as another child born to a Japanese mother and an American serviceman (Buck, 1972). Buck was not only known to be outspoken about transracial adoptions as viable, but she wrote in *Today's Health* that "love is color blind" (Buck, 1972, p. 23), underscoring the simplicity of love rather than addressing the complexities of the social environment of the day characterized by deep racial inequalities and racism. Fundamentally, Buck advocated for adopting children of color when transracial adoptions were deeply criticized both by adoption professionals as well as members of the general public (Buck, 1972).

The most startling development for Buck was the position of the National Association of Black Social Workers that the adoption of Black children by White families was a form of genocide (Briggs, 2012; National Association of Black Social Workers, 1972). This statement, ultimately a political position confronting unfair adoption practices in the United States, specifically targeted impoverished families of color and the removal of children from their racial groups and placing them with White families. Not only was this a confrontation of differences in race and culture, but it was a direct statement on and resocialization of children as an attack on the ancestry and culture of Black children. It was also a confrontation of the failure to assist Black families, recognizing their strengths and capacity to care for their children rather than forcibly removing them. Removing children from Black families has too often been related to problems in which poverty and racial inequality are underlying causes of family distress.[5] Thus, race entered concerns over ICA early on in its formalized history as well as the counter response of color blindness (Yngvesson, 2010).

Buck was so committed to her cause that she opened her own agency called *Welcome House*—the earliest adoption agency on record dating back to 1949 and focusing solely on transracial adoptions. In time, the agency placed over 7,000 children into adoptive families from 28 different countries (Welcome House, n.d.). Among her many accomplishments, Buck was quite proud of her work in adoption, and reflecting upon her work in 1964 she said, "Parenthood has nothing to do with color, race, or religion. It has to do with a far deeper likeness of mind, and heart, and soul" (Welcome House, n.d.). Today, many parents who have built their families through intercountry adoption share this sentiment (Pertman, 2001).

World War II as a turning point and a conception of refugee children

Buck's adoption of children from a war zone was one of thousands that began to take place as a result of World War II (Selman, 2009, 2012b). At that time, an unknown but significant number of children were displaced throughout Europe, South Korea, Japan, and elsewhere. Informal care arrangements were common as community members came together to respond to orphaned and vulnerable children, and sometimes these arrangements became de facto adoptions. These solutions were intended for the short term as families stepped forward to care for children in guardianship arrangements as a response to a global crisis rather than a motivation to build their family through adoption. In fact, "no one expected the child to take on the identity of her/his new family, nor that she/he adopt the religion, nationality, and culture of her/his new home" (Fonseca, Marre and San Román, 2015, p. 180).

Mobilizing on behalf of the orphaned and vulnerable children of war became a cause of concern whose most prominent champion was First Lady Eleanor Roosevelt who, at the request of her husband, took active leadership on the 1940 United States Committee for the Care of European Children (Teaching Eleanor Roosevelt, n.d.). This early initiative secured the safety of Jewish and other children brought to the United States as a reprieve from war. In this humanitarian approach to remove children from war zones, child–family reunification was the long-term expectation. Fundamentally, this child-rescue plan was viewed to be a short-term solution to the crisis of war and the need to safeguard the wellbeing of children in need of refuge.

Child adoption finally began to be included in immigration law when the 1948 Displaced Persons, Refugees and Orphans Act was passed by the US Congress, which allowed for 4,000 war orphans to immigrate to the United States. Eventually, these original quotas were exceeded as new laws were developed to respond to the growing crisis (Davis, 2011). The data indicate a peak beginning slowly from 1948 to 1953 during which an estimated 5,800 European children were adopted by American families (Selman, 2009). Eventually, by 1957, it was estimated that a sum total of 19,084 children were adopted internationally by United States citizens through special wartime legislation (Weil, 1984; Davis, 2011). Most of these children originated from Korea, Greece, Japan, Italy, Germany, and Austria (Weil, 1984).

Children were also sent elsewhere to those countries that were open to receiving the children of war. For example, 70,000 Finnish children were taken in as foster children and many were adopted by families in Sweden (Nelson, 2015; Selman, 2009) and the children of the United Kingdom were sent into foster-care arrangements with varying levels of quality in Britain and elsewhere (Rusby & Tasker, 2009). Some children were sent to foster families in the United States and countries of the Commonwealth, like Australia and Canada, for temporary safeguarding. Many children eventually returned home and some of these "temporary" solutions became de facto adoptions in time. Sadly, other children were exploited for the purpose of child labor.

The movement of children from Europe to the Americas was not without controversy due to concerns about such labor exploitation. For example, the movement of the "orphans of Tenegru" was greatly contested; the Polish children's transport crossed multiple continents, eventually settling permanently in Canada. In the end, the settlement of the children became an international incident. The Canadian government and the International Refugee Organization's motivations were questioned, with allegations including speculation that the children would be used for slave labor on Canadian farms (Taylor, 2009). According to Taylor, who provides a detailed history of this particular migration, settlement of the children required interventions at the highest levels of government and the United Nations. In the end, the Catholic Church was important in negotiating an agreement for these 126 children (Taylor, 2009).

As children scattered across the globe as a result of war, the practical matter of meeting their day-to-day needs was undeniably a crisis situation. Birth records as well as other family documentation were simply lost in the haste of evacuation. Today, such evacuation and place-ment of children into new families would not meet contemporary human rights guidelines set by the United Nations (Boéchat, 2013; Dambach & Baglietto, 2010; Doyle, 2010; United Nations, 2009). However, at this time in history, those engaged in moving children to other coun-tries for safety were acting as pioneers in human rights intervention during a worldwide crisis.

At this juncture, the children were actually considered refugees by many of those who advocated on their behalf. In the United States, the 1953 Refugee Relief Act opened the doors for more immigrants; however, that particular legislation was oriented to adults who could verify family ties and an employment opportunity in the United States. When President Eisenhower signed the legislation, he said, "In enacting this legislation, we are giving a new chance in life to 214,000 fellow humans. This action demonstrates again America's traditional concern for the homeless, the persecuted and the less fortunate of other lands" (Eisenhower, 1953, p. 1). Like the earlier Displaced Persons, Refugees and Orphans Act, this follow-up legislation also had quotas as indicated by the President's comments upon signing the bill into law.

Eleanor Roosevelt steps in to help rescue the children of war

The most influential human rights pioneer was Eleanor Roosevelt; she herself was particularly sensitive to orphaned and vulnerable children as both of her parents had died by the time she was 10 years old. Roosevelt was subsequently raised by her grandmother who eventually sent the young Eleanor to Britain to attend boarding school (Roosevelt, 2000). This experience of living abroad certainly influenced Roosevelt's humanitarian sensibilities that came to be an immense asset while first lady in an otherwise isolationist period of US history. Roosevelt's dedication to the children displaced by war was such that she personally checked in on the progress of medical evaluations and the logistics of settling the children.[6]

Eleanor Roosevelt advocated for changes in immigration policy and law in order to clear the way to relocating refugees of war to other countries, and she was particularly concerned about the quotas set forth in the laws of the day (Roosevelt, 2001). Roosevelt was known for action and her greatest accomplishment was her integral leadership in the drafting of the United Nations Declaration of Human Rights (UNDHR), which was passed soon after World War II in 1948. In this work, she was able to express her humani-tarian views, advocating for people who must flee conflict areas for safety, among other concerns.

For refugees, UNDHR states that people have the right to free movement (Art. 13) and seek asylum (Art. 14), and the right to their nationality or to change nationality (Art. 15). Furthermore, the UNDHR recognizes that universally, family is a fundamental unit of society that must be protected (Art. 16) with specific mention of motherhood as a social protection issue (Art. 25). These major ideas, newly formed in the late 1940s, are now recognized and accepted as universal, and their relevance continues to play out as we consider how families are formed globally. It should be noted that adoption of children is not mentioned in the UNDHR, and that concept was not integrated and globally agreed upon until much later in the 1980s when the Convention on the Rights of the Child (CRC) was drafted and then coming into force in 1990 (Roby, 2007; Roby & Maskew, 2012). We will turn our attention to the CRC and the specific articles related to intercountry adoption in Chapter 3 as we look more clearly at human rights instruments and implications for adoption practices.

South Korea: over time the most significant country of origin

As human rights agreements were being forged, including the UN more clearly defining child rights in the follow-up Refugee Convention of 1951, South Korea emerged as an important and paradigm-shifting international adoption country by the mid-1950s (Bergquist, Vonk, Kim, & Feit, 2007). In the long view, South Korea is overall the most significant country of origin globally, beginning with the first adoptions documented in 1953 (Davis, 2011). From 1953 to 1962, it is estimated that 4,162 children were adopted in the United States due to the Korean War (Kim, 2007). Today well over 150,000 South Korean children have been adopted internationally, the majority by US families, but many have also been adopted into families in Canada, Australia, and other Western European countries such as Sweden (Bergquist et al., 2007; Fronek, 2006; McGinnis, 2012; Hübinette, 2005; Selman, 2012b,Yngvesson, 2010).

What began with "war orphans" shifted over time, and for many years the extreme poverty and shame of illegitimacy in the post-conflict country fueled the ICA system (Bergquist et al., 2007; Kim, 2007; Fronek, 2006). Korea has added cultural dimensions related to shame and stigma; children who are born out of wedlock have historically been marginalized and those children often lived without a sense of social place in society (Kim, 2007). This is evidenced by the family registries (family "hojeok") which document the family relationships that hinge on the paternal relationship in recognizing a child's rights to family name and inheritance. A lack of paternal bloodline has historically been a deep source of shame, and those children have faced serious stigma in their day-to-day lives. While the treatment of illegitimacy has been slowly changing and contraception is easily available today as women have greater autonomy over their reproductive health, the persistent importance of paternal bloodlines and family names remains a significant underlying dynamic in terms of norms and social acceptance. Additionally, "after the Korean War, cultural beliefs in ethnic homogeneity, discrimination toward children born outside of wedlock, post-war chaos, poverty, social upheaval and decline of traditional Korean society contributed to the continuation of intercountry adoption practice" (McGinnis, 2006, p. 162). As a result of the Korean War, the post-conflict relationship between the United States and South Korea flourished and intercountry adoptions were one area of partnership (Sarri, Baik, & Bombyk, 1998).

The most celebrated adoptions from the war-torn nation were those completed by Harry and Bertha Holt. The deeply religious couple adopted eight Amerasian babies fathered by US soldiers. The couple actively advocated in the policy arena to repeal the Refugee Relief Act, aiding in the passage of new US legislation that made ICA of Amerasian children possible on a large scale in a relatively expedient process (Bill for Relief of Certain War Orphans). In 1956, funded with their own resources, Holt International Children's Services was founded in their name (Bergquist et al., 2007). Not only did evangelical and other Christians rush to adopt from Korea, but US military families were also given priority for child placement, thereby raising questions about neocolonialism in a post-conflict context (Gailey, 2000).

In South Korea today, ICAs have been a source of controversy for a number of years including problematic birth-mother homes. The country's supply of very young children to families around the world became particularly pronounced during the Olympic Games, hosted in Seoul in 1988, and the government made promises to step up social services and make contraception more readily available (Davis, 2011). McGinnis (2006) points out that reports of child trafficking in the early 1980s, corruption of government officials, and adoption agencies "hastily sending children not available for adoption overseas (which ended the practice of sending abandoned children for international adoption), led the government in 1989 to enact a policy that would terminate international adoptions by 1996" (p. 164), with exceptions for some children (for example, mixed-race or disabled children). Domestic adoptions became a priority and tax incentives were put in place to raise awareness of and promote the adoption of Korean children by Korean families (McGinnis, 2006; Sarri et al., 1998; Hübinette, 2005).

> In 1994 with continuing low rates of domestic adoption, this policy would again be abandoned. In 1996 the South Korean government revised its adoption law, currently known as the Special Law on Adoption Promotion and Procedure. The new law called for an annual decrease of international adoptions by 3 to 5 percent, with an eventual phasing out by 2015.
>
> *(McGinnis, 2006, p. 165)*

Small revisions have been made to the law in the years since[7] and in 2013 a major revision included the involvement of the court in the adoption process (McGinnis, personal communication, February 25, 2016). Since then the number of children adopted internationally has, on average, been around 2,000 children annually (Selman, 2015). A decade later, the practice was still persisting with a significant number of children still being sent abroad as adoptees and President Kim Dae-Jung announced, during his inauguration in 1998, that international adoption would be one of his focal issues (McGinnis, 2012). The issue is periodically raised as part of a political debate with some candidates promising to end ICA during the national elections. Closing down the system has yet to occur, but steps towards ending the ICA system remain a stated priority. Fundamentally, many South Koreans find the practice of ICA to be an embarrassment, especially in a now-vibrant economy with national pride in prosperity and advancement.

Policy and procedural changes have occurred, and most recently in 2009, domestic adoptions in the country outnumbered ICAs[8] for the first time and this has been the trend every year since (Selman, 2012b; Selman, 2015). This shift is considered a positive step forward in a country that has strengthened its child welfare systems rather than simply resorting to the solution of sending children overseas as adoptees while neglecting to build a consistent system of child protection and family support. Intervening in an orphaned or vulnerable child's life meant sending them abroad as the first response rather than providing social care oriented to preserving their family life (Fronek, 2006; Sarri et al., 1998). However, social service systems have been built and continue to emerge, including foster care and domestic adoption programs. And while there is still an over-reliance on institutional care, social progress with clear movement towards domestic solutions to orphaned and vulnerable children's needs is precisely the vision of those who have developed human rights instruments such as the Convention on the Rights of the Child (Roby & Maskew, 2012) and adoption-specific human rights agreements and laws that will be discussed later in this book.

A watershed moment in history: the Vietnam Babylift

Looking back on the historical timeline again, another war marks a shift in ICA; the most celebrated and controversial child-rescue event in wartime history was the Vietnam Babylift. During the fall of Saigon in 1975, in the last phases of the war in Vietnam, some 3,000 children were removed by airlifts funded largely by the United States but also by Canada, Australia, and Western European countries (Bergquist, 2009, 2012; Fronek, 2012). President Ford on

April 4, 1975, authorized 2 million dollars for emergency evacuation and ordered US military and civilian aircraft to conduct the airlift. The actions were under the oversight of the US Agency for International Development, which eventually released a detailed report of the endeavor, documenting the logistics and outcomes of the airlifts (US Agency for International Development, 1975). To date, the Babylift is the largest mass evacuation of children for adoption (Bergquist, 2009, 2012), and the use of military planes for the evacuation of children for adoption was not only unprecedented but such an action has never been repeated since.

At the time, the Babylift was largely celebrated in the mass media as a rescue mission, and the idea of such a rescue entered into the public consciousness, including the ethical dilemmas of leaving Amerasian children behind (Sachs, 2010). There were credible and well-founded fears for the wellbeing of the children airlifted. As such, organizations like Catholic Relief Services, Pearl Buck's Welcome House, and Holt International Family Services sprang into action with countless volunteers and large financial donations backing the effort to remove and resettle Vietnamese children (Bergquist, 2009, 2012). Many of these "war orphans" were placed with US families as well as some Canadian, Australian, and Western European families (Fronek, 2012). These children were never expected to be returned to Vietnam as the intent was not temporary refuge. Rather, they were seen by primarily US caregivers and orphanage volunteers as adoptees even as they were very publicly being airlifted to lives with new families. Photographs of this event serve as a reminder as news stories captured emotional scenes of children being brought to safety (see www.adoptvietnam.org; Sachs, 2010).

While many argued that the rescued children were spared from almost certain death, one group of religious leaders and academic scholars took the position that the child removal was immoral, even taking out a full-page advertisement in the *New York Times* denouncing the airlift. These intellectuals viewed the Babylift as a "salve our conscience" about an unjust war. Indeed, many viewed the child rescue as political theater during a very contentious period— using "war orphans" as one more act of propaganda—especially during a losing conflict for the US (Sachs, 2010). In addition, politicians weighed in on the decision to evacuate children for adoption, some in open applause and others with concerns. Then senator Walter Mondale, chairman of the Labor and Public Welfare Committee, Subcommittee on Children and Youth, was quoted as saying that "Americans by-passed [domestic adoptions] in a rush for Vietnamese [children]" (Joe, 1978, p. 2).

In Vietnam, controversy and outrage ensued as not all children truly met the criteria of being orphans as decisions were made in haste without the full knowledge of the children's social histories or making diligent attempts to locate able family (Sachs, 2010). The US was accused of stealing a generation of children. As a result, a variety of court cases were brought in the US, with a prominent one being the *Nguyen Da Yen et al.* v. *Kissinger* class-action lawsuit filed on the grounds that the children were being unconstitutionally detained (Bergquist, 2009). In the end, the legal case was unsuccessful, due in part to the fact that it was determined that the children's best interests were not to be again removed from their new adoptive families (Bergquist, 2009, 2012).

Other sources of controversy in Vietnam itself included sentiments that the evacuated children were the spoils of war. War correspondent Gloria Emerson reported that upon the fall of Saigon, one Vietnamese military officer said, "It is nice to see you Americans taking home souvenirs of our country as you leave—china elephants and orphans…Too bad some of them broke today, but we have plenty more." This statement was made when the very first evacuation aircraft crashed upon departure, killing 180 passenger children and caregivers (Bergquist, 2009). Coupled with such visual images as President Gerald Ford meeting the "first" plane of children to arrive in the US from Vietnam in San Francisco in April 1975, these sentiments underscore the criticism that intercountry adoption is an act of neocolonialism and cultural imperialism in which countries like the United States enjoy the resource of young and desirable children through less than humanitarian means.

Without a doubt, most of the women and children who were left behind experienced serious social and economic consequences as Vietnam plunged into another war with neighboring Cambodia and experienced a ten-year economic slowdown. The actual number of Amerasian births is unknown, numbering in the thousands, and they were seen as a problem by the US government as evidenced in the 1971 report entitled "The Department of Defense Report Regarding Children Born out of Wedlock in Countries Where U.S. Armed Forces Are Assigned" (US Department of Defense, 1971).

This Department of Defense report begins with a statement that US command does not condone "immoral behavior" (p. 1) while downplaying the issue of unknown numbers of children of "mixed parentage" (p. 1). The numbers of such children were likely underreported by the department, which stated the following:

> A recent survey of 120 orphanages with a total orphanage population of 18,000 children indicates a range of 350–400 children or about 2.08 percent were of possible U.S. parentage. Another survey of a representative number of institutions for children in Vietnam shows that children with possible U.S. parentage account for approximately 2.6 percent of the total. A United Press media report indicated that less than one-half of one percent of the children in Vietnamese orphanages are thought to be Vietnamese-American.

In the close of this relatively brief report, the Department of Defense responds to the problem with the following telling statement: "We take pride in the fact that the American serviceman, through his generosity in all foreign lands, has adopted many of these alien children" (p. 2). This assertion was made without clear evidence of said adoptions, and this paternalistic position inevitably was one element of the decision making related to executing the Vietnam Babylift.

Operation Babylift adoptees themselves have expressed mixed feelings about their own experience as they have navigated life with a difficult start. Some report that their own personal histories are complicated with notions of rescue and racial and cultural difference (Willing et al., 2015). Some adoptees have reported their experiences with gratitude. For example, Bree Cutting Sibbel writes of her experience saying that "adoption is one of those rare gifts that touches many lives and can bring great rewards" (Sibbel, 2006, p. 448). In general, many adoptees echo Sibbel's sense of gratitude, even while recognizing that their own adoptions have many unanswered questions and even questionable circumstances while others have challenged the practice as they interrogate their own origins and human rights (see Borshay Liem, 2000; Kim, 2010). Bert Ballard, a Babylift adoptee and intercountry adoption researcher, might sum up the effects of the Babylift best:

> The Babylift was a chaotic and politically charged event that represents the complex, multi-dimensional, grief-stricken, and miraculous experience of intercountry adoption. Young American women were making decisions under harrowing circumstances and misinformation about children in their care that made sense then, politicians and countries were waging a public battle over whose we really were with each side claiming victory, and the costs of those choices are borne by us, the adoptees, as

we lost our personal histories and connections. Yet, for most of us our lives have been enriched through family, love, and opportunities that would not have been there had it not been for the Babylift. There is anger, there is hurt, there is gratitude, and there is growth. Above all, there is loss that cannot be forgotten or overcome, but can be understood and a beginning point to learn and grow. Indeed, it has a set a tone by which future ICAs have been judged and evaluated, both in how it was handled and its long-term effects.

(Ballard, personal communication, 2016)

In the years since the Babylift, Vietnam has had an unstable history of ICAs. Prior to the latest US moratorium on ICAs from Vietnam, the US Department of State (2008) released a deeply concerning report, announcing that adoption agencies had created financial incentives among centers of institutional care in Vietnam, which in turn had increased the number of abandoned children (e.g. children mysteriously being left abandoned near residential care institutions), creating "orphans" and ultimately a growing number of irregular adoption practices. The report goes on to state that "credible reports from orphanage officials that [adoption] facilitators are deliberately staging fraudulent desertions [child abandonments] to conceal the identity of the birth parents" (US Department of State, 2008, p. 2). Upon investigation, a pattern of abandonment was found in some areas of the country that were remarkable, including individual police officers repeatedly finding children abandoned, raising concerns about the legitimacy of the abandonment reports and corruption of some police officers. The concerns were serious enough for the United States to take a proactive approach in closing the system down until more safeguards could be built in. The moratorium that ensued has been lifted only since 2013 when Vietnam began strategic improvement of their own governmental system regarding adoptions, announced a reopening of ICAs for special needs children with only a few agencies carrying out the adoptive placement of children abroad (US Department of State, 2015), but they are also open to adoptions to other countries like Ireland and France.

It is noteworthy that this particular US report about Vietnam is known by adoption practice insiders to have upset Vietnam officials—as a dishonoring name-and-shame report. Some have speculated that the report actually resulted in a delayed resumption of adoptions between the two countries as a result of a relationship rift in the aftermath of the report.

Latin America: civil conflict and tough economic times

Early adoptions from Latin America began largely in the 1970s when North American missionaries in Colombia and Ecuador and elsewhere started to adopt children. From the early 1980s until the early 1990s, Latin America, as a region, began to see a significant and rapid rise in intercountry adoptions and the parallel problems of illicit practices (Ngabonziza, 1991; Herrmann & Kasper, 1992; Pilotti, 1993; Selman, 2012b). Lovelock (2000) points out that Latin America was a critical turning point in moving from intercountry adoption as a humanitarian solution to solve the demand for infant adoption. The availability of contraception, including the *Row* v. *Wade* decision making abortion legal in the United States, along with social acceptance of single parenthood left a gap for those wanting to adopt a healthy infant (Freundlich, 1998, 2000). This is the era in which the search to find children for families rather than finding families for children emerged (Davis, 2011) with significant consequences that undoubtedly continue to reverberate today on a global scale.

Several countries in Latin America stand out in terms of conflict and poverty, including the various forces of the Cold War. Guatemala and El Salvador are two Central American countries with well-documented child adoption fraud with an array of child and family rights violations (Briggs & Marre, 2009; Dubinsky, 2010); Mexico, Honduras, Peru, and Brazil are among countries that also had significant problems in the ICA system during the Latin American era (Fonseca, 2009; Herrman & Kasper, 1992; Pilotti, 1993).

Brazil, located in the heart of South America, was once a relatively active country of origin beginning in the 1970s, with children being sent around the world to the United States, Western Europe, and Israel (Fonseca, 2009; Jaffe, 1991; Scheper-Hughes, 1995). Scandal eventually erupted and by the early 1990s alarming documentation of force, fraud, and coercion began to emerge. Anthropologist Scheper-Hughes' field notes captured some of the problems[9] first hand. For example, in an interview of a children's home director, Scheper-Hughes (1990, p. 62) documents that:

> Mrs. C. [home director] was not surprised when I raised the question of traffic in babies, and she was prepared to answer. It was true, she said, that some aspects of the adoption process were murky. Sometimes she, herself, fought with parents or other guardians over the release of children…Some birth mothers do not want to sign the legal adoption papers releasing their children even though they know that this would be best for the child and that they themselves are in no position to care for another child. Other women abandon their babies freely to the home, but then they are too ashamed to sign the formal documents. They do not want any official record of their having given away a child. In such cases, Mrs. C. admitted to exerting some pressure on the mothers.

Scheper-Hughes (1995, p. 13) further illustrates the idea of child abduction for adoption with an intermediary orchestrating the process of force, fraud, and coercion.

> When Maria Lourdes, the mother of five sickly and malnourished children living in a miserable hovel in the Alto do Cruziero was asked by her boss [patrona] if she could "borrow" Maria's four-year-old, Maria readily agreed. The woman, for whom Maria washed clothes, said she wanted the little "blond" just for her amusement. Maria sent her daughter off just as she was: untidy, barefoot, and without a change of clothing. The patrona promised to return the child the following morning. Two nights passed and when still her daughter was not returned, Maria became worried but she did not want to anger her boss by appearing mistrustful…[When Maria's husband learned that his daughter was missing he] went off in a frantic search. At the house of the patrona he learned that the child had already been given to a missionary who directed a "children's home" that specialized in overseas adoption.

Fonseca's research (2009) confirms problems in Brazil's system in the early years, in which payment to birth mothers for child sales into adoption was a serious and persistent problem; some of the activities rose to the level of abduction into adoption. Fonseca points out that investigative media found intermediaries involved in the problem of adoption fraud, many of whom were greatly enriched by unethical financial gains that were ultimately human sales. Lawyers, judges, nuns, priests, and others have been implicated in force, fraud, and coercion. Fonseca (2009) notes that these individuals were once considered "child savers," but in time the terminology shifted to "child traffickers" for those who were sensitive to the human rights violations that were being reported. Brazil eventually strengthened its child-protection laws with a strong child rights emphasis; in fact, today Brazil's laws are considered to be an exemplar of child rights. As a result, adoption in Brazil is highly regulated and intermediaries are no longer allowed to operate as they did previously with little oversight and impunity (Abreu, 2009).

Civil conflict created fertile ground for ICA. El Salvador's two-decade civil war (1970–90) resulted in an estimated 75,000 Salvadorans killed and an additional half million people left internally displaced. There were also nearly a million refugees, many relocating to the United States, Canada, and elsewhere (US Institute for Peace, 2001). The conflict left an unknown number of forced separations and disappearances of children for placement in residential care institutions, internal or domestic adoptions, and ICAs; in the case of the latter, children were sent mainly to the United States, Italy, France, and Honduras (Pro-Búsqueda, 2002).

Documentation of the atrocities that took place related to the illegal adoptions of children from El Salvador has been so profound and threatening to those who have something to hide, that in November 2013 the offices of a small non-governmental organization (NGO) called Pro-Búsqueda were attacked and destroyed as a result of arson (*Democracy Now!*, 2013). To outsiders, the organization appeared innocuous as it simply assists families of origin to locate their children abducted into adoption during the war years. However, in the course of documenting oral testimonies and case investigations of missing persons, the organization amassed significant documentation of illegal ICA networks during the war years.

Pro-Búsqueda's evidence in El Salvador indicates that unscrupulous entrepreneurs were charging up to $10,000 per adoption, an enormous sum during the war years (Pro-Búsqueda, 2002). Among the illicit activities beyond forced separation were the falsified documents (child laundering) necessary to fully carry out child abduction into adoption. Among other organizations, the Red Cross has been implicated in some of those cases (Pro-Búsqueda, 2002). Today, over 300 lost children and their biological families have been reunited with the investigative and psychological support of Pro-Búsqueda. The reunions are highly emotional; scenes of tearful family reunions have caught international media attention, which further underscores the atrocities carried out during the war years (Mónico & Rotabi, 2012). Pro-Búsqueda's documentation was precise and detailed, ultimately offering a glimpse into the horrific conditions of war (Pro-Búsqueda, 2002).

Incriminating records have been used as the organization made statements in high-profile human rights advocacy efforts. For example, testimonies were given before the Inter American Human Rights Court; specifically, several high-profile cases were heard there as a result of Pro-Búsqueda's advocacy work (Mónico & Rotabi, 2012). Within El Salvador, the small NGO was also relatively powerful, reminding current politicians and government bureaucrats of their obligation to help families find each other as a part of the peace and reconciliation process for healing.

Pro-Búsqueda has enjoyed support of some critical members of the Catholic Church since its inception as well as many human rights defenders in El Salvador (Pro-Búsqueda, 2002). It is not entirely clear why the organization was ransacked and records set ablaze, but human rights defenders in El Salvador recognize that the documents could possibly have been used effectively against former government and military officials who have been enjoying an environment of impunity since the war years. Cases of abduction into adoption have the potential to challenge the amnesty that the war criminals of El Salvador have enjoyed in the years since the Peace Accords in 1992.

The abduction of children for adoption during the war years has become a crime that could be prosecuted years later as children reach the age of maturity and, as young adults, lodge legal complaints. In other words, after the war these children were not returned to their families of origin, and as a result, the crime was ongoing after the cutoff date for pardons in the truth and reconciliation process (Briggs & Marre, 2009). Active steps to hold those guilty accountable in El Salvador was a threat to the political elites (many being retired military officials) who continued to maintain power and privilege in post-war society. In addition, while Pro-Búsqueda was attacked and critical records were destroyed, family reunification and legal advocacy work has continued (*Democracy Now!*, 2013).

Neighboring Guatemala has a similar history, as documented by their truth and reconciliation process at the end of the Civil War (1960–96). Military officers and their wives were actors in child abduction into adoption during the war years (Dubinsky, 2010; REMHI, 1999). The resulting controversy is an undercurrent as Guatemala struggles in its post-conflict era. Illicit adoptions during the war continue to capture the attention of the press and general consciousness of the people of Guatemala. For example, in February 2015, allegations were made against an elite government official implicated in illegal adoptions during the conflict. The *Boston Globe* published an opinion piece titled "Diplomat should be removed from UN over inquiry" (Reynolds, 2015), which documents the fact that Guatemala's highest-ranking appointee to the United Nations devised, during the war years, "a shrewd scheme where the children's biological parents signed a document granting custody of their children…[and] tourist visas were then issued for the infants and in just two months they were on a plane to Canada." The press piece goes on to document that the individual in question "was imprisoned after the police raided a hotel in Guatemala City where four Canadian women were preparing to leave the country with five Guatemalan babies, but he was released after a short time" (Reynolds, 2015).

Guatemala and El Salvador are just two examples of civil war and illicit adoptions. There are other examples in the region such as Argentina (Rotabi, 2012). In that conflict, women who were detained as dissidents have now been documented to have given birth while imprisoned and then killed upon labor and delivery; their children were then placed as "adoptees" with families in Argentina (Brysk, 1994). The problem was so profound that in July 2012, Argentinean General Jorge Rafael Videla was sentenced to 50 years in prison for his role in crimes against humanity during that war (Caistor, 2013). Among the crimes that featured prominently in his trial were illegal child adoptions.[10] At this point, the problems with illicit adoptions from Latin America were such that many countries in the region (Herrmann & Kasper, 1992), with some exceptions like Guatemala, passed strict laws to prohibit their children leaving as intercountry adoptees (Dubinsky, 2010). The history of Guatemala, including an adoption boom and then moratorium that occurred after the war years, will be covered in detail in Chapter 4.

China's one-child policy

China has been one of the most significant countries of origin. Some 88,000 Chinese children, mostly girls, were adopted into United States families alone between 1992 and 2014 (Selman, 2015). Families in other countries such as Canada and the United Kingdom have also received thousands of Chinese girl children as adoptees (Dowling & Brown, 2009; Johnson, 2012). They have come to symbolize the "lucky girls" who were spared sex-selective abortion and then were abandoned and adopted due to China's one-child policy (Hopgood, 2010; Johnson, 2016; Smolin, 2011). This dynamic created a particular child-rescue narrative inclusive of issues related to the boy preference and the plight of girl children. It should be noted that this conception of *preference* has been challenged with convincing evidence as Kay Johnson's (2016) field research indicates that many Chinese families wanted their girls, hid their girl children from interrogating government officials, made secret arrangements for their girls to go to rural families in informal care arrangements, and so forth. Johnson's (2016) evidence indicates a complicated scenario rather than a straightforward "boy preference" and the resulting abandonment of girls.

For many years in the United States, China was not only a top country of origin of children but it was also exceptionally popular due to expediency and a process that appeared to be well organized and ethical (Johnson, 2012, 2016; Smolin, 2011), reaching its peak in 2005, with 14,484 Chinese children adopted globally, of which 7,906 Chinese children were adopted by US citizens. The rate has declined steadily since, and by the year 2014 less than 3,000 Chinese children were adopted globally to 17 countries, including Italy and Spain. Of these, 2,040 went to the United States (Selman, 2015). Interestingly, China's "rise and fall" is a close composite and direct indicator of the overall rise and fall of adoption globally, with the exception of an unusual peak, related to Guatemala.[11]

Reasons for the dramatic decrease vary, including stricter controls of who can adopt— prospective parents must meet specific criteria of age, weight, and other characteristics (Dowling & Brown, 2009)—and a ban on gay and lesbian adoptions and restrictions on individuals with a mental health treatment history or people who are considered to be obese (Goodno, 2015; Dowling & Brown, 2009). Also, China prioritized the adoption of "special needs" children; that is, a focus on children with medical and/or emotional challenges and older children or sibling groups. Bureaucratic delays have emerged and prospective parents now wait five or more years for a Chinese adoption. What was once a very popular ICA country became a country with a trickle of children available for adoption. All of these changes coincide with recent increases in domestic adoptions and an improved economy, just as in the case of Korea today, with more Chinese families adopting domestically (Johnson, 2012, 2016; Vich, 2013; see Figure 1.2).

Looking back, it is clear that China's adoption boom really took off in 1995 with 2,130 children adopted by US citizens (compared to 787 in 1994 and less than 100 in 1991). Adoption agencies enjoyed a relatively easy process, known to be quick compared with other countries. Adoption services were advertised boldly, and the pervasive narrative was that the expedient process was due to China's one-child policy for population control and the resulting large-scale abandonment of girl children into massive residential care institutions.

In the early days, China was also celebrated as a highly ethical country with an efficient bureaucracy that was partly related to the establishment of the China Center for Adoption Affairs in 1996 to act with government oversight of the practice. Most children adopted internationally were girls, and their health, on the whole, was considered to be relatively good (Johnson, 2012). Prospective parents made required financial donations (US$3,000 in recent years) to residential child institutions as a part of the formal process. For many of those adopting, the financial transparency was considered a strength of Chinese adoptions compared with other countries that have a history of mismanagement of charitable donations, often enriching a few—such as residential care institution directors—while failing to truly serve the children left behind. However, the reality is that these "donations" are really an area of risk for fraud and China, like other countries, has not been immune to illicit adoptions.

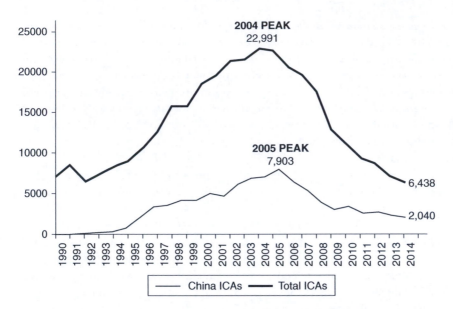

FIGURE 1.2 Total number of intercountry adoptions to the United States compared to flow of children from China (fiscal years 1990–2014)
Source: Author's own research

A 2010 headline in the *Los Angeles Times* was "Some Chinese parents say their children were stolen for adoption" and the article stated that "In some rural areas, instead of levying fines for violations of China's child policies, greedy officials took babies, which would each fetch $3,000 USD in adoptions." The article outlined alarming child-removal tactics of bureaucrats claiming to be acting within the guidelines of the one-child policy. Young children were forcibly separated from their families and placed into institutions in a manner that made them appear to be abandoned. "Parents who say their children were taken complain that officials were motivated by the $3,000 per child that adoptive parents pay orphanages," stated the *Los Angeles Times*. In what is now commonly called the Hunan Scandal (Meier & Zhang, 2008), a number of government officials were implicated. Kay Johnson, an expert on ICA from China, writes that the scheme was "highly organized [with] profit-driven practices that were declared by the Hunan court to constitute illegal child trafficking. One institution director and nine traffickers were found guilty of 'buying and selling children' and sent to prisons…over a dozen Hunan orphanages were implicated" (Johnson, 2012, p. 113). This particular scandal highlights the fact that China is not without its own problems of illicit adoptions and underlying ethical dilemmas even with such a large population and reputation for the need to intervene for girl children.

The one-child policy has consistently been pointed to as the culprit of the problems in China, but the reality is far more complex (Johnson, 2012; Smolin, 2011; Subramanian & Lee, 2011). In the fall of 2015, China changed the one-child policy and now families are allowed two children without government interference (Johnson, 2016). The change in intercountry adoption patterns as a result of this policy shift is not yet known.

China's influence on recent ICA history cannot be overstated. The challenges that have surfaced related to gender, identity, racism, transracial families, culture keeping, kinship, cultural identity (Richards, 2014) and adoptee and adoptive family issues are not unlike other adoptee groups that have come before them, especially Koreans (see Dorow, 2006; Volkman, 2005). More than any other country, the influx of adopted "lucky girls" from China (Hopgood, 2010) has generated attention to post-placement challenges and spawned a whole industry of resources, camps, books, therapeutic interventions, and communities, many of them insular and attending only to those with direct connections to Chinese adoption. Indeed, even with the decrease in adoptions from China, today they remain a dominant influence in shaping the experience of what adopting can look like after placement.

Cambodia: a legal case study of child sales and "laundering"

Cambodia is an important case study of adoption fraud, as documentation in this particular case outlines the many steps in force, fraud, and coercion in illicit adoptions. The story begins with two sisters, both US citizens, who founded Seattle Adoptions International. What began with what some argue were good intentions ended in prosecution by the US federal government (US District Court, Western District of Washington at Seattle, 2004).

US Federal Marshall Richard Cross, who was sent to Cambodia to investigate the case, has been exceptionally open about the facts of the case while also sharing some of his personal views. He said that this particular case was one of the most disturbing in his career, in which he has witnessed the worst of human behavior (personal communication, October 2006). The story, presented below, is based on Cross' own version of events and illuminates the multiple elements of organized crime that were necessary to execute the force, fraud, and coercion in this particular illicit child-sales scheme (Cross, 2005).

Lauryn Galindo, a central player in Cambodian adoption fraud, had a long-term history of involvement in Cambodia, ranging over a decade. She claims to have been in the country engaging in humanitarian work in a range of activities—eventually she took on intercountry adoption for employment. Galindo referred to herself as an "adoption facilitator," although she was not a trained child welfare professional. Her sister, Lynn Devin, was a trained and a licensed professional counselor (State of Washington) and was the director of Seattle Adoptions International, running the agency from a spare room in her home. In time, the two sisters placed over 700 children into adoptive families and millions of dollars changed hands (Cross, 2005).

It is impossible to know just how many of the adoptions were ethical versus illicit due to Galindo's own confession of sloppy paperwork. Because Galindo and Devin both pleaded guilty to federal charges of conspiracy to commit visa fraud and money laundering in 2004, the full extent of their illegal actions are not known as a result of plea bargains. However, approximately a dozen cases were fully verified by investigators to have illicit practices (Cross, 2005). This handful of cases were those investigated in depth for the purpose of evidence for prosecution—the investigators eventually stopped further investigation as a pattern of wide-scale fraud was established.

Cross (2005) describes the activities of the two sisters as follows. Devin operated the adoption agency, which appeared to be fiscally sound and involved in legitimate adoptions and humanitarian activities in Cambodia. On paper, the agency appeared to be not only legitimate, but the humanitarian actions claimed by the agency were quite compelling. However, the truth is that Galindo used her contacts within the Cambodian government to move cases along in a manner which may be called "expediting" the process with the argument that swift action was essential in preventing a child from further suffering in what she called an "orphanage." To orchestrate the scheme, Galindo admitted to paying bribes or "tips," as she called the practice in one media interview. In this process, a "false paper trail" was created. "The children's true identities were erased. They [the children] were given new names and histories. This information was placed on birth certificates and adoption-related documents. These documents were then used to obtain legitimate Cambodian passports" (Cross, 2005, p. 10). These falsified documents were then passed along to unsuspecting adoptive parents who applied for the children to be adopted as orphans under the US Department of State guidelines for immigration.

Apparently, children were not difficult to secure, as the investigation, called "Operation Broken Hearts" revealed that Galindo collaborated with a number of Cambodians who recruited birth families for child sales and abduction. These individuals are called birth-mother recruiters, and in general, the transaction would take place in the following manner: a poor Cambodian mother, father, or extended family would be approached by a recruiter, a critical role in this fraudulent activity. Sometimes the child's mother and other family members would be shown photos of happy, healthy Cambodian children living with their adoptive families in the United States. Typically, the recruiter would make promises about the wonderful future awaiting her child. Reportedly, the false promises made to the families included the following:

- A reputable humanitarian organization will provide food and medical care for your child in Cambodia.
- Your child will be able to attend a boarding school in Cambodia.
- You can regularly visit your child in Cambodia.
- You can reclaim your child at any time and even children living abroad will return to Cambodia. (This particular false promise was made to those families who agreed for their child to be taken to a second country.)

Once a child was secured, the next step would entail medical testing for HIV and other health conditions. With a confirmation of good health, the negotiated payment and child-relinquishment signatures would follow (Cross, 2005). Apparently, it was not uncommon for legal documents of consent to be written in English and verbally translated into the birth mother's native language. Immediately following signature, some children would be secreted to a location where they would be housed while awaiting ICA. Investigator Cross recounted the conditions of some of these waiting locations to be like "stash houses" used in drug trafficking—he found filthy and sometimes unattended and sometimes naked infants soiled in their own waste. Cross shared that the conditions of these homes would be considered to be animal cruelty by US standards. Apparently prior to the prospective family pick-up, the children would be moved to an institution and presented to their families after being bathed and clothed appropriately.

Reportedly Galindo paid recruiters a US$50 commission for each child that he or she located in the villages (Cross, 2005). Their work was like that of independent contractors or "freelance locators" who were compensated for a successful relinquishment of a healthy and desirable child. This approach, a contingency-payment system, further fueled adoption fraud as a recruiter's income was based on the number of children secured for ICA.

Once potential parents were matched with a child and before they departed the United States, adoptive families would be instructed by the sisters to carry US$3,500 in crisp hundred-dollar bills. They were told that the money would be used as donations for humanitarian aid purposes in Cambodia. Well-intentioned families, experiencing the highly emotional process of adopting a child, were led to believe that the money would help in the care of the children left behind in the institution. Unfortunately, this claim could not have been further from the truth.

Groups of 20 parents would typically travel to Cambodia to pick up the children, handing the cash directly to Galindo. The evidence clearly indicated that Galindo was not using the money for humanitarian purposes, and in fact she was laundering the money in multiple locations including offshore banks in Singapore, real-estate investments, and other luxury items. This evidence came to light when the investigators discovered that many of Galindo's bank deposits were in perfect increments of US$3,500. In the end, the US Internal Revenue Service seized much of these ill-gotten assets, including a $1.5 million beachfront home in Hawaii and a luxury automobile valued at US$75,000 (Cross, 2005). These items of conspicuous consumption are mentioned to underscore the value system of Galindo who professed humanitarian aid work while enriching herself and ultimately becoming a millionaire as Cambodian families and children suffered the consequences of her crimes as they lived in extreme poverty.

The term "stash house" is frequently used for the trafficking of drugs. Using this term to describe the facts of the Galindo and Devin case underscores the federal marshall's view that the activity was not only a human rights abuse but also a form of human trafficking (Cross, 2005). However, Galindo and Devin never were charged with human trafficking as the laws were inadequate to pursue that pathway; ultimately they were charged with financial offenses related to tax fraud (Cross, 2005; Smolin, 2004, 2006). Seizure of assets by the Internal Revenue Service was perhaps the most fitting of immediate punishment for a woman like Galindo. Driven by greed, this punishment was critical as she lost both her riches and community status. The latter, status as an "orphan rescuer," was clearly enjoyed by Galindo, and she argued her case to the end—she clearly saw herself as doing good things for children in poverty. Her confusion of the facts was truly stunning.

When the US federal authorities moved forward to prosecute the two sisters for their illegal activities, Devin agreed to testify against her sister, Lauryn Galindo, for a lesser sentence. She made this agreement with prosecutors partly because she herself was largely unaware of Galindo's activities on the ground in Cambodia (Cross, 2005). For these illegal activities, Galindo was sentenced to 18 months in prison, which illustrates the inadequate legal system that interfaced with her crimes. Part of the problem is that many of the crimes took place in another country and the prosecution largely rested on money laundering and immigration fraud. The laws, as that time, were simply inadequate to prosecute on the grounds of child trafficking into adoption.

It is important to note that some US families were informed that their child's case had conclusive evidence of adoption fraud. However, Cambodian families had no such official communication or opportunity for redress or restitution. There were initially concerns for the immigration status of the children in the US; in the end the US Department of Justice determined that no action would be taken that would jeopardize the residency of the children involved in the case (personal communication, Cross, October 2006). While these children are afforded the opportunities of US citizenship today, some of them most certainly will be faced with the realities of their adoption being carried out under the dark shadow of Devin and Galindo's illicit activities. The reconciliation of their past, for some, will be difficult and painful as they intersect with the reality of global poverty, desperation, and their own complex stories.

Legal scholar and ICA expert David Smolin (2006) has extensively analyzed the case of Cambodia and elsewhere and describes how "child laundering" is executed in illicit adoptions.

> The term "child laundering" expresses the claim that the current intercountry adoption system frequently takes children illegally from birth parents, and then uses the official processes of the adoption and legal systems to "launder" them as "legally" adopted children. Thus, the adoption system treats children in a manner analogous to a criminal organization engaged in money laundering, which obtains funds illegally but then "launders" them through a legitimate business.
>
> *(Smolin, 2006, p. 115)*

In the case of Cambodia, the prosecution of Galindo and Devin is most informative of just how a child's identity may be recrafted to fit the criteria necessary for removal from their community and family life. Trish Maskew is a legal and adoption-practice expert who was personally involved in the reform efforts in Cambodia. She points out that Seattle Adoptions International was just one agency caught in the criminal investigations (Maskew, 2004). There were other individuals and agencies involved in exploitation related to child sales and laundering, including European adoption professionals representing prospective families in Western Europe. In fact, Seattle Adoptions International was just the tip of the iceberg; there were many unscrupulous entrepreneurs involved in laundering children from Cambodia with reports of wrongdoing at the highest levels of Cambodia's government. For example, the prime minister's wife is alleged to have misused her position with the Red Cross and engaged in illicit adoption practices (Goodno, 2015). This individual of status in Cambodia, along with others, were not held accountable for their actions.

In the case of Galindo, the United States was particularly aggressive in the investigation of wrongdoing. In fact, Cambodia became the first case in which the US government closed down a country, placing US-citizen adoption transactions in the small Asian country on moratorium and stopping some adoptions during their process. Ceasing adoptions mid-stream during their processing brings considerable pressure from US citizens, but the problem was so serious that the United States Department of State took this unprecedented step to cease the illicit adoptions (Maskew, 2004; Smolin, 2006). In the broader landscape, Cambodia, and especially Galindo's complicity, serve as negative examples for ICA, and Cambodia is closed to adoptions to the US today.

The Operation Broken Hearts case serves as a critical and thorough example of *how* adoption fraud and illicit adoptions, in general, are carried out. The documentation is quite detailed due to prosecution and Federal Marshall Rick Cross' willingness to speak publicly about the investigation. When one considers the crimes related to child laundering, it is important to recognize that falsifying paperwork (e.g. birth certificate, etc.) to obscure a child's background is a clear violation of a child's right to her identity as per the Convention on the Rights of the Child. Specifically, Article 8 "guarantees the right of the child to preserve her identity and this includes nationality, name and family relations as recognized by law without unlawful interference." We will continue to look at child rights violations throughout the book as this particular aspect of human rights abuses strikes at the very core of the idea of *vulnerability* and the importance of social protections to ensure *human dignity*.

Child "rescue" in the face of disaster: Haiti's earthquake

In early 2010, Haiti was crippled by a 7.0-magnitude earthquake, which led to the deaths of well over 200,000 people (Telegraph, 2010) and added an unknown number of unparented children already in the country. Based on past historical events, human-trafficking scenarios, including adoption fraud, are of immediate concern for international NGOs and other national and international players during natural disasters, especially in low-resource countries such as Haiti (Better Care Network, 2010; Doyle, 2010; International Social Services, 2010).

In the aftermath of the Haiti earthquake, members of an American Baptist mission group named the New Life Children's Refuge (NLCR), headed by Laura Silsby, tried to illegally remove 33 Haitian children between the ages of 2 months to 12 years from Haiti to the Dominican Republic (BBC News, 2010) with the purpose of permanent adoptions to the United States, according to an NLCR planning document (NLCR, n.d.; BBC, 2010). However, despite the ongoing crisis and chaos in Haiti at the time, the NLCR group was stopped at the Dominican Republic border because they lacked the appropriate paperwork to remove the children in their possession from Haiti. The group members were later arrested in Haiti and were accused of attempted child trafficking. Former US president Bill Clinton made a comment to the international media, while visiting Haiti to assess the crisis, that it was all just a "misunderstanding" and eventually US President Obama negotiated for the return of the accused traffickers, and with the exception of Silsby, the other members returned to the United States relatively quickly (Associated Press, 2010; CNN, 2010; Cook & Snider, 2010).

Silsby served a nearly three-month jail sentence in Haiti before being released and returning to the United States as an unfairly persecuted hero to some of those in the Baptist and evangelical communities. After the abduction attempt, all 33 children were eventually reunited with family members; in this case, not one of the 33 children was found to be a true or bona fide orphan (Australian Broadcasting Corporation, 2010). In fact, they were not even living in the earthquake zone. Reportedly, many of the families who had been duped by Silsby and the missionary group were quite distressed and relieved to be reunited with their children.

Although the Haitian Prime Minister initially accused the Baptist group as being human traffickers, some of the parents of the children later testified in court that they had willingly relinquished the children to the group, which is why the initial accusation that the group was attempting human trafficking was dropped by the Haitian government. Families agreed to the relinquishments apparently under conditions of fraud after they were reportedly assured by Silsby and her agents that the children would receive a free education, that the parents would be able to visit them in the Dominican Republic, and that they would one day return to their family members in Haiti (CNN, 2010). This is in sharp contrast to a planning document written by the group that stated the ultimate goal to be a "rescue operation" with adoption to families in the United States (BBC, 2010). In fact, Silsby had constructed a rather elaborate plan with donors for the construction of a children's home with a variety of first-class services to include vacation-quality housing for those prospective adoptive parents waiting for their adoption paperwork to clear in the Dominican Republic (NLCR, n.d.).

One can easily see how during this time of chaos in Haiti when people could not acquire even the most basic necessities for their children, parents would agree to temporarily allow their child to be transported to a safer location where there is a promise of food, healthcare, and education. However, as in the cases previously discussed, Haitians do not share the Western notion of adoption, and the idea of a cessation of the legal relationship between parent and child is simply not a conception for most Haitians. Silsby and her group seized upon an opportunity of misunderstanding during a time of chaos and extreme vulnerability (Associated Press, 2010; Rotabi & Bergquist, 2010; Selman, 2011), and the scenario that unfolded is a poignant illustration of why the initiation of intercountry adoptions should not be permitted during humanitarian crises (United Nations, 2009). Nonetheless, by the end of May 2010, at least 2,000 intercountry adoptions of Haitian children had been completed by families in the United States, France, and elsewhere (Boéchat, 2013; Selman, 2011), in which just over half were completed as a result of some special provisions quickly enacted by the United States in the days following the earthquake, as we will explore next (Reitz, 2010).

A closer look: sanctioned government intervention in Haiti and the case of the United States

Some organizations took a cautioned stance against removing children (Better Care Network, 2010) and for a search (family tracing) to link lost children to their families to begin internally through a systematic process (International Committee of the Red Cross, 2010), while International Social Services called for a cessation of adoption activities for Haitian children during the chaos in the days and months after the earthquake (Boéchat, 2013; Dambach & Baglietto, 2010). Other organizations such as the International Red Cross echoed these concerns in their own disaster response communications to the general public (International Red Cross, 2010). However, hundreds of prospective adoptive parents who were already in the process of a Haitian adoption demanded their government's intervention; this was particularly true of US citizens who had the paperwork to support their grounds that adoptions had been initiated prior to the earthquake. While pleas for government intervention ensued, some adoption-agency directors and case workers flew into Haiti on private planes immediately after the quake as they already had adoptions underway (Armistead, 2010). The case was compelling, as international news broadcast images of dazed and confused Haitians among the rubble, including disturbing photos of children wandering around without adult caretakers.

One agency director, Lucy Armistead of All Blessings International adoption agency, has spoken quite publicly about her own experience in Haiti as she was one of the first adoption-agency personnel on the ground there. From a first-person perspective, she talks about the rules that were quickly put into place by the US immigration officials in order to determine which children were appropriate for removal (Armistead, 2010). Basically, any child for whom an adoption file had been opened prior to the quake and had a match with prospective parents in the United States met the criteria for approved removal from Haiti. Whitney Reitz (2010), the bureaucrat that made the late-night decision to proceed with this plan, reflected on it as being the "right" thing to do as she clearly saw the decision to be an act of child rescue.

However, even with US government support, as Armistead points out, the destruction was such that moving among the residential childcare institutions or *crèches* to identify appropriate children was very difficult; finding the children and also double checking records also had challenges because of the chaos. It was heart wrenching, but some children simply did not meet the criteria when the timeline of adoption application and the disposition of the case were examined. Armistead herself faced difficult decisions on the ground, working within the criteria set forth, and she left many children behind—hoping to continue to work on their cases at a later date (Armistead, 2010).

As children were loaded onto private planes, there were inevitable challenges to the rules. In one highly publicized case, the Governor of Pennsylvania was personally involved as two young women, originally from his state, had been running a *crèche*/children's home (Armistead, 2010; Rotabi, Armistead, & Mónico, 2015). They refused to leave the country without all of the children in their care coming along—they had gone to the airport with all of the children, even those who did not meet the criteria for immigration, and refused to board the plane until all of the children were allowed to depart. It was a relatively brief standoff, as the planes sat on the tarmac in position for near immediate takeoff (Armistead, 2010; Rotabi et al., 2015). There were offers by others staying in Haiti to take responsibility for the children (Armistead, 2010; Rotabi, et al., 2015), but the sisters refused, saying that they simply would not leave any children behind.

Reportedly, amid this drama, a phone call was made to the White House (Armistead, 2010; Rotabi et al., 2015). It has been said that President Obama himself did not take the call, but the highest levels of his staff were aware that the plane was departing with children who did not meet the criteria for immigration. Little more is known, but the international news did question the overreach of the governor. A handful of children were left in legal limbo, and as a result of their status found themselves in a residential children's home in Pennsylvania, staying there for well over a year while a permanent plan was put into place (Arce & O'Brien, 2011; Gurman & Schmitz, 2010). While one may argue situational ethics, this scenario further underscores the cavalier attitude of those in power who feel justified as "rescuers" or "saviors" while others may call these individuals "robbers" or "kidnappers" (Selman, 2011; Economist, 2010). These questions were reminiscent of other evacuations, including the Vietnam Babylift (Fronek, 2012; Fronek & Cuthbert, 2012).

While less is known about other countries, including France and other Western European countries, and their removal of children in haste (Boéchat, 2013; Selman, 2011), inevitably they had their own drama in deciding which children to "take home" and which children to "leave behind," for it is an unthinkable task.

Finally, the situation that played out in Haiti sounds somewhat similar to the 2007 "Zoe's Ark" incident and the attempted removal of children from Chad (Bergquist, 2009, 2012; Hancock, 2007). In this case, French charity workers attempted to evacuate children to Europe where they had already identified families ready for foster care and adoption. While in Haiti, the removal of children was government sanctioned with some rules for necessary paperwork, the evidence was clear that the Zoe's Ark team had engaged in illicit activities and without any form of approval for child removal. In fact, it was reported that some children were lured away with candy; in other cases there were promises to parents that their children were being taken to the capital city for educational purposes, and extraordinary lengths were taken in bandaging children to make them appear to be in need of medical care (Bergquist, 2009, 2012; Hancock, 2007). After being sentenced to eight years of hard labor in a Chadian court on kidnapping charges, the French government intervened by arranging for their citizens to return to France, where the charity workers were pardoned, as many saw them as heroes of a botched child-rescue effort. Just as was the case in Haiti with US government involvement, the French government ultimately rescued their own citizens from hard prison time—thereby rescuing the so called "rescuers" or saviors. They were anything but honorable, as many parents reported that they were led to believe that the children would go temporarily to Europe and receive an education with the full expectation that their children would return to Africa (Mezmur, 2010).

Restitution as an attempt to recognize and restore human rights

In the examples thus far, on the whole there has been a lack of financial restitution for those who have experienced the loss of their child as a result of illicit adoption practices. For example, in Cambodia the aggressive legal investigation and prosecution did not result in restitution. However, financial restitution is not entirely unheard of. The Samoan Islands and the Magdalene Laundries in Ireland serve as landmark cases for restitution.

The Samoan Islands: probation and financial restitution

In 2009, a case of illicit adoptions in the Samoan Islands had many of the same characteristics as the Cambodian scandal orchestrated by Seattle Adoptions International. However, the agency was Utah based and run by married couple Scott and Karen Banks, who claimed to be involved in a religious mission through their agency Focus on Children (Davis & Longhini, 2009). The case was not unlike Cambodia as many of the birth families thought that their children would return to Samoa and some reported being told that the children were going to be in an "educational foster program" (Davis & Longhini, 2009). The Banks were convicted of a number of federal crimes to include wire fraud, mail fraud, and money laundering and they were barred from ever engaging in adoption work again in the future. The difference from the Cambodia prosecution was that the judge, in the case of Samoa, allowed for the Banks and others implicated in the agency wrongdoing to pay restitution of US$100,000 into a trust with five years of probation rather than serve jail time for their crimes (Davis & Longhini, 2009; Roby, 2012). This was a remarkable and innovative legal decision to avoid any further trauma for the children with an orientation to meeting the best interests of the child through an alternative approach made available through restitution.

According to Jini Roby (2012), the executor of the restitution trust, the money is used to pay for activities that encourage the children to remain in touch with their families in Samoa, to pay for communication and some travel back to the Samoan Islands. Some of the funds are used for reunions and activities, such as social gatherings for the children and their families, developed as a means of support and reconciliation. To meaningfully aid this process, funds have also been used for translation during phone calls, delivery of photos and letters, and for outreach to both birth and adoptive families.

It is uncommon for an adoptive family to return the child to her family once it is learned that the adoption process was illicit. However, one young girl was returned to her Samoan family as the result of a heartbreaking decision made by the adoptive family when they learned that their adoptive daughter was much loved and wanted back in Samoa. While the decision was difficult, the family felt that there was no other pathway (Davis & Longhini, 2009). This is an unusual case and certainly not the norm—most adoptive families simply find the idea of returning a child back to their family of origin to be unthinkable.

Ireland: the Magdalene Laundries and restitution

In Ireland, the Magdalene Laundries were operated from the 18th to the late 20th centuries under the authority of the Roman Catholic Church. In Ireland, at least 30,000 girls and women were forced into slave labor, working long hours cleaning laundry from which the church profited greatly. The conditions were such that in 2013 a formal apology was made and "The Irish government...agreed to pay up to 58 million euros to hundreds of women forced to work at the Catholic Church's notorious Magdalene Laundries after a report found that a quarter of them were sent there by the Irish state" (Humphries, 2013). Some of these survivors were adolescent girls sent to the laundries while pregnant—sent for punishment or repentance and remediation, as they were unwed mothers and seen to be immoral. They were forced to work in the laundries to pay for their room and board as well as the medical costs of childbirth (Sixsmith, 2009).

The spotlight in 2013 was particularly heated as the film *Philomena* chronicled a true story about one woman who searched for her son; the young boy was adopted by a US family and the film captured the deep pain and need to know about the health and safety of a child lost through illicit adoption. However, the resulting scrutiny was not the first time that practices of the Catholic Church were called into question. In 1952 "several embarrassing international incidents" brought to light the fact that thousands of Irish children were being sent out of Ireland for adoption overseas, particularly to the United States (Maguire, 2006, p. 132). The Church is known to have sent children for adoption by US Catholic families rather than allowing the children be adopted by Protestant families in Ireland closer to home (Maguire, 2006). Because the documentation was poor and some of it was intentionally destroyed, the absolute numbers of children sent into intercountry adoption from Ireland is unknown today (Sixsmith, 2009).

Ireland is not the only country to "apologize" for the past injustices in adoption practices. Australia leads the world in apology for forced adoptions (Fronek & Cuthbert, 2013). This is as a result of the fact that in Australia, not only did unwed mothers suffer the injustices of fraudulent and forced adoptions, but their indigenous Aborigine population was targeted for child removal (Quartly, Swain & Cuthbert, 2013).[12] Fronek and Cuthbert (2013) have presented the "need to frame its [Australia's] apology to all of those people harmed by forced adoption practices to include intercountry adoption, in particular, overseas mothers who have no ready access to the Australian government to press their claims for themselves" (p. 3). There is also movement amongst adoptees themselves who are advocating on behalf of birth mothers. For example, reportedly in Denmark there is currently a movement amongst some Korean adoptees for restitution, demanding that the Denmark government provide financial compensation to the known birth mothers in Korea (Vora, 2016). If such restitution were to be established, it would be a first to result from adoptee advocacy.

Spain: a shift from being a country of origin to a top receiving country

Not unlike Ireland, Spain has also had significant adoption fraud problems when they were a country of origin for intercountry adoption. As in Ireland, there is evidence of some wrongdoing by leaders within the Catholic Church and others during this era of Spain sending children into intercountry adoption in significant numbers (Shubert, 2012). However, during the 1990s, Spain transformed into a receiving country for international adoptees (Briggs & Marre, 2009), second only to the United States in 2004 and in recent years Spain and Italy have been the most active European countries receiving children for intercountry adoption (Selman, 2015). Patterns of adoption to Spain are indicated in Table 1.1, indicating China, Russia, Ethiopia, and Colombia as top countries of child origin.

The dilemma today in Spain is the fact that the sheer number of people who have applied to adopt (including an application fee) has far exceeded the realistic capacity of the adoption agencies to deliver. That is, there are far too many "waiting" individuals and couples given the current flow of children thereby creating a demand that is lopsided. By the end of 2012, there were 23,000 Spanish adoption applications awaiting a child; in 2013 only 1,188 adoptions took place; and the figures dipped lower in 2014 to 824 adoptions (San Román, personal

TABLE 1.1 Countries of origin for children sent to Spain as international adoptees (2000–2014)

Area/country of origin	2000	2001	2002	2003	2004	2005	2006	2007	2008	2009	2010	2011	2012	2013	2014	Total
All adoptions	3,062	3,428	3,625	3,591	5,541	5,423	4,472	3,648	3,156	3,006	2,891	2,573	1,669	1,188	824	48,097
ASIA	686	1,107	1,586	1,194	2,577	2,854	2,041	1,269	865	724	1,016	978	714	423	428	18,462
China	475	941	1,427	1,043	2,389	2,753	1,759	1,059	619	573	584	677	447	293	229	15,268
EUROPE	1,493	1,569	1,395	1,915	2,111	1,727	1,567	1,460	1,304	1,236	1,039	833	552	416	227	18,844
Russia	496	652	809	1,157	1,618	1,262	1,290	955	899	868	801	712	479	350	161	12,509
AFRICA	32	31	51	163	268	278	374	545	656	784	578	537	403	283	92	5,075
Ethiopia	0	0	12	107	220	227	304	481	629	722	508	441	302	260	79	4,292
AMERICA	905	721	593	679	585	564	490	374	331	262	258	225	14	66	77	6,271
Columbia	414	319	271	285	256	240	260	174	189	160	174	148	74	25	39	2,964

Source: Ministerio de Sanidad, Servicios Sociales e Igualdad, n.d.

communication, May 1, 2016). This kind of pressure is not only a problem in agency functioning, but the resulting sense of urgency to meet targets holds the potential of fueling fraudulent and poor practices on the ground.

In conclusion

The history of intercountry adoption from a human rights perspective is mixed, and while there have been many ethical adoptions of truly orphaned and vulnerable children, sadly there have been far too many cases of poor practices and exploitation. In contemporary practices, unscrupulous entrepreneurs have been too frequently enriched and those acting as "saviors" are applauded while children's identities are forever altered. In Nepal, where adoption scandals highlighted how identities of children have been changed to make them appear to meet the criteria of being orphaned, these children have been called "paper orphans" (Huygens, 2013). The term underscores the construction of a child's family status through fraudulent paperwork related to identity (e.g. birth certificate) and immigration requirements. The fraud is carried out through a variety of actors, often including those who run institutions ("orphanages") and others who appear to be professionals engaged in legitimate child welfare work but were being enriched by illicit practices (Smolin, 2006).

The term "paper orphans" also illustrates the circumstances of children and their families living in extreme poverty in Nepal, a social environment that made for fertile ground for serious adoption fraud. Just like many other cases, many of the families living in the highlands of Nepal did not understand the concept of adoption and thought their children were in the care of a respectable organization that would provide for the child's education and other basic needs—they never expected to be permanently separated from their children.

Reflecting on this sad reality, we cannot simply ignore the rights of children legitimately living in residential childcare institutions or on the streets or other dire circumstances, especially their child rights to grow to and develop to their fullest potential within a family environment. This particular right is identified in the preamble of the Convention on the Rights of the Child—the most agreed-upon human rights instrument in the world (Roby & Maskew, 2012). Even with concerted efforts to improve the lives of children, with gradual change oriented to child rights and safe environments for children, millions of children still live in residential care institutions (Williamson & Greenberg, 2010). Some of these environments are better than others and there are actually some small-scale homes that are managed with a family-like approach to care. Sadly, most children continue to languish in large and impersonal residential care facilities, suffering neglect such that their long-term growth and development are impaired (Bakermans-Kranenburg et al., 2008; Juffer & Van IJzendoorn, 2012).

Children who stay for long periods in impersonal institutional circumstances live in serious and persistent emotional pain that is simply unimaginable (Nelson, Fox & Zeanah, 2013). This fact should not be underestimated in terms of human rights dimensions when considering adoption as a solution to these children languishing without parental or extended family care. However, evidence revealed that children who have been institutionalized frequently have biological families, and what appears to be willful abandonment into residential care is often a function of their desire for the child to have their basic needs met—including educational needs—in the face of extreme poverty (Williamson & Greenberg, 2010). Again, it is important to underscore that the vast majority of children living in institutions have at least one living parent, which refutes the misuse of the term "orphan" (Rotabi & Bunkers, 2011). How to intervene for these children and the implications for intercountry adoption practice have been a source of debate (see Ballard et al., 2015; Bartholet & Smolin, 2012; Gibbons & Rotabi, 2012), highlighting the complexities of not only the phenomena but also the want and need to build a family through alternative means.

The history we have presented thus far excludes Russia and the former Soviet Union where large-scale childcare institutions have been the norm. We will look at this human rights dimension of residential care facilities when we consider the unique issues related to intercountry adoption, specifically from Romania and Russia, as the practice there and elsewhere so clearly interfaces with politics. We next consider illicit practices in Guatemala and India as we take a closer look at human trafficking and force, fraud, and coercion in illicit adoptions, including child abduction into adoption. Also, we consider the United States and that country's system, including changes in agency policy, processes, and procedures as a result of reform. Then, the final frontier of Africa and the serious and persistent problems there are discussed. Social protections and a legal framework to address illicit adoptions are considered, including international private law and human rights instruments. We then turn to global surrogacy as a relatively new and emergent practice for building families as we look at the perspectives of the surrogate mothers themselves.

Notes

1   We mainly use the term *residential care facility* or *institution* as the term *orphanage* is a misnomer given the fact that most children living in these settings have one or both parents as well as extended family.

2   There are overinflated estimates of the world's "orphans" because children with one living/lone parent have been included in that count by some. By this definition, "single orphans" are estimated to be as many 153 million children globally. A fraction of this sum are "double orphans" (both parents deceased) and living in institutional care; the US government (2010) estimates there are 17.8 million such children. Single orphans typically live with their surviving parent and the vast majority of double orphans are absorbed into their extended family systems (Roby, 2012).

3   Children leaving their family life and being taken to another country dates back much earlier to the late 1800s and early 1900s in which thousands were shipped from the United Kingdom to other countries such as Canada and the United States for labor. This movement was obviously not intercountry adoption, but it is historically noteworthy as we consider the movement of children from one country to another.

4   This particular aspect of history is overlooked because there is so little documentation; Pearl Buck wrote about her own adoption thereby documenting that particular case. There were relatively few such adoptions and, at this juncture in history, there was no formal process of adoption paperwork, etc. for the purpose of child immigration and so forth. Some may argue that this movement of children was not actually intercountry adoption based on today's standards, but we wanted to note this early activity as the great rise in adoptions by Christian families—often assisted by faith-based adoption agencies—is remarkable in contemporary history. Importantly, the notion that children were in need of being "saved" from their impoverished—financially, emotionally, relationally, etc—conditions partly originated with Buck and residues of that narrative continue to drive both religious and non-religious motives to adopt today.

5   For an expanded discussion see Briggs' (2012) book entitled *Somebody's children: The politics of transracial and transnational adoption*.

6   Karen Rotabi's mother-in-law, Elizabeth Martin, observed Eleanor Roosevelt checking in on the medical evaluations of the children who had arrived from Europe.

7   Minor revisions took place in 1999 and 2000.

8   It should be noted that South Korea now institutes a quota system that is designed such that intercountry adoptions may not exceed domestic adoptions.

9 Scheper-Hughes began her study focused on rumors of organ theft in Brazil. In her field notes, she captured adoption practices in which children were sold and abducted into intercountry adoption. She also reports that parents were so frightened by child abduction into adoption that some families would lock their own children indoors to secure their safety.

10 It should be noted that the illicit adoptions that took place during Argentina's war years appear to have been carried out without a significant number of children leaving the country. Intercountry adoptions on a large scale were not as dynamic as found in El Salvador and Guatemala.

11 Intercountry adoption expert, Peter Selman, points out that adoptions from Colombia are essentially a mirror image of the global rise and fall of adoption (personal communication, February 22, 2016). China's most active year for intercountry adoption was actually 2005 with 14,484 adoptions sent to 15 receiving states of which 55 percent of children were sent to the United States.

12 The US shares this history as the Indian Child Welfare Act (1978) was passed to protect indigenous peoples and the forcible removal of their children for foster care and adoption.

References

Abreu, D. (2009). Baby-bearing storks: Brazilian intermediaries in the adoption process. In D. Marre & L. Briggs (Eds), *International adoption: Global inequalities and the circulation of children* (pp. 138–53). New York: New York University Press.

Arce, R. & O'Brien, S. (2011, January 13). Most have homes, but some Haitian orphans still in shelters. *CNN*. Retrieved from http://edition.cnn.com/2011/US/01/11/haiti.us.orphans/index.html

Armistead, L. (2010, September). Reflections on orphan rescue in Haiti: Critical thinking post-disaster. Paper presented at the Intercountry Adoption Summit, Ontario, Canada.

Associated Press. (2010, April 28). Lesser charge for missionary. New York Times. Retrieved from http://query.nytimes.com/gst/fullpage.html?res=9F01E3D61F38F93BA15757C0A9669D8B63

Australian Broadcasting Corporation. (2010, March 15). All "trafficked" Haiti quake orphans have parents. *Australian Broadcasting Corporation News*. Retrieved from www.abc.net.au/news/stories/2010/03/18/2849365.htm

Baden, A. L., Gibbons, J. L., Wilson, S. L., & McGinnis, H. (2013). International adoption: Counseling and the adoption triad. *Adoption Quarterly*, 16(3/4), 218–37.

Bakermans-Kranenburg, M. J., Van IJzendoorn, M. H., & Juffer, F. (2008). Earlier is better: A meta-analysis of 70 years of intervention improving cognitive developments in institutionalized children. *Monographs of the Society for Research in Child Development*, 73, 279–93. doi: 10.1111/j.1540-5834.2008.00498.x

Ballard, R. L., Goodno, N., Cochran, R., & Milbrandt, J. (Eds). (2015). *The intercountry adoption debate: Dialogues across disciplines*. Newcastle upon Tyne: Cambridge Scholars Publishing.

Bartholet, E. & Smolin, D. M. (2012). The debate. In J. L. Gibbons & K. S. Rotabi (Eds), *Intercountry adoption: Policies, practices, and outcomes* (pp. 233–51). Farnham: Ashgate Press.

BBC News. (2010, February 5). Profile: New Life Children's Refuge. *BBC*. Retrieved from http://news.bbc.co.uk/2/hi/americans/8490843.stm

Beimers, D. (2006) "I am the better woman for having my two Black children": An account from Pearl S. Buck. In K. S. Stolley & V. L. Bullough (Eds), *The Praeger handbook of adoption* (pp. 116–17). Greenport, CT: Praeger.

Bergquist, K. J. S. (2009). Operation Babylift or Babyabduction: Implications of the Hague Convention on the humanitarian evacuation and "rescue" of children. *International Social Work*, 52(5), 621–33. doi: 10.1177/0020872809337677

Bergquist, K. J. S. (2012). Implications of the Hague Convention on the humanitarian evacuation and "rescue" of children. In J. L. Gibbons & K. S. Rotabi (Eds), *Intercountry adoption: Policies, practices, and outcomes* (pp. 43–54). Farnham: Ashgate Press.

Bergquist, K. J. S., Vonk, M. E., Kim, D. S., & Feit, M. D. (2007). *International Korean adoption: A fifty-year history of policy and practice*. Binghamton, NY: Haworth Press.

Better Care Network. (2010). Child protection working group guiding principles: Unaccompanied and separated children following the Haiti Earthquake January 2010. Retrieved from http://better-carenetwork.org/bcn/details.asp?id=21563&themeID=1005&topicID=1033

Boéchat, H. (2013, July). The grey zones of intercountry adoption: Where adoptability rules are circumvented. Paper presentation at the Fourth Intercountry Adoption Research Conference, Bilbao, Spain.

Borshay, Liem, D. (2000). First person plural. Video. San Francisco, CA: Center for Asian American Media.

Briggs, L. (2012). *Somebody's children: The politics of transracial and transnational adoption.* Durham, NC: Duke University Press.

Briggs, L. & Marre, D. (2009). *International adoption: Global inequalities and the circulation of children.* New York: New York University Press.

Brysk, A. (1994). *The politics of human rights in Argentina.* Stanford, CA: Stanford University Press.

Buck, P. S. (1955, September). The children waiting: The shocking scandal of adoption. *Woman's Home Companion*, 129–32. Retrieved from http://pages.uoregon.edu/adoption/archive/BuckTCW.htm

Buck, P. S. (1972, January). I am the better woman for having my two Black children. *Today's Health*, 64, 21–2. Retrieved from http://pages.uoregon.edu/adoption/archive/BuckIBW.htm

Caistor, N. (2013, May 17). Obituary: General Jorge Rafael Videla: Dictator who brought terror to Argentina during the "dirty war". Independent. Retrieved from www.independent.co.uk/news/obituaries/general-jorge-rafael-videla-dictator-who-brought-terror-to-argentina-in-the-dirty-war-8621806.html

Cartwright, L. (2003). Photographs of "waiting children": The transnational adoption market. *Social Text*, 21(1), 83–109.

Cheney, K. E. (2014). Giving children a "better life"? Reconsidering social reproduction and humanitarianism in intercountry adoption. *European Journal of Development Research*, 26, 247–63.

Cheney, K. E. (in press). *Crying for our elders: African orphanhood in the age of HIV and AIDs.* Chicago, IL: University of Chicago Press.

CNN. (2010, February 19). Freed missionaries from Haiti "glad to be home". Retrieved from www.cnn.com/2010/WORLD/americas/02/19/haiti.border.arrests/index.html

Cook, L. & Snider, S. (2010, March 17). Haitian kids allegedly taken by Americans reunited with families. *CNN*. Retrieved from http://articles.cnn.com/2010-03-17/world/haiti.baptists.children_1_laura-silsby-haitian-officials-orphanage?_s=PM:WORLD

Cross, R. (2005, April 15). Operation Broken Hearts: Transcript of Richard Cross video. Lecture given at Samford University, Birmingham, AL. Retrieved from http://cumberland.samford.edu/files/rushton/Richard_Cross_transcript.pdf

Dalen, M. (2012). Cognitive competence, academic achievement, and educational attainment among intercountry adoptees: Research outcomes from the Nordic countries. In J. L. Gibbons & K. S. Rotabi (Eds), *Intercountry adoption: Policies, practices, and outcomes* (pp. 199–210). Farnham: Ashgate Press.

Dambach, M. & Baglietto, C. (2010). *Haiti: "Expediting" intercountry adoptions in the aftermath of a natural disaster.* Geneva: International Social Service. Retrieved from www.iss-ssi.org/2009/assets/files/Haiti%20ISS%20final-%20foreword.pdf

Davis, K. & Longhini, D. (2009, December 12). The lost children [48 Hours Mystery]. New York: *CBS.*

Davis, M. A. (2011). *Children for families or families for children: The demography of adoption behavior in the U. S.* Rotterdam: Springer.

Democracy Now! (2013, November 15). Democracy Now! on attack at Pro-Búsqueda. Retrieved from www.youtube.com/watch?v=HTmocI0abVs

Dorow, S. (2006). *Transnational adoption: A cultural economy of race, gender, and kinship.* New York: New York University Press.

Dowling, M. & Brown, G. (2009). Globalization and intercountry adoption from China. *Child and Family Social Work*, 1–10. doi: 10.1111/j.1365-2206.2008.00607.x

Doyle, J. (2010). Misguided kindness: Making the right decisions for children in emergencies. Retrieved from Save the Children website: http://reliefweb.int/sites/reliefweb.int/files/resources/1481589D74C062C4C12577FF003BCCFC-Full_report.pdf

Dubinsky, K. (2010). *Babies without borders: Adoption and migration across the Americas.* Toronto: University of Toronto Press.

Economist. (2010, February 6). International adoption: Saviours or kidnappers? Economist. Retrieved from www.economist.com/node/15469423

Eisenhower, D. W. (1953, August 7). Statement by the President upon signing the Refugee Relief Act of 1953. Retrieved from www.presidency.ucsb.edu/ws/?pid=9668

Fonseca, C. (2009). Transnational connections and dissenting views: The evolution of child placement policies in Brazil. In D. Marre & L. Briggs (Eds), *International adoption: Global inequalities and the circulation of children* (pp. 154–73). New York: New York University Press.

Fonseca, C., Marre, D., & San Román, B. (2015). Child circulation in a globalized era: Anthropological reflections. In R. L. Ballard, N. H. Goodno, R. F. Cochran, Jr., & J. A. Milbrandt (Eds), *The Intercountry Adoption Debate: Dialogues across Disciplines* (pp. 157–93). Newcastle upon Tyne: Cambridge Scholars Publishing.

Freundlich, M. (1998). Supply and demand: The forces shaping the future of infant adoption. *Adoption Quarterly*, 2(1), 13–46.

Freundlich, M. (2000). Market forces: The issues in international adoption. In M. Freundlich (Ed.), *Adoption and ethics* (pp. 37–66). Washington, DC: Child Welfare League of America.

Fronek, P. (2006). Global perspectives in Korean intercountry adoption. *Asia Pacific Journal of Social Work and Development*, 16(1), 21–31.

Fronek, P. (2012). Operation Babylift: Advancing intercountry adoption into Australia. *Journal of Australian Studies*, 36(4), 445–58. doi: 10.1080/14443058.2012.727845

Fronek, P. & Cuthbert, D. (2012). History repeating…Disaster-related intercountry adoption and the psychosocial care of children. *Social Policy and Society*, 1–14. doi: 10.1017/S1474746412000103

Fronek, P. & Cuthbert, D. (2013). Apologies for forced adoption practices: Implications for contemporary intercountry adoption. *Australian Social Work*, 66(3), 402–14.

Gailey, C. W. (2000). Race, class and gender in intercountry adoption in the USA. In P. F. Selman (Ed.), *Intercountry adoption: Developments, trends and perspectives* (pp. 295–314). London: British Association of Adoption and Fostering.

Gibbons, J. L. & Rotabi, K. S. (Eds). (2012). *Intercountry adoption: Policies, practices, and outcomes*. Farnham: Ashgate Press.

Goodno, N. H. (2015). The Hague: An endless balancing act of preventing intercountry adoption abuses and finding permanent homes for orphans. In R. L. Ballard, N. Goodno, R. Cochran, & J. Milbrandt (Eds), *The intercountry adoption debate: Dialogues across disciplines* (pp. 207–38). Newcastle upon Tyne: Cambridge Scholars Publishing.

Gurman, S. & Schmitz, J. (2010, January 19). Rescue mission bringing Haitian orphans to Pittsburgh. Pittsburgh Post Gazette. Retrieved from www.post-gazette.com/pg/10019/1029290-455.stm

Hancock, S. (2007, November 23). Air firm was told UN, France backed Zoe's Ark. *Reuters*. Retrieved from www.reuters.com/article/latestCrisis/idUSL23512519

Herman, E. (2008). *Kinship by design: A history of adoption in the modern United States*. Chicago, IL: University of Chicago Press.

Herrmann, K. (2010). Reestablishing the humanitarian approach to adoption: The legal and social change necessary to end the commodification of children. *Family Law Quarterly*, 44(3), 409–29.

Herrmann, K. & Kasper, B. (1992). International adoption: The exploitation of women and children. *Affilia*, 7(1), 45–58. doi: 10.1177/088610999200700104

Hopgood, L. (2010). *Lucky girl*. New York: Algonquin Books.

Hübinette, T. (2005). The orphaned nation: Korea imagined as an overseas adopted child in Clon's abandoned child and Park Kwang-su's Berlin report. *Inter-Asia Cultural Studies*, 6(2), 227–43.

Humphries, C. (2013, June 26). Ireland agrees compensation for Magdalene Laundries survivors. *Reuters*. Retrieved from www.reuters.com/article/us-ireland-laundries-compensation-idUSBRE95P18420130626

Huygens, F. (2013). *Paper orphans* [Documentary film]. Thames Ditton: Journeyman Pictures.

International Committee of the Red Cross. (2010). Haiti earthquake: No effort must be spared in reuniting children with their families. Retrieved from www.icrc.org/web/eng/siteeng0.nsf/htmlall/haiti-earthquake-interview-020210

International Social Services. (2010). Earthquake in Haiti: Intercountry adoption cases. Retrieved from www.iss-ssi.org/2009/assets/files/news/haiti_position%20CIR_ENG.pdf

Jaffe, E. D. (1991). Foreign adoptions in Israel: Private paths to parenthood. In H. Altstein & R. J. Simon (Eds), *Intercountry adoption: A multinational perspective* (pp. 161–79). New York: Praeger.

Joe, B. (1978). In defense of intercountry adoption. *Social Service Review*, 52(1), 1–20.

Johnson, K. A. (2012). Challenging the discourse of intercountry adoption perspectives from rural China. In J. L. Gibbons & K. S. Rotabi (Eds), *Intercountry adoption: Policies, practices, and outcomes* (pp. 103–18). Farnham: Ashgate Press.

Johnson, K. A. (2016). *China's hidden children: Abandonment, adoption, and the human costs of the one-child policy*. Chicago, IL: University of Chicago Press.

Joyce, K. (2013). *The child catchers: Rescue, trafficking, and the new gospel of adoption*. New York: Public Affairs.

Juffer, F. & Van IJzendoorn, M. H. (2012). Review of meta-analytical studies on the physical, emotional, and cognitive outcomes of intercountry adoptees. In J. L. Gibbons & K. S. Rotabi (Eds), *Intercountry adoption: Policies, practices, and outcomes* (pp. 175–86). Farnham: Ashgate Press.

Kim, E. J. (2010). *Adopted territory: Transnational Korean adoptees and the politics of belonging*. Durham, NC: Duke University Press.

Kim, H. (2007). Mothers without mothering: Birth mothers from South Korea since the Korean War. In K. J. S. Bergquist, M. E. Vonk, D. S. Kim, & M. D. Feit (Eds), *International Korean adoption: A fifty-year history of policy and practice* (pp. 131–53). New York: Haworth Press.

Los Angeles Times. (2010, January 24). Some Chinese parents say their babies were stolen for adoption. Retrieved from http://articles.latimes.com/2009/sep/20/world/fg-china-adopt20

Lovelock, K. (2000). Intercountry adoption as a migratory practice: A comparative analysis of intercountry adoption and immigration policy and practice in the United States, Canada, and New Zealand in the post WWII period. *International Migration Review*, 34(3), 907–49.

Maguire, M. (2006). The Catholic Church and adoption: Lessons learned from Ireland. In K. S. Stolley & V. L. Bullough (Eds), *The Praeger handbook of adoption, 1* (pp. 131–4). New York: Praeger.

Maskew, T. (2004). Child trafficking and intercountry adoption: The Cambodian experience. *Cumberland Law Review*, 35, 619–38.

McGinnis, H. (2006). From the ashes of war: Lessons from 50 years of Korean international adoption. In R. A. Javier, A. L. Baden, F. A. Biafora, & A. Camacho-Gingerich (Eds), *Handbook of adoption: Implications for researchers, practitioners, and families* (pp. 160–70). New York: Sage Publications.

McGinnis, H. (2012). All grown up: Rise of the Korean adult adoptee movement and implications for practice. In J. L. Gibbons & K. S. Rotabi (Eds), *Intercountry adoption: Policies, practices, and outcomes* (pp. 293–300). Farnham: Ashgate Press.

Meier, P. J. & Zhang, X. (2008). Sold into adoption: The Hunan baby trafficking scandal exposes vulnerabilities in Chinese adoptions to the United States. *Cumberland Law Review*, 39, 87–130.

Mezmur, B. N. (2010, June). The sins of the saviors: Trafficking in the context of intercountry adoption from Africa. Paper presented at the Special Commission of the Hague Conference on Private International Law, The Hague, Netherlands. Retrieved from https://assets.hcch.net/upload/wop/adop2010id02e.pdf

Miller, L. C. (2012). Medical status of internationally adopted children. In J. L. Gibbons & K. S. Rotabi (Eds), *Intercountry adoption: Policies, practices, and outcomes* (pp. 187–98). Farnham: Ashgate Press.

Ministerio de Sanidad, Servicios Sociales e Igualdad. (n.d.). Adopción internacional [Intercountry adoption]. Retrieved from www.msssi.gob.es/ssi/familiasInfancia/adopciones/adopInternacional/home.htm

Mónico, C. & Rotabi, K. S. (2012). Truth, reconciliation and searching for the disappeared children of civil war: El Salvador's search and reunion model defined. In J. L. Gibbons & K. S. Rotabi (Eds), *Intercountry adoption: Policies, practices, and outcomes* (pp. 301–10). Farnham: Ashgate.

Moore, R. (2009). *Adopted for life: The priority for adoption for Christian families and churches*. Wheaton, IL: Crossway Books.

National Association of Black Social Workers. (1972, April). Policy on preserving families of African ancestry. NABSW Conference, Nashville, TN.

Nelson, C. A., Zeanah, C. H., Fox, N. A., Marshall, P. J., Smyke, A. T., & Guthrie, D. (2007). Cognitive recovery in socially deprived young children: The Bucharest Early Intervention Project. *Science*, 318, 1937–40.

Nelson, C., Fox, N., & Zeanah, C. (2013). Anguish of the abandoned child. *Scientific American*, 308, 62–7.

Nelson, K. Z. (2015). War children, evacuation and state politics during WWII: A local case of sick Finnish children in Sweden. In T. Skelton, C. Harker, & K. Horschelmann (Eds), *Geographies of children and young people. Conflict, violence and peace* (pp. 1–21). New York: Springer Reference.

New Life Children's Refuge (NLCR). (n.d.). Haitian orphan rescue mission. Retrieved from www. esbctwinfalls.com/clientimages/24453/pdffiles/haitnlcrhaitianorphanrescuemission.pdf

Ngabonziza, D. (1991). Moral and political issues facing relinquishing countries. *Adoption & Fostering*, 15(4), 75–80.

O'Connor, M. K. & Rotabi, K. S. (2012). Perspectives on child welfare: Ways of understanding roles and actions of current USA adoption agencies involved in intercountry adoptions. In J. L. Gibbons & K. S. Rotabi (Eds), *Intercountry adoption: Policies, practices, and outcomes* (pp. 77–88). Farnham: Ashgate Press.

Pertman, A. (2001). *Adoption nation: How the adoption revolution is transforming America*. New York: Basic Books.

Pilotti, F. J. (1993). Intercountry adoption: Trends, issues and policy implications for the 1990s. *Childhood*, 1, 165–77. doi: 10.1177/090756829300100305

Pro-Búsqueda. (2002). *El día mas esperado: Buscando a los niños desaparecidos de El Salvador* [The most awaited day: Searching for the disappeared children of El Salvador] (2nd ed.). San Salvador: UCA Editors.

Quartly, M., Swain, S., & Cuthbert, D. (2013). *Market in babies: Stories of Australian adoption*. Melbourne: Monash University Publishing.

Reitz, W. (2010). Reflections on the special humanitarian parole program for Haitian orphans. *New York Law School Law Review*, 55, 791–8. Retrieved from www.nylslawreview.com/wp-content/uploads/sites/16/2013/11/55-3.Reitz_.pdf

REMHI (Recuperación de la Memoria Histórica). (1999). *Guatemala never again!* Maryknoll, NY: Orbis.

Reynolds, L. (2015, February 20). Diplomat should be removed from UN over inquiry. Boston Globe. Retrieved from www.bostonglobe.com/opinion/2015/02/20/guatemalan-diplomat-should-removed-from-over-child-trafficking-probe/MPScQrpLDijTghU1i46UrN/story.html

Richards, S. (2014). Stories of paper and blood: Narratives of belonging in families with daughters adopted from China. Unpublished PhD thesis, Institute of Education, University College London.

Roby, J. L. (2007). From rhetoric to best practice: Children's rights in intercountry adoption. *Children's Legal Rights Journal*, 27(3), 48–71.

Roby, J. L. (2012). Justice served? Restitution as a remedy in fraudulent Samoan adoption cases. Society for Cross-Cultural Research Annual Meeting, Las Vegas, NV.

Roby, J. L. & Maskew, T. (2012). Human rights considerations in intercountry adoption: The children and families of Cambodia and Marshall Islands. In J. L. Gibbons & K. S. Rotabi (Eds), *Intercountry adoption: Policies, practices, and outcomes* (pp. 55–66). Farnham: Ashgate Press.

Roosevelt, E. (2000). *Autobiography of Eleanor Roosevelt* (reprint ed.). Jackson, TN: DeCapo Press.

Roosevelt, E. (2001). *My day: The best of Eleanor Roosevelt's acclaimed newspaper columns 1936–1962*. New York: MJF Books.

Rotabi, K. S. (2012). Fraud in intercountry adoption: Child sales and abduction in Vietnam, Cambodia, and Guatemala. In J. L. Gibbons & K. S. Rotabi (Eds), *Intercountry adoption: Policies, practices, and outcomes* (pp. 67–76). Farnham: Ashgate Press.

Rotabi, K. S. & Bergquist, K. J. S. (2010). Vulnerable children in the aftermath of Haiti's earthquake of 2010: A call for sound policy and processes to prevent international child sales and theft. *Journal of Global Social Work Practice*. Retrieved from www.globalsocialwork.org/vol3no1/Rotabi.html

Rotabi, K. S. & Bunkers, K. M. (2011). In the era of reform: A review of social work literature on intercountry adoption. *Sage Open*. doi: 0.1177/2158244011428160. Retrieved from http://sgo.sagepub.com/content/early/2011/11/14/2158244011428160.full#aff-1

Rotabi, K. S., Armistead, L., & Mónico, C. C. (2015). Sanctioned government intervention, "misguided kindness," and child abduction activities of U.S. citizens in the midst of disaster: Haiti's past and its future as a nation subscribed to the Hague Convention on Intercountry Adoption. In R. L. Ballard, N. Goodno, R. Cochran, & J. Milbrandt (Eds), *The intercountry adoption debate: Dialogues across disciplines*. Newcastle upon Tyne: Cambridge Scholars Publishing.

Rusby, J. S. M. & Tasker, F. (2009). Long-term effects of British evacuation of children during World War 2 on their adult mental health. *Aging and Mental Health*, 13(3), 391–404.

Sachs, D. (2010). *The life we were given: Operation Babylift, international adoption, and the children of war in Vietnam*. Boston, MA: Beacon Press.

Sarri, R., Baik, Y., & Bombyk, M. (1998). Goal displacement and dependency in South Korean–United States intercountry adoption. *Children and Youth Services Review*, 20(1/2), 87–114.

Scheper-Hughes, N. (1990). Theft of life. *Society*, September–October, 57–62.

Scheper-Hughes, N. (1995). Organ stealing: Fact, fantasy, conspiracy, or urban legend? Paper presented at Securing Bodily Integrity for the Socially Disadvantaged: Strategies for Controlling the Traffic in Organs for Transplantation Conference, Bellagio, Italy.

Selman, P. (2009). The rise and fall of intercountry adoption in the 21st century. *International Social Work*, 52(5), 575–94. doi: 10.1177/0020872809337681

Selman, P. (2010, July). The global decline of intercountry adoption: Is this the beginning of the end? Paper presented at the 4th International Conference on Adoption Research, Leiden, Netherlands.

Selman, P. F. (2011). Intercountry adoption after the Haiti earthquake: Rescue or robbery? *Adoption & Fostering*, 35(4), 41–9.

Selman, P. F. (2012a). The global decline in intercountry adoption: What lies ahead? *Social Policy & Society*, 11(03), 381–97.

Selman, P. F. (2012b). The rise and fall of intercountry adoption in the 21st century: Global trends from 2001 to 2010. In J. L. Gibbons & K. S. Rotabi (Eds), *Intercountry adoption: Policies, practices, and outcomes* (pp. 7–28). Farnham: Ashgate Press.

Selman, P. F. (2013, July). One million children moving: The demography of intercountry adoption. Paper presented at the 4th International Conference on Adoption Research, Bilbao, Spain.

Selman, P. F. (2015). Global trends in intercountry adoption, 2003–2012. In R. L. Ballard, N. Goodno, R. Cochran, & J. Milbrandt (Eds), *The intercountry adoption debate: Dialogues across disciplines* (pp. 9–48). Newcastle upon Tyne: Cambridge Scholars Publishing.

Shubert, A. (2012, April 26). Stolen babies scandal haunts Spain. *CNN*. Retrieved from www.cnn.com/2012/04/25/world/europe/wus-spain-stolen-babies/index.html

Sibbel, B. C. (2006). Operation Babylift: A first-person narrative. In K. S. Stolley & V. L. Bullough (Eds), *The Praeger handbook of adoption, 1* (pp. 447–8). New York: Praeger.

Sixsmith, M. (2009). *The lost child of Philomena Lee: A mother, her son and a fifty-year search*. London: Macmillan.

Smolin, D. M. (2004). Intercountry adoption as child trafficking. *Valparaiso University Law Review*, 39, 281–325.

Smolin, D. M. (2006). Child laundering: How the intercountry adoption system legitimizes and incentivizes the practices of buying, trafficking, kidnapping, and stealing children. *Wayne Law Review*, 52, 113–200.

Smolin, D. M. (2011). The missing girls of China: Population, policy, culture, gender, abortion, abandonment, and adoption in East Asian perspective. *Cumberland Law Review*, 41(1), 1–65.

Subramanian, S. & Lee, D. J. (2011, October 19). China: Blackmarket babies. Retrieved from http://pulitzercenter.org/reporting/china-children-stolen-sold-orphanage-adoption

Taylor, L. (2009). *Polish orphans of Tengeru: The dramatic story of their long journey to Canada 1941–1949*. Toronto: Dundurn Press.

Teaching Eleanor Roosevelt Glossary. (n.d.). United States Committee for the Care of European Children. Retrieved from www.gwu.edu/~erpapers/teachinger/glossary/uscom.cfm

Telegraph. (2010, February 4). Haiti earthquake: Death toll reaches 200,000. Telegraph. Retrieved from www.telegraph.co.uk/news/worldnews/centralamericaandthecaribbean/haiti/7152315/Haiti-earthquake-death-toll-reaches-200000.html

United Nations. (2009). Guidelines for the alternative care of children. Human Rights Council, Eleventh Session Resolution 11/7. Retrieved from http://ap.ohchr.org/documents/E/HRC/resolutions/A_HRC_RES_11_7.pdf

US Agency for International Development. (1975). Operation Babylift report, 1975. Retrieved from Adoption History Project, http://darkwing.uoregon.edu/~adoption/archive/AIDOBR.htm

US Department of Defense. (1971). The Department of Defense report regarding children born out of wedlock in countries where U.S. Armed Forces are assigned. Retrieved from http://pages.uoregon.edu/adoption/archive/DoDstatement.htm

US Department of State. (2008). Summary of irregularities in adoptions in Vietnam. Retrieved from http://vietnam.usembassy.gov/irreg_adoptions042508.html

US Department of State. (2015, January 8). Additional information on the operation of the U.S.–Vietnamese Special Adoption Program. Retrieved from http://travel.state.gov/content/adoptionsabroad/en/country-information/alerts-and-notices/vietnam15-01-08.html

US District Court, Western District of Washington at Seattle. (2004). *Plea agreement: United States of America* v. *Lauryn Galindo*. Retrieved from www.pear-now.org/reference/USvsGalindoPlea.pdf

US Government. (2010). Fifth annual report to Congress on PL 109–95. World's vulnerable children. Retrieved from: http://pdf.usaid.gov/pdf_docs/PDACU307.pdf

US Government Accountability Office. (2005). Foreign affairs: Agencies have improved the intercountry adoption process, but further enhancements are needed. Publication No. GAO-06-133. Retrieved from www.gao.gov/new.items/d06133.pdf

US Institute for Peace. (2001). From madness to hope: The 12-year war in El Salvador. Report of the Commission on the Truth for El Salvador. UN Security Council, Annex, S/25500, 1993, 5–8. Retrieved from www.usip.org/files/file/ElSalvador-Report.pdf

Vich, J. (2013, July 8). Realities and imaginaries on the Chinese transnational adoption program. Paper presented at the Fourth International Conference on Adoption, Bilbao, Spain.

Volkman, T. A. (2005). *Cultures of transnational adoption*. Durham, NC: Duke University Press.

Vora, K. (2016, May). Contracting care: Indian commercial surrogacy as life support. Gujarat/Guatemala: Marketing care and speculating life. Ithaca, NY: Cornell University.

Weil, R. H. (1984). International adoptions: The quiet migration. *International Migration Review*, 18(2), 276–93.

Welcome House. (n.d.). Welcome House: A historical perspective. Retrieved from www.psbi.org/page.aspx?pid=384

Williamson, J. & Greenberg A. (2010). Families, not orphanages: Better Care Network working paper. Retrieved from http://bettercarenetwork.org/IAI/details.asp?id=23328&themeID=1003&topicID=1023

Willing, I., Kolbe, A. D., Golding, D., Holtan, T., Wolfgang, C., Allen, K. M., Chau, A., Sharp, L., & Nhat, M. (2015). *Vietnamese adopted: A collection of stories*. Melbourne: CQT Media and Publishing and Gazillion Strong.

Yngvesson, B. (2010). *Belonging in an adopted world: Race and identity in transnational adoption*. Chicago, IL: University of Chicago Press.

Young, A. (2012a). Choosing intercountry adoption: An Australian study of motivations and attitudes of intending and recent adoptive parents. *Australian Journal of Social Work*, 47(2), 221–41.

Young, A. (2012b). Developments in intercountry adoption: From humanitarian aid to market-driven policy and beyond. *Adoption & Fostering Journal*, 36(2), 67–78.

2

THE POLITICS OF ADOPTION FROM ROMANIA TO RUSSIA AND WHAT WE KNOW ABOUT CHILDREN LANGUISHING IN RESIDENTIAL CARE FACILITIES

FIGURE 2.1   Children play at a residential care institution fence
Source: Photo courtesy of Tony Bradley

Fundamentally, intercountry adoption is political when it comes to systems critique and reform. The response by politicians during times of crisis is not unlike the stereotypical "baby kissing" of political campaigns; there is arguably not a higher-profile opportunity for a politician to underscore his or her commitment to family life intersecting with poverty and doing the right thing as per the popular notion of what is "right" in terms of intervention. Adoption is exceptionally popular where notions of child rescue are the narrative, whereas adoption can be quite controversial in some countries such as South Korea, as we have already illustrated.

Two obvious cases from the former Soviet Union highlight the political dimensions underlying intercountry adoptions: Romania and Russia. The social and political forces of these countries interface with the West, with a complicated Cold War history and relatively new pressures related to the European Union in the case of Romania. For Russia, new conflicts in the post-Cold War era have complicated intercountry adoption relations. Beginning with Romania and then looking at Russia, the political forces are part of the story that combines with a somewhat parallel course of the emergence of empirical evidence about child development of those children living in institutional care. Greater awareness about the needs of institutionalized children has added fuel to the intercountry adoption phenomena.

Stalinist Policy: the case of Romania

Institutional care of children has long been a feature of the social system in Soviet Bloc countries including Romania, dating back to at least World War II. When President Nikolae Ceauşescu came to power in 1966, his vision included the Stalinist pronatalist idea that Romania's population and economic growth went hand in hand to achieve prosperity for a nation (Nedelcu & Groza, 2012). Because the birth rate was low, in 1966 the government issued Decree 770, outlawing abortion for women under 40 with fewer than four children. Women were required to give birth to at least five children, and Ceauşescu viewed children to be the property of the state. Ceauşescu reportedly proclaimed that "Anyone who avoids having children is a deserter who abandons the laws of national continuity" (Steavenson, 2014, p. 1).

Birth control was banned, and the birth rate began to climb, eventually doubling. Motherhood was seen as an obligation or duty to the state. Fundamentally, the growth of a proletariat population—those who would carry out the labor of the state in agriculture, factories, and so forth—was highly oppressive for all, with women bearing the burden to reach population targets. The struggle to meet the basic needs of their children was a real dilemma for Romanian parents. As a result, institutional care of children became a necessity. Ceauşescu's position was that the state could raise children better than the family, and in these care settings children could be socialized to carry out his Communist vision. Sadly, "social orphans" became a part of Ceauşescu's legacy—an unfortunate social norm of abandoning children to massive institutions emerged in this era. Those institutions at this time have been called "prison-like," and terms like "warehousing children" have been used to describe the abhorrent, miserable conditions.

By the mid- to late 1980s, the economic system began to fail undeniably, and while all Romanians were strongly affected, the most vulnerable to suffer were the children who were institutionalized with inadequate food, heat, and other basic necessities as they were confronted with bitter winters and other harsh conditions. As is the case with institutional living, the daily lives of the social orphans were highly regimented. Every major task was scheduled; children were often toileted all at the same time among other daily routines of eating, sleeping, and so on. The population of institutionalized children in Romania is estimated to have been at least 150,000 by the late 1980s. It is believed that over 16,000 of these children were dying annually as a result of treatable diseases (Groza, Illeana, & Irwin, 1999). While it cannot be verified because of inadequate records, it has been estimated that 50 percent or more of these children were Roma,[1] even though Romany people constituted less than 20 percent of Romania's population. This disproportionate number of Roma children living in state institutions was a product of not only a repressive social policy for all individuals and families, but also of a social environment in which the Romany people were marginalized and oppressed because they were considered to be mentally unfit and deviant (Steavenson, 2014).

As President Ceauşescu's rule came to a dramatic end with the revolution and his execution during the final days of 1989, the international media displayed shocking images of children languishing in state institutions (Nedelcu & Groza, 2012). The documentary evidence was startling as most of the children were suffering from a variety of medical and emotional conditions related to malnutrition and extreme neglect. Lack of physical and mental stimulation from nurturing and caretaking adults was common, and televised images included children tied to beds and other alarming images underscoring neglect (Ruggiero, 2007). Children rocking back and forth and even self-protecting in fetal positions from a lack of sensory and social stimulation was common (Beckett et al., 2002). Some of the conditions observed were psychotic, and failure to thrive was common as child growth and development were stunted (Ruggiero, 2007). International outrage erupted when the world suddenly learned of this particularly cruel aspect of Ceauşescu's brutal regime.

As a result, a new wave of international adoptions began almost overnight in 1990 at a time when Romania's adoption laws were ambiguous, at best (Nedelcu & Groza, 2012). People flew to Romania set on the idea of adopting with literally little or no planning, convinced that they could help. Most of those who adopted were individuals and couples from Western Europe, Canada, and the United States. From 1990–1 alone, an estimated 10,000–15,000 or more children from Romania were adopted internationally (Ruggiero, 2007). This period of hasty adoptions resulted in record keeping focused mainly on the age of the child at the time of adoption with no consistent documentation of medical and emotional needs. Thus records of race, ethnicity, or special needs of the children adopted are non-existent, and families departed Romania with little knowledge about their newly adopted child. Today, long-term outcomes of the children and their adoptive families scattered throughout the world have been called into question as international media has exposed troubling stories about children with exceptional special needs and their overwhelmed adoptive families (Ruggiero, 2007).

Table 2.1 indicates the total number of adoptions to US citizens as well as the age of the child at the time of adoption. These data were drawn from "orphan visa" record keeping by the US Department of State and indicate that adoptions from Romania began with at least 50 percent of those children leaving as infants in the first two years, and then there was a clear decline as there was a shift to children aged 1–4 years old, with a peak of 85 percent of such children in 1997.

The rapid and chaotic rise of international adoptions, at a high of 2,552 children adopted by US citizens alone in 1992, eventually led to serious problems or "irregularities" in Romania. For example, one couple from Britain was found leaving Romania with an infant who lacked the appropriate paperwork for adoption. The press followed the story vigorously as multiple questions were raised amid fears that people were simply leaving Romania with children—worries were that some had nefarious purposes of child trafficking. Other lesser known incidents during the early years included an American military family residing in Germany at the time. When this particular family attempted to return to the United States, the children's paperwork was inadequate for immigration and the family reportedly sent the children back to the institution in Romania.[2] These and other incidents related to poor and fraudulent practices in the early years were the result of a reckless time in Romania's adoption history. During those early years, it was not uncommon for prospective parents to personally walk through institutions to select children in a manner similar to choosing a product based on desirability of physical attributes, such as eye color. The problems were so severe that Romania's early child adoption activities resulted in the first shutdown of adoptions in 1991 (Nedelcu & Groza, 2012).

Reforms were based on new legislation,[3] and the system reopened in 1993. Romania continued to send children abroad as adoptees even as more scandals began to emerge that suggested that

TABLE 2.1 Total Romanian adoptions by US citizens 1990–2013 with age of child

Year	Total	% Male	% Female	% Age 0–1	% Age 1–2	% Age 3–4	% Age 5–12	% Age 13–17
1990	90	37	63	50	41		9	
1991	2552	46	54	56	39		5	
1992	145	51	49	32	54		14	
1993	88	50	50	9	63		27	
1994	197	39	61	13	57		30	
1995	260	45	55	12	70		18	
1996	554	49	51	8	84		8	
1997	558	47	53	3	85		12	
1998	388	45	55	10	76		15	
1999	611	53	47	20	49	17	12	3
2000	1119	50	50	27	42	16	14	2
2001	777	53	47	26	37	19	17	2
2002	169	42	58	1 child	45	17	30	8
2003	200	45	55	5	50	17	24	6
2004	57	39	61	1 child	36	49	11	4
2005	2		100				100	
2006	0							
2007	3	2 children	1 child				3 children	
2008	2			1 child			1 child	
2009	5	3 children	2 children				5 children	
2010	0							
2011	0							
2012	0							
2013	0							
2014	3	2 children	1 child		1 child			

Note: In 2005 a moratorium was instituted, and any adoptions thereafter are unusual cases.
Data from the United States are used as a representation of the age dynamics. While this is not a full picture of Romanian children being sent to other countries globally, these data are a good snapshot of the trends. Percentages across the years do not always equal 100 because of rounding.
Source: United States Department of State at www.adoption.gov and Ruggiero (2007)

many of the children were not really orphaned. US Embassy field investigations in 1994 uncovered "incidents where Romanian mothers believed that they were merely 'loaning' their children to foreign parents and not relinquishing them permanently" (Carro, 1994, p. 135). Even when it was questioned whether the exceptionally young children leaving Romania were appropriate for ICA, prospective parents continued to rush to adopt. However, in time Romanian ICAs became increasingly difficult and eventually impossible in most cases (Nedelcu & Groza, 2012).

Criticism of an adoption "marketplace" became increasingly common, and when Romania set forth to join the European Union, a new child-protection law was passed in order to be congruent with other EU state practices (Yemm, 2010). The new law included abolishing fees for adoption and established an 18-month residency period for prospective parents, effectively instituting a de facto moratorium. Cessation of sending children overseas as adoptees was sharply criticized in the United States and seen as reactionary rather than rational (Yemm, 2010); claims of undue pressure to keep adoptions open were lodged including comments from prominent members of the US Congress.

Reports from multiple congressional delegations that have resulted reinforce the notion of rescue and intercountry adoption as humanitarian intervention. Adoption fraud is largely ignored in these diplomatic interfaces in terms of public comments, a tactic that became common as US politicians began to make public remarks about adoptions in this region and elsewhere. However, change in Romania was underway and the political stance of the United States (and even pleadings of prospective adoptive parents whose cases were left in limbo) had little effect, except that the pro-American approach may have actually further inflamed the situation as Romania was moving forward to join the European Union.

With a new law in Romania came a shift to domestic foster care and adoption as internal solutions were sought. The gains in this area of domestic childcare systems development have been significant. Today a system of care has been developed and there are more opportunities for non-institutional care in Romania than ever before (Nedelcu & Groza, 2012). Although childcare institutions still exist, care solutions have shifted to other interventions such as foster care in which foster parents are trained and supported as a long-term placement for children in a family environment. Some of these children have gone on to become adopted by their foster families. Children who need care outside of their family have become a domestic priority as the country continues to strengthen its child-protection system and develop alternatives to residential care institutions.

Policies related to intercountry adoption certainly ebb and flow and, at the time of this writing, Susan Jacobs, who serves as the United States Global Ambassador for Children, was beginning discussions with Romania related to the possibility of a more liberalized policy related to intercountry adoption. Specifically, the United States has expressed its position that Romanian children should be allowed for adoption beyond the restrictions currently in place limiting the practice to Romanian citizens residing abroad (US Department of State, 2015). This position touches upon concerns about finding adoptive families for Roma children as discrimination still persists today (Roth & Toma, 2014). While there is no evidence of a shift in policy, at this time anything is possible as the political seas shift and change and pressure is applied to reopen intercountry adoptions from Romania to the US and beyond.

Russia: large-scale institutions, scandal, and significant shifts in adoption policy

Russia, like Romania, has a history of large childcare institutions (Schmidt, 2009). Also like Romania, Russia has been undergoing a shift away from large-scale institutional care of children to smaller group homes and foster care while child-protection policy and legislation have been strengthened (Agafonova, 2012; Mikhaylova, 2012; Spivak, 2012). However, those changes have been relatively slow and in 2011, at least 110,000 children were still living in state institutions in Russia (Al Jazeera, 2012). A very pointed moratorium imposed by Russia on adoptions by US families after years of controversy has now slammed the door on intercountry adoptions between the two nations. This change, occurring at the end of 2012, was dramatic. For the United States, Russian adoptions were a top source of children, with well over 50,000 children having been adopted by American families, and others going to Western Europe, Canada, and elsewhere (Al Jazeera, 2012; Dembosky, 2012; Selman, 2012). A variety of factors including poor practices and shocking deaths of adoptees are at the heart of the problems between the two countries. What went wrong?

Approximately six months prior to the moratorium, Russia's child rights ombudsman Pavel Astakhov spoke at the Russian–American Child Welfare Forum in Chicago (Rotabi, 2012). While at this meeting, Astakhov talked about the need for collaboration while addressing the diplomatic tensions between the two nations; he pointedly stated that intercountry adoptions and negotiations between Russia and the United States are not "political games" (Rotabi, 2012).

Astakhov, an attorney with celebrity status in Russia, is known to be provocative and often raises issues in a televised talk-show format. At times, he has lambasted the United States for the treatment of Russia's adoptees. Because Russia legally recognizes these children as retaining their citizenship combined with the obvious old tensions between the two countries, the controversy has taken on its own life in the Russian media.

At the Chicago forum, Astakhov was characteristically blunt as he underscored the 19 documented deaths of intercountry adoptees at the hands of US citizen parents. He said that these were the "official" numbers and that there were actually higher estimates made by human rights organizations in Russia. Even with such a negative framing of the Russia–US adoption scenario, Astakhov did say there was hope for new agreements and improved practices as a result of more stringent rules. Very shortly after this public commentary in the summer of 2012, the Russian parliament finally ratified a bilateral agreement crafted to improve adoptive placement practices, largely focusing on adoption agencies in the United States and strengthening practices as an enhanced prevention measure (Rotabi, 2012).

Interestingly, this ratification came after Astakhov's trip to the United States had resulted in added frustration. As child-rights ombudsman, he has repeatedly stated that he should be allowed to visit and check on Russian-adoptee health and well-being. The blocking of such action in the past had infuriated Astakhov as well as others back in Russia. Astakhov left Chicago on a trip to visit adoptees at a well-known and private residency-based rehabilitation program that caters to troubled Russian adoptees. He expected to gain entry to this facility called "The Ranch" in Montana; however, reportedly he was barred entry (Nehamas, n.d.). In Astakhov style, he was in the company of a Russian television news crew that captured him being denied access. In this provocative media moment, Astakhov questioned why children would be isolated from society and asked if this was some sort of detention facility—underscoring his view of a lack of transparency by the United States and raising the embedded human rights questions of removing children from society. In one news story about this incident, it was reported that Astakhov left the entrance of The Ranch and went to the local county attorney's office. It is not clear exactly what occurred there, and this particular local government official said that he refused to allow the encounter to be filmed because he "suspected a publicity angle." In the end, Astakhov has insisted that this particular treatment facility is a violation of child rights and he has demanded that the home be closed (Nehamas, n.d., p. 1).

It is impossible to know how this refusal to allow entry to an official of Russia influenced diplomatic matters, but it certainly did not help build good will or suggest any new environment of transparency in the treatment of Russian adoptees. When the word "moratorium" was applied to Russia–United States intercountry adoptions (Al Jazeera, 2012), it was a surprise. While Russia's parliament had periodically raised intercountry adoption problems in the past, this swift action was not predicted, especially given concerted diplomatic efforts to improve practices and soothe troubled relations. When President Vladimir Putin signed the new legislation, he made comments emphasizing his disgust at the intercountry adoption of Russian children to the United States. Responding to the fact that he was blocking thousands of children from better lives in the United States, Putin responded: "There are lots of places in the world where living standards are higher than they are here. And what? Are we going to send all our children there? Perhaps we should move there ourselves?" Putin also raised Israel as an example country that does not send its children abroad as adoptees, even in conditions of compromised security. The Israelis "always fight for their national identity," said Putin. "They form a single fist and fight for their language and their culture" (Al Jazeera, 2012). Raising national pride in this evocative manner when addressing intercountry adoption problems was new rhetoric for Putin, but not all that surprising as Russian nationalism has been a feature of his regime.

This particularly political moment of finally instituting a moratorium was a culmination of many years of problems, including a completely unrelated human rights abuse incident in Russia that resulted in the death of a prominent individual in a Russian prison in 2012. When the United States publicly condemned Russia for its treatment of this particular prisoner (a lawyer investigating tax fraud of Russian officials) and raised human rights concerns and prisoner treatment,[4] Russia was incensed. Russia's parliament moved swiftly. The adoption moratorium came when some Russian officials were publicly named and barred from travel visas to the United States due to tax fraud. Regardless of the cause of the political standoff, in the end the United States' criticism was seen as cavalier, given the number of deaths of Russian adoptees who most frequently died from head injuries and other conditions related to non-accidental causes (Hegar, Verbovaya, & Watson, 2015). The Russian media had been following those cases—questioning human rights—and what was perceived in Russia as a failure to prosecute abusive adoptive parents.[5] Tensions were high and those organizing against intercountry adoption in Russia seized upon an opportunity to move along their agenda for ICA moratorium[6] for the US when the strain between the two countries reached a peak.

Ironically, when Putin lashed out with his public commentary when signing the law, he stressed Israeli adoption policy as an exemplar. However, he failed to acknowledge that Russian children have been adopted by Israeli families for a number of years. Today, the practice still exists as a result of bilateral agreements with countries like Spain. In this case, it was a matter of controversy when Spain signed the new bilateral agreement that included a ban of gay individuals and same-sex couples from adopting. However, with this compromise came the reopening of adoptions between Spain and Russia in the spring of 2015 (San Román, personal communication, April 10, 2016). It should be noted that Russia's ban on gays and lesbians from adopting its citizen children is not unique. This discriminatory stance is the pervasive position globally as same-sex couples or individuals who are openly gay have been systematically barred from intercountry adoption, with minor exceptions such as Colombia (Davis, 2011; Briggs, 2012).

Looking back to understand the moratorium: four cases of Russian adoptees

Four cases of Russian–US adoptions with tragic outcomes are discussed in this chapter. The first is not the case of a death, but rather intense media coverage surrounding the rights of an adoptive child and family obligations once the child has been adopted. On April 8, 2010, seven-year-old Artyom "Justin" Saveliev, a Russian adoptee, was put on a plane in the US and sent, unaccompanied, to Moscow. Artyom had only a backpack to meet a waiting taxi driver at the Russian airport. Instructions to the driver were to take the child to the adoption authorities with a note that said:

This child is mentally unstable. He is violent and has severe psychopathic issues/behaviors. I was lied to and misled by Russian orphanage workers and director regarding his mental stability and other issues…After giving my best to this child, I am sorry to say that for the safety of my family, friends, and myself…I am returning him to your guardianship and would like the adoption disannulled.

(Banfield & Netter, 2010b)

The media frenzy that followed led to outcries for justice in both countries. As the story unfolded, we learned that the child's adoptive mother, Torry Hansen, was a professional nurse who lived in rural Tennessee, and her own mother (Artyom's adoptive grandmother) was also involved in the case. It is believed that the family did not seek help although it was ostensibly accessible; Tennessee-based Vanderbilt University has a respected clinic where the child could have received treatment for a range of problems and the family could have sought support.[7] According to the adoption agency that made the child placement, Hansen also did not request help and support from the case managers (World Association for Children and Parents, 2010). It also appears that the home-study provider (a separate organization), which approved Hansen's ability and readiness to parent, may have acted questionably as she was clearly not ready to parent this particular child; the required follow-up visits should have identified problems and a case plan should have been developed for a family in crisis. It is also not clear how this home-study provider was involved in Hansen's planning for another adoption. According to the media, Hansen was actively pursuing another adoption with a different agency to replace Artyom (Banfield & Netter, 2010a).[8] One may argue that the home-study provider should have been aware, to some degree, of the highly irregular scenario that was playing out.

Professionals in Russia have now said that Artyom was evaluated and he does not suffer from psychological problems as Hansen asserted—apparently the adoptive mother was afraid that the child may try to kill her (Banfield & Netter, 2010b). Fundamentally, it is impossible to know exactly what happened in this case, partly due to the political nature of the incident as well as legal liabilities, but clearly Hansen's actions placed the child's health and safety at serious risk and she was never held legally accountable for endangerment due in part to jurisdictional issues (Rotabi & Heine, 2010). However, Hansen has been court ordered by a Tennessee judge to pay child support for Artyom in the sum of US$150,000 (Hall, 2012), a legal precedent.

In the second case, a young child died in Virginia in 2008, and the neglect and then the legal outcome outraged many Russians concerned about intercountry adoption and their citizen children. Briefly, the toddler died of heat exposure; his father had forgotten him and left him in a car for nine hours during extreme summer heat. Charged with manslaughter, the child's adoptive father was found to be not guilty. The US press reported that the father, during hearings, was tearfully remorseful (Weingarten, 2009). The case left many in the United States wondering how a father could live with his negligence.

The sentence appeared to Russians to lack accountability, and the Russian press was very pointed and even sensationalist about the lack of a homicide sentence. This particular case was a bitter example of different perspectives on criminality and negligence. Most recently, in the closure/moratorium of Russian adoptions, this particular case has been pointed to as an example of human rights abuses against Russian children, acts of abuse that are perceived to lack the appropriate punishment for the adoptive parent when it comes to prosecution for wrongdoing. In fact, when the Russian parliament voted to cease adoptions to the United

States in late 2012, reportedly the bill was unofficially titled in this particular child's Russian name, Dmitri Yakovlev.

The third case, of extreme child exploitation and torture, is one of the most outrageous stories of intercountry adoption malpractices in the history of the United States. The sad case of Masha A. is actually an example of human trafficking that was heard when the young woman testified before a US Congressional Committee hearing on child pornography (US House of Representatives, 2006). Allen painfully recounted her horrific treatment at the hands of her "adopted" father Matthew Mancuso, who was called a "pedophile" in this testimony. Testimony revealed that adoption services failed to protect her from Mancuso. The home-study investigator failed to interview Mancuso's adult stepdaughter, who likely would have reported her own sexual abuse if the adoption home-study investigator had bothered to conduct such an interview. Sadly, Masha A. was failed throughout the process and the little girl kept wondering why no one came back to check on her. In the meantime, thousands of pornography images were circulated of the child as Mancuso profited from his illicit activities (US House of Representatives, 2006).

Sadly, in the first month of the US adoption shutdown in 2013, the Russians placed the name of a twentieth child who died in the home of his adoptive family. Maxim K. was a toddler who, according to his autopsy results in Texas, died as a result of abdominal injuries that were "self-inflicted" (Al Jazeera, 2013). Obviously, the media attention to this case—in Russia and the United States—highlighted again all of the problems and further agitated the political scenario playing out.

One element missing from the discourse is an honest discussion about what has gone wrong with Russian adoptions to the United States. Yes, in some cases agencies have acted irresponsibly, most especially in the egregious case of Masha A., and follow-up care has been inadequate in this and other cases. However, what has failed to be discussed publicly are the many physical and mental health problems of Russian adoptees in general (Hawk & McCall, 2011; Miller et al., 2006; Miller et al., 2007). For some children the problems are profound, and many adoptive families are ill-equipped to handle the special needs without significant and expensive professional help, including intensive mental healthcare that can require lengthy and residency-based treatment (Stryker, 2010).

Adoption dissolution: mental illness, rehoming, and Russian outrage

A remarkable case that unfolded after the Russian–US intercountry adoption moratorium accentuates a number of important issues about adoptee health and safety. In 2014, a New York couple filed a court request to dissolve their adoption of two children from Russia (Traster, 2014). The children, adopted at the ages of six and eight through two different US-based agencies, were thought to be siblings. Beginning family life with the hope that is characteristic of intercountry adoptions, the adopting couple was distressed to learn that the children had a range of psychological problems, reportedly stemming from sexual and other abuse in institutional care. After a DNA test, the children were determined not to be siblings and the couple began to question their adoption agencies and lack of care in their case. The couple, feeling overwhelmed and unprepared to care for the children began to fear for their own lives because of the children's extreme anger and violent behavior. They applied to a New York State court for adoption nullification. The children were reportedly placed in the care of state-funded mental health institutions for serious disorders as the case was deliberated. The couple claims the adoption agencies represented the children as "healthy and socially well-adjusted" (Traster, 2014, p. 1).

The judge overseeing the case took extraordinary steps to keep the case open to the public because he considered the information to be in the public interest. This step was resisted by the adoption agencies that requested closed hearings (Traster, 2014). The judge not only kept the case open, but the proceedings became quite provocative when the judge found that he had to address attempts by Russian authorities to intervene, in a manner that the judge considered to be intimidating. The *Daily Mail* of the UK began to follow the case, and one of the headlines captures the outrageous political turn the case took: "Kremlin agents 'intimidated' American couple trying to void adoption of 'dangerous' Russian children by contacting parents on unlisted phone number—leaving them in 'state of fear'" (Bates, 2014).

In this press piece, Astakhov once again had a stage on which to raise critical issues, including the problem of families rehoming children. This particular practice was attempted by this couple as they tried to "undo" their adoption by negotiating for someone else to take over care of the adopted children. Rehoming the children was struck down as a solution by the judge who said it was no different from child trafficking, and he banned such activity in his jurisdiction. According to the *Daily Mail*, Astakhov reportedly asked for immediate access to the children and raised the following points in the story (Bates, 2014):

- The children "remain two underage citizens of Russian Federation."
- They are protected by Russian laws. The Russian consul has a right to meet them, to access them.
- Russian authorities were not given access to their citizen children despite repeated attempts.

Astakhov also accused the adoptive parents of "covering their inconsistency by blaming the poor children, who have already been placed in a psychiatric clinic. This is despicable" (Bates, 2014, p. 1). Raising questions about the children's mental health diagnosis, Astakhov said that he considered the children to be labeled and imprisoned in mental institutions. Furthermore, reportedly Astakhov said: "They want not merely to surrender the children, they are seeking to cancel adoption, alleging the children's diagnoses were somehow concealed from them... This is utter nonsense." Finally, Astakhov said, "The American couple had a complete [adoption] dossier[9] on each child and had the right to consult any doctor. They could have sought additional medical opinions if they had wished" (Bates, 2014, p. 1).

With the skill of grandstanding as he interfaced with the media, Astakhov has never responded to any of the problems on the Russian side of the equation. Large-scale institutions and inhumane conditions are simply not a part of his open discourse about the problems that adoptees have experienced. Further, the high rate of fetal alcohol syndrome and other pre and perinatal exposures are simply silenced in Astakhov's commentary (Miller et al., 2006). The finger pointing is always at the United States rather than a self-reflective discourse about the multiple problems in Russia and the implications for children. However, the problems are well known, and many United States adoption professionals would quietly admit that they don't want to touch Russian adoptions and they seek children elsewhere. Russian adoptions have a reputation for children with serious special needs, in many cases, and a history of disruption and adoption dissolution. Combined with a notorious history of adoption fraud in which bribery is a known expectation in moving the paperwork along for the child's departure from the country (Pertman, 2001), Russian adoptions simply became a risky proposition for many adoption agencies. For example, it was not uncommon for prospective adoptive parents to travel into Russia with $10,000 USD in crisp $100 bills to bribe officials in the many links of the intercountry adoption chain.[10] Sometimes families are told that these are "expediting fees," but in reality cash transactions are always highly suspect in intercountry adoption scenarios. This unfortunate reality of hard cash changing hands, on such a large scale in Russia, has led some to question if the Russian mafia actually has connections to intercountry adoption. There is no conclusive evidence of this particular element of organized crime and even investigating such an allegation would be hazardous.

One area of evidence is the fact that many of the children who have been adopted from Russia have required extraordinary medical and psychological services (Miller et al., 2006, 2007). One United States adoption-agency director with a sole Russian program permanently closed his agency doors a number of years before the moratorium, even though his program was still viable. This director, a seasoned clinical social worker, said that it became clear to him that the Russians were sending the children with the greatest challenges abroad. He believed that many of the children who were identified to be good candidates for adoption were those that the institution directors simply wanted to be rid of—children with serious behavioral problems and thus the most difficult children to manage in an institutional setting. Privately, he reported that he simply no longer had the stomach for the multiple forms of corruption and poor practices in Russia. On ethical grounds, he quietly closed his agency and took up an interest in mental health treatment of adoptees experiencing difficulties in the United States.

Child-development research evidence and institutional childcare

In recent years, there has been an incredible shift in information about the health of children living in institutions, shedding light on the biological and environmental factors that contribute to psychosocial growth. Sensationalism and political activity aside, child adoption from Romania and Russia has resulted, to some degree, in important research on child development and the effects of institutionalization on children. Fundamentally, living in institutional care can cause lifelong and harmful effects on children's cognitive, socioemotional, and physical development (Bakermans-Kranenburg, Van IJzendoorn, & Juffer, 2008; Nelson, Zeanah, & Fox, 2007a). Evidence now indicates that children who are deprived of family care, living life in institutional settings like those found in Russia, Romania, and elsewhere, have seriously stunted growth patterns and some essentially stop growing and even die in this emotionally harsh environment.

Substantial research evidence has also demonstrated that the negative effects are more severe the longer children are in care and the earlier they enter care (Browne, 2009). Furthermore, there is a "sensitive period" that is a critical time in which a child must receive intimate emotional and physical contact (Nelson et al., 2007a, 2007b; Sonuga-Barke, Edmund, Kreppner, & Leiden Conference on the Development and Care of Children without Permanent Parents, 2012; Bakermans-Kranenburg et al., 2008). Sensory deprivation related to extreme neglect results in outcomes that are startling. Losses in physical growth, cognitive abilities, and the ability to attach to a caregiver are some of the concerns (Juffer & Van IJzendoorn, 2012; Pollak et al., 2010).

Critically important is the reciprocal relationship between a child and a caregiver. The interpersonal connection is essential in supporting brain development and emotional growth. A lack of caregiver–child connection for sustained periods is linked to attachment disorders, which have a range of symptoms related to a child's ability to form healthy relationships

(Howe, 2006; Roberson, 2006). Antisocial behavior is found in radical attachment disorder, a known problem among some previously institutionalized and later adopted children (Stryker, 2010). This most serious of attachment problems found in the disorder include significant behavioral problems such as poor impulse control and in the worst cases the desire to harm others (Howe, 2006; Roberson, 2006). The above legal case, in which the parents reported fearing for their own safety, is likely an example of radical attachment disorder.

Research also shows the detrimental effect that growing up in residential care has on people after they leave. Rates of suicide, depression, and unemployment are extremely high in young adults who leave residential care (Family Health International Children's Investment Fund & UNICEF, 2010). Furthermore, children who grow up in institutions are at a high risk for recruitment into human trafficking as they lack family support during adolescence and early adulthood years. In sum, the negative outcomes related to institutional care of children is damning, and this evidence enters the discourse when considering adoption policy, especially when large-scale institutions are a part of the equation. The children's recovery in the context of family life is particularly compelling and the evidence about a child languishing in an institution is clear—every day that a child languishes in care, more biological, psychological, and social function damage is the result.

For example, the reversibility of developmental delays found in institutionalized children was an important finding in the Bucharest Early Intervention Project. Institutionalized children were randomly assigned to ongoing standard care (remaining in an institution) or foster care at a mean age of 21 months. When tested at 54 months of age, children in foster care had significantly higher IQs (Nelson et al., 2007b). These investigations and others demonstrate the resilience of children, but also imply some limits to recovery. As a result, intervening with children is considered to be best and most effective earlier rather than later (Bakermans-Kranenburg et al., 2008), thereby creating a dilemma in how long children remain in care when an intercountry adoption placement may be immediately possible. Called the "time paradox" (International Reference Centre for the Rights of Children Deprived of Their Family, 2015), the issue of a timeline for due diligence in planning for family reunification (principle of subsidiarity) versus the importance of moving children out of institutional care as quickly as possible is a significant and persistent issue.

Conclusion

There may be nothing more compelling than children languishing in institutional care, especially considering the need for humane alternatives. Intercountry adoption is only one alternative that has historically served very few children who are in need of family-based care globally.[11] The fantasy of simply fixing the problem with an idyllic family life in a middle- to upper-class family in a high-resource country and the multiple forces at play are difficult grounds to navigate ethically. Then, when adoption fraud and poor practices rise up to a crisis point in these countries, or the countries to where the children are sent (e.g. rehoming children and child deaths in the US), the door inevitably faces closure as the system is reformed. The push and pull that results is a recurring story as each country unravels as a result of problems in practice. Sadly, children who are truly appropriate for intercountry adoption live with the negative consequences when the door closes to that opportunity.

Those who remain in institutional care have serious psychological and medical consequences that are far ranging for them personally, as well as for society as a whole. The implications for those families who adopt children with the resulting challenges can be profound, both positively and negatively. Each case is unique and some children are good matches for intercountry adoption while other children need alternatives that are socially just, with a commitment to a sense of family life as per their rights as children (Preamble, Convention on the Rights of the Child).

Russian Child Rights Commissioner Pavel Astakhov, who was featured prominently in this chapter, resigned from his post in July, 2016 amid controversy related to outrageous comments on television. Reportedly, in an opening question of a televised interview, Astakhov asked some young girls who had survived a drowning (in which other many other children died), "how was the swim?". Also, Astakhov is known to have legally supported a forced child marriage that resulted from the rape of a young girl. There have been other suggestions of wrongdoing across a rather questionable career. A quick scan of his Wikipedia entry also indicates a plagiarized dissertation for doctoral studies. Many in Russia and elsewhere see Astakhov as two-faced and only interested in attention seeking and political gain rather than a commitment to child rights. Today, he is now recognized to be a notorious lawyer and former public official with a highly questionable record (Savitskaya, 2016).

Notes

1 Roma people are frequently called "gypsies" as a pejorative term, indicating societal discrimination against the group.
2 Randy Barlow, an adoption professional with expert knowledge of military families in Europe, recounted this to the author as personal communication.
3 In June 1993, Romania passed the Judicial Declaration of Child Abandonment in which the Romanian Committee on Adoption was given a clear mandate, including oversight of adoptions rather than allowing prospective parents to select a child for adoption.
4 The Magnitsky Act was passed by the US Congress in 2012.
5 Some cases have been prosecuted with the outcome of incarceration while other cases have gone without a criminal investigation.
6 The moratorium was only placed on US adoptions. Other countries continued to negotiate their own bilateral agreements to secure their relationship with Russia.
7 Because this particular adoptive mother was a professional nurse, her background was a point of discussion quietly amongst adoption professionals. For example, did she seek care and still feel overwhelmed by the child? Just how much help did she ask for? Due to confidentiality, some of the answers remain unknown.
8 It should be noted that this particular child is not the first to be sent back to Russia without professional oversight of the process of adoption dissolution. However, this case resulted in press attention as the child's wellbeing was so clearly at risk.
9 A *dossier* is the detailed file of a child's social and medical history. The quality of information provided by Russia has never been questioned publicly for this case or any other. It is unlikely that Russia will concede to inadequate or poor records.
10 For many countries in Western Europe and elsewhere, citizens engaging in bribery overseas is illegal. For US citizens, federal law applies.
11 This is not only true today, but it was true when intercountry adoption was at an all-time high of 45,000 children being adopted globally in 2004.

References

Agafonova, N. (2012, June). Developing regional models of family care for orphaned and abandoned children: Krasnodar. Paper presented at the Second Russian–American Child Welfare Forum of the American Professional Society on the Abuse of Children Annual Colloquium, Chicago, Illinois.

Al Jazeera. (2012, December 28). Putin signs anti-U.S. adoption bill. Retrieved from http://m.aljazeera.com/story/20121228111918186278

Al Jazeera. (2013, March 2). Adopted Russian child's death "accidental". Retrieved from www.aljazeera.com/news/europe/2013/03/201332790559700.html

Bakermans-Kranenburg, M. J., Van IJzendoorn, M., & Juffer, F. (2008). Earlier is better: A meta-analysis of 70 years of intervention improving cognitive development in institutionalized children. *Monographs of the Society for Research in Child Development*, 73(3), 279–93.

Banfield, A. & Netter, S. (2010a, April 13). Mom in adoption scandal was trying for second child. *ABC News: Good Morning America*. Retrieved from http://abcnews.go.com/GMA/mom-russia-adoption-scandal-child/story?id=10358887

Banfield, A. & Netter, S. (2010b, April 12). Adopted boy sent back to Russia showing no signs of violent behavior, Russian officials say. *ABC News: Good Morning America*. Retrieved from http://abcnews.go.com/GMA/adopted-boy-back-russia-sign-mentan-issues-problems-officials/story?id=10349424

Bates, D. (2014, November 12). Kremlin agents "intimidated" American couple trying to void adoption of "dangerous" Russian children by contacting parents on unlisted phone number—leaving them in "state of fear". Daily Mail Online. Retrieved from www.dailymail.co.uk/news/article-2832038/Kremlin-agents-intimidated-couple-trying-void-adoption-Russian-children-contacting-unlisted-phone-number-leaving-state-fright.html

Beckett, C., Bredenkamp, D., Castle, J., Groothues, C., O'Connor, T. G., & Rutter, M. (2002). Behavioral patterns associated with institutional deprivation: A study of children adopted from Romania. *Developmental and Behavioral Pediatrics*, 23(5), 297–302.

Briggs, L. (2012). *Somebody's children: The politics of transracial and transnational adoption*. Durham, NC: Duke University Press.

Browne, K. (2009). The risk of harm to youth children in institutional care. Save the Children. Retrieved from www.kinnected.org.au/assets/resources/23.The_Risk_of_Harm.pdf

Carro, J. L. (1994). Regulation of intercountry adoption: Can abuses come to an end? *Hastings International and Comprehensive Law Review*, 121, 121–47.

Davis, M. A. (2011). *Children for families or families for children: The demography of adoption behavior in the U. S.* Rotterdam: Springer.

Dembosky, L. (2012, June). Opening plenary remarks: Department of State representative's response to the Russian Child Rights Commissioner. Presented at the Second Russian–American Child Welfare Forum at the American Professional Society on the Abuse of Children Annual Colloquium, Chicago, IL.

Family Health International Children's Investment Fund & UNICEF. (2010). Improving care options for children through understanding institutional child care and factors driving institutionalization. Family Health International. Retrieved from www.fhi.org/en/CountryProfiles/Ethiopia/res_eth_institutional_care.html

Groza, V., Illeana, D. F., & Irwin, I. (1999). *A peacock or crow? Stories, commentaries and interviews on Romanian adoptions*. Bedford, OH: Williams Custom Publishing.

Hall, K. M. (2012, July 13). Judge upholds child support in Russian adoption. *Associated Press*. Retrieved from http://bigstory.ap.org/article/judge-upholds-child-support-russian-adoption

Hawk, B. N. & McCall, R. B. (2011). Specific extreme behaviors of postinstitutionalized Russian adoptees. *Developmental Psychology*, 47, 732–8.

Hegar, R. L., Verbovaya, O., & Watson, L. D. (2015). Child fatality in intercountry adoption: What media reports suggest about deaths of Russian children in the US. *Children and Youth Services Review*, 55, 182–92.

Howe, D. (2006). Development and attachment psychotherapy with fostered and adopted children. *Child and Adolescent Mental Health*, 11(3), 128–34.

International Reference Centre for the Rights of Children Deprived of Their Family (2015). *Manifesto for ethical intercountry adoption*. Geneva: International Social Services.

Juffer, F. & Van IJzendoorn, M. H. (2012). Review of meta-analytical studies on the physical, emotional, and cognitive outcomes of intercountry adoptees. In J. L. Gibbons & K. S. Rotabi (Eds), *Intercountry adoption: Policies, practices, and outcomes* (pp. 175–86). Farnham: Ashgate Press.

Mikhaylova,V. (2012, June). Training and psychological support for foster families. Paper presented at the Second Russian–American Child Welfare Forum at the American Professional Society on the Abuse of Children Annual Colloquium, Chicago, IL.

Miller, L. C., Chan, W., Litvinova, A., Rubin, A., Comfort, K., Tirella, L., … Boston-Murmansk Orphanage Research Team. (2006). Fetal alcohol spectrum disorders in children residing in Russian orphanages: A phenotypic survey. *Alcoholism, Clinical and Experimental Research*, 30, 531–8.

Miller, L. C., Chan, W., Litvinova, A., Rubin, A., Tirella, L., & Cermak, S. (2007). Medical diagnoses and growth of children residing in Russian orphanages. *Acta Paediatrica*, 96, 1765–9.

Nedelcu, C. & Groza,V. (2012). Child welfare in Romania: Contexts and processes. In J. L. Gibbons & K. S. Rotabi (Eds), *Intercountry adoption: Policies, practices, and outcomes* (pp. 91–102). Farnham: Ashgate Press.

Nehamas, N. (n.d.). Russian official says Montana ranch abuses adoptees: Kremlin to ask U.S. to close rural home for troubled kids. *Latitude News*. Retrieved from www.latitudenews.com/story/pavel-astakhov-criticizes-ranch-for-kids-montana-adoption-russia/

Nelson, C. A., Zeanah, C. H., & Fox, N. A. (2007a). The effects of early deprivation on brain-behavioral development (pp. 197–218). In D. Romer & E. Walker (Eds), *Adolescent psychology and the developing brain: Integrating brain and prevention science*. New York: Oxford University Press.

Nelson, C. A., Zeanah, C. H., Fox, N. A., Marshall, P. J., Smyke, A. T., & Guthrie, D. (2007b). Cognitive recovery in socially deprived young children: The Bucharest Early Intervention Project. *Science*, 318, 1937–40.

Pertman, A. (2001). *Adoption nation: How the adoption revolution is transforming America*. New York: Basic Books.

Pollak, S. D., Nelson, C. A., Schlaak, M. F., Roeber, B. J., Wewerka, S. S., Wiik, K. L., Frenn, K. A., Loman, M. M., & Gunnar, M. R. (2010). Neurodevelopmental effects of early deprivation in postinstitution-alized children. *Child Development*, 81(1), 224–36.

Roberson, K. (2006). Attachment and caregiving behavioral systems in intercountry adoption: A review of the literature. *Children and Youth Services Review*, 28(7), 727–40. doi: 10.1016/j.childyouth.2005.07.008

Rotabi, K. S. (2012, October). The Second Russian-American Child Welfare Forum: Opening remarks of the Russian child rights commissioner about intercountry adoption, responses, and the spirit of child protection collaboration between the two nations. Retrieved from www.soc-mag.net/?p=994

Rotabi, K. S. & Heine, T. M. (2010). Commentary on Russian child adoption incidents: Implications for global policy and practice. *Journal of Global Social Work Practice*. Retrieved from www.globalsocial-work.org/vol3no2/Rotabi.html

Roth, M. & Toma, S. (2014). The plight of Romanian social protection: Addressing the vulnerabilities and well-being of Romanian Roma families. *International Journal of Human Rights*, 18(6), 714–34.

Ruggiero, J. A. (2007). *Eastern European adoption: Policies, practice and strategies for change*. New York: Aldine Transaction.

Savitskaya,Y. (2016, 4 July). Russia's Children's Right's Commissioner is stepping down but we'll remember him for these 7 things. Global Voices. Available from https://globalvoices.org/2016/07/04/russias-childrens-rights-commissioner-is-stepping-down-but-well-remember-him-for-these-7-things/

Schmidt,V. (2009). Orphan care in Russia. *Social Work and Society*. Retrieved from www.socwork.net/2009/1/special_issue/schmidt

Selman, P. (2012). The rise and fall of intercountry adoption in the 21st century: Global trends from 2001 to 2010. In J. L. Gibbons & K. S. Rotabi (Eds), *Intercountry adoption: Policy, practice, and outcomes* (pp. 7–28). Farnham: Ashgate Press.

Sonuga-Barke, Edmund, J. S., Kreppner, J., & Leiden Conference on the Development and Care of Children Without Permanent Parents. (2012). The development and care of institutionally reared children. *Child Development Perspectives*, 6, (2), 174–80.

Spivak, A. (2012, June). Main challenges in revising child protection legislation in Russia. Paper presented at the Second Russian–American Child Welfare Forum of the American Professional Society on the Abuse of Children Annual Colloquium, Chicago, IL.

Steavenson, W. (2014, December 10). Ceausescu's children. Guardian. Retrieved from www.theguardian. com/news/2014/dec/10/-sp-ceausescus-children

Stryker, R. (2010). *The road to Evergreen: Adoption, attachment therapy, and the promise of family life.* Ithaca, NY: Cornell University Press.

Traster, T. (2014, October 26). Couple wants to void adoption of "mentally ill" Russian orphans. New York Post. Retrieved from http://nypost.com/2014/10/26/li-couple-ask-judge-to-void-adoption-of-russian-children/

US Department of State. (2015). Statement of Ambassador Michele Thoren Bond, Assistant Secretary for Consular Affairs before the Senate Judiciary Committee on November 18, 2015. Retrieved from www.judiciary.senate.gov/imo/media/doc/11-18-15%20Bond%20Testimony3.pdf

US House of Representatives. (2006). Sexual exploitation of children over the internet: Follow-up issues to the Masha Allen adoption: Hearings before the Subcommittee on Oversight and Investigations of the Committee on Energy and Commerce of the House of Representatives, 109th Cong., Second Session. Retrieved from http://frwebgate.access.gpo.gov/cgi-bin/getdoc.cgi?dbname=109_house_hearings&docid=f:31471.pdf

Weingarten, G. (2009, March 8). Fatal distraction: Forgetting a child in a backseat of a car is a horrifying mistake. Is it a crime? Washington Post. Retrieved from www.washingtonpost.com/wpdyn/content/article/2009/02/27/AR2009022701549.html

World Association for Children and Parents. (2010). Child returned to Russia FAQs. Retrieved from www.wacap.org/LinkClick.aspx?fileticket=1XRPTkz9cnc%3d&tabid=36

Yemm, L. M. (2010). International adoption and the "best interests" of the child: Reality and reactionism in Romania and Guatemala. *Washington University Global Studies Law Review,* 9, 555–74.

3

POVERTY, BIRTH FAMILIES, LEGAL, AND SOCIAL PROTECTION

FIGURE 3.1   Mother and baby embrace in Guatemala
Source: Photo credit Karen S. Rotabi

To begin this discussion, it is important to understand that research into international birth families, as a group, is largely non-existent. Scholars and activists recognize that little empirical evidence exists on international birth mothers (Högbacka, 2014) and they are essentially "silenced" (Riben, 2007; Rotabi & Bunkers, 2011; Wiley & Baden, 2005). This assertion is made because there is limited literature that explores intercountry adoption from the birth-family perspective (Mónico, 2013); countless studies have focused almost exclusively on the positive child-development outcomes of intercountry adoption with a blind eye to the causes and consequences of the practice, particularly the family history of the child prior to adoption (Rotabi & Bunkers, 2011). Research carried out by proponents of adoption most frequently ignores the family of origin in their framing of intercountry adoption—almost as if the "orphanage" is the only source of a child without any consideration of the many ways in which a child enters the global adoption equation.

The research that is available, with strong empirical evidence about women in impoverished countries, includes three important studies in the Marshall Islands, in the Tamil region of India, and South Africa. These studies provide important insight into how birth mothers typically view ICA, specifically full-break adoptions in which no further contact is expected by the adopting family due to a legal child adoption decree that ceases legal rights between the biological family and the adoptee (Högbacka, 2014; Richards, 2014a). Before we turn to these studies and countries, we first consider birth mothers in the United States, because a downturn in the availability of healthy young children there as well as in Canada and Western Europe is an important part of the story that we have yet to tell.

What we know about birth mothers in the United States

Well over 10 million women in the United States have surrendered, or relinquished, their children for adoption (Day, 1994). Fessler (2006) carried out a series of important interviews with 100 US birth mothers and found disturbing practices in the time period of the adoptions reviewed. Called the "girls who went away," Fessler documented the shame and stigma of unplanned pregnancies, particularly for young and unwed mothers during a time that is now called the "Baby Scoop Era" which took place from 1945 to 1973 (Gailey, 2010; Quartly, Swain & Cuthbert, 2013[1]). These young women often found themselves sent to a home before their pregnancy became physically obvious. Frequently, they would live with other young women in similar circumstances. The time in the home and out of community sight was considered by many to be the best way to spare the mother and child the shame of an illegitimate birth. Fessler's interviews found significant levels of grief many years later as these women frequently felt taken advantage of and sometimes reported outright force, fraud, and coercion. Fessler presented multiple cases of questionable and fraudulent adoption "relinquishments"—that is, the legal agreement, upon the birth mother's consent and signature, for the child to enter into adoption. These accounts are consistent with cases of adoption fraud, carried out in "birth-mother homes" and other circumstances that have been exposed in investigations in the United States (Gailey, 2010). While some adoption agencies still house birth mothers, such as Gladney Child Adoption Services just outside of Dallas, Texas, the practice has changed as there is now greater awareness of adoption ethics, stronger laws, and a greater sense of self-determination and exercise of rights. While there are still abuses, women are now more able to act upon their own decision in a social context that is far more supportive of single or lone motherhood. And, when they do choose adoption as the best option, mental-health aftercare is theoretically available in many communities although this is variable with inconsistencies to include limited training of mental health professionals in grief associated with adoption loss.

The ability to exercise rights and self-determination was not the case for the women Fessler (2006) interviewed. She found that many birth mothers expressed feelings of shame, guilt, regret, doubt, anger, and helplessness after their child was adopted. The environment of secrecy and deceit as well as denial, blame, and uncertainty was a frequent story. These birth mothers, most of whom had been very young when they relinquished their infants, said they believed they had no choice but to surrender their children. Since unmarried mothers were generally shunned in the community—by birth fathers and their own families—they often felt that surrendering their infant to adoption was "what society demanded" (Fessler, 2006, p. 13). After the pregnancy, the young girls and women were expected to go back to their day-to-day lives and just forget the whole experience. They were expected not to speak of the ordeal and to pretend as if nothing happened—they simply went away. Today, we know that the resulting trauma was significant, and many women have longed to know about the well-being of their child. Quite simply, unresolved grief is a common experience for many birth mothers (De Simone, 1996; Gailey, 2010). Some mothers have found that the opportunity to finally meet their child has been a source of comfort, and reunions are more and more common. However, many women never really reconcile their experience or meet their child (Riben, 2007).

Today, domestic adoptions of infants in the United States are extremely expensive, often arranged by private attorneys who have been known to charge US$50,000 and more. Of course, this fee for adoption underscores the scarce supply of healthy infants in what has been called a "marketplace" or "industry" (Freundlich, 2000; Riben, 2007). This "shortage" of infants for adoption dates back to the 1970s (Landes & Posner, 1978) and has been a significant factor in the United States. As we discussed in Chapter 1, it coincides with the availability of contraceptives, especially the birth–control pill as well as legalization of abortion. As the availability of young and healthy children changed, and there was a greater consciousness of institutionalized children due to media coverage of the massive Romanian institutions in the late 1980s and the "abandoned girls" of China, the shift to these and other countries to meet the need began (Richards, 2014b).

Finally, it is important to identify that today the US women who most frequently relinquish their infants into adoption are college students who recognize that timing for motherhood is the problem; often they want to finish their education and pursue career and other opportunities available to them (McRoy, as discussed in Rotabi, 2014). Their plan for adoption is characterized by a high level of self-determination, in total contrast to the women Fessler (2006) interviewed. Times have changed, and women are exercising a great deal of autonomy over their decision making as they consider their future with an unplanned pregnancy. In addition, although we are not looking at birth fathers here (as they are even more invisible than birth mothers), they, too, have begun to increasingly exercise their own autonomy with far greater involvement in the adoption decision today (Coles, 2011).

Just as many prospective adoptive parents have turned to impoverished countries to seek healthy young children, now we will look at research that has been carried out in adoptions in the Marshall Islands, India, and South Africa.

Marshall Islands

After a series of illegal acts and ICA scandals were reported, Roby and Matsumura (2002) carried out important and ground-breaking research in the Marshall Islands, a Pacific island nation with small clusters of people living in communities with strong family networks and traditional life and culture. Interviews were carried out with 73 birth mothers in 2001. Most of the mothers in the sample had other children. Importantly, relinquishment decisions were found to be financial; mothers reported they had no means of support for ordinary care of the child. The roles of grandmothers were also considered, and it was found that they were often helping with childcare. A significant number of birth mothers reported that they experienced pressure from their own mothers to relinquish the child into ICA to relieve some of the caregiving burden in large families.

Roby and Matsumura (2002) state that these dynamics took place in communities with high birth rates and limited social services. Financial assistance in the form of food or subsistence payments is essentially non-existent in the island nation. Furthermore, abortion services are not available because abortion is illegal. These factors were complicating reasons for relinquishment; ultimately poverty and the related social forces, combined with a lack of government support services, were the social context that framed birth-mother decisions.

Roby and Matsumura's (2002) observations include cultural conceptions related to the continuity of the parent–child relationship. Fundamentally, child adoption does not terminate the relationship in Pacific Islander culture, because informal care in the Marshall Islands has existed for centuries to meet the needs of orphaned and vulnerable children within the extended family and kin group. Roby and Matsumura found that birth mothers often believed that their child would return at the age of maturity and the child was viewed as a link or bridge between two families. In a collectivist society, the child may even be viewed as a "gift" to the new family. In reciprocity, the act of "giving a child" would provide for and help the birth family financially, resulting in a particularly complicated ethical dilemma when this concept is applied to ICA. In Roby and Matsumura's (2002) study, the authors posed the question "If I give you my child, aren't we family?" and this question reverberates throughout all of the research with birth families. This idea of "gift child" clashes with international standards of practice when money is exchanged (above and beyond ordinary fees) to encourage the adoption. Adoption ethics, in general, are framed to prevent the sales of children into adoption, including the use of incentives for birth-mother relinquishment (Babb, 1999). Incentives may be at the immediate time of decision making about the future of the child (time of relinquishment), but also may include promises of financial support in the future. Such promises may include remittances (which may include pledges to give scholarships to the adopted child's siblings left behind, etc.). As we continue in our discussion, the idea of a gift or "gift child" arises in later chapters related to global surrogacy and ideas of reciprocity.

Tamil region of India

Pien Bos (2007) carried out ethnographic research in the Tamil region of India, an investigation taking place over two years and including interviews with birth mothers and others involved in the adoption transaction. Her in-depth research found that the shame and discrimination related to children being born out of wedlock, combined with extreme poverty in a traditional society, were important factors that ultimately led to child intercountry adoptions (Bos, 2007). As has been the case elsewhere, birth mothers in this region of India did not see the mother–child relationship being terminated, and their hope was for a continued familial relationship.

It is also important to point out that Bos (2007) found that birth-mother homes were a part of the story for some of the women interviewed. Like the women in earlier times in the United States, Bos found women who reported coercion in the relinquishment process with the home administrators exerting a great deal of pressure for the signature that is necessary for child relinquishment. For example, Bos (2007, p. 143) described the following case in southern India.

> When Rekha [birth mother] delivered a healthy young baby boy, she immediately changed her mind. Since she has two daughters but no son, she wanted to keep this baby instead of relinquishing him…She had approached the social worker of the non-governmental organization [arranging the adoption] to discuss reversing her decision but the outcome of this meeting was disappointing for Rekha. In her words, the social worker "shouted at her" and made it clear that she could not rescind on the relinquishment that she had already agreed to. Soon after this debacle, Rekha left the institution, according to her room mate, crying, upset, and empty handed.

The boy preference was another important finding in Bos' (2007) study as she reported that married Indian couples were also relinquishing girl infants into adoption because they only wanted a son.

South Africa

In another ethnographical study, Högbacka (2012) interviewed 32 Black South African women who had relinquished children into the ICA system. Looking at the trade-offs and dilemmas that birth mothers face, Högbacka points out that previous research indicates that "maternal commitment is contingent on the particular social and economic circumstances" (p. 143–4). She frames maternal commitment as being consistent with evolutionary theory and the principle of survival of the fittest. As follows, when a mother perceives a child as being weak and unlikely to survive, there is a maternal ambivalence and/or a maternal withdrawal. Högbacka explored this idea when asking women about their motivations to relinquish a child into adoption under difficult social conditions. Högbacka found this ambivalence to be complex as related to intercountry adoption. In her findings, Högbacka identified that:

> In the South African context, the high value placed on children along with the importance of the extended family and traditional child fosterage, all influence the meanings of child relinquishment. As a large number of children do not live with their birth mothers all the time or are raised by kin or non-kin at some point, adoption tends to be viewed not as a permanent erasing of ties. Most of the birth mothers I interviewed saw inter-country adoption as a way to provide their children with better opportunities. It will be shown that for many, motherhood does not end with the relinquishment of the child.
>
> (Högbacka, 2012, p. 144)

Högbacka also found that most of the birth mothers she interviewed lived in extreme poverty, and problems like homelessness were a reality for many of them. "Everyday life was a matter of survival" (p. 147), and the basic necessities were the focus of day-to-day living in an environment where unemployment is common and malnutrition is rampant. Under these circumstances, most women reported that they did not see any option other than adoption as there were no temporary care measures available. In addition, they did not see the adoption as a complete legal break, as they longed to be reunited, hoping for the child to remain in contact. As a result, these mothers and the larger biological family are vulnerable to misunderstandings and a wide range of illicit activities in the ICA transaction. Fundamentally, the idea of a "clean break" adoption that is promoted in the Global North is largely incongruent with traditional and collectivist societies in the Global South as the idea of a total severance of the child's tie to their family group (the blood tie) is simply not a concept (Richards, 2014a; Högbacka, 2014).

Protections: international private law

In all of these country case examples, the birth mothers' position has been that of vulnerable women living in extreme poverty with little or no social support, including no government subsistence in times of unemployment and crisis (Högbacka, 2014). As such, inherent issues of social justice have been identified related to the intersection of privilege and poverty (Fronek, Cuthbert, & Willing, 2015; Hollingsworth, 2003; Quarty et al., 2013; Roby, Rotabi, & Bunkers, 2013), and birth mothers and biological families must have special protections given their vulnerability to exploitation—including child sales and abduction into intercountry adoption (Ballard, Goodno, Cochran, & Milbrandt, 2015; Briggs & Marre, 2009; Rotabi & Gibbons, 2012; Selman, 2000).

The Hague Convention on Intercountry Adoption

The 1993 Hague Convention on Protection of Children and Co-operation in Respect to Intercountry Adoption (henceforth referred to as the Hague Convention on Intercountry Adoption or simply the HCIA) was developed and established to provide social protections for orphaned and vulnerable children and their families who interface with intercountry adoption (Hague Conference on Private International Law, 1993, 2008). The best interests of the child is a guiding principle, as identified in the Preamble, and as Goodno (2015) points out, the Hague Convention has three main objectives, identified in Article 1:

1. safeguards principle: [which] is necessary to prevent the abduction, sale of, and traffic in children;
2. co-operation principle: [requiring] effective co-operation between…[contracting states] to ensure that safeguards are applied effectively; and
3. competent authorities principle: [requiring] only competent authorities, appointed or designated in each State, [to] be permitted to authorise intercountry adoptions.

(Goodno, 2015, p. 218)

The best interests of the child are of paramount consideration (Cantwell, 2014) and fundamentally, the HCIA intent is to prevent child trafficking into intercountry adoption within a child-rights approach to care that clearly acknowledges the strengths of the family, kin group, and community of origin and their inherent capacities to care for their children (Hague Conference on Private International Law, 1993, 2008).

Currently, just over 90 countries have ratified the Convention. More than 20 years after the initial agreement, scholars in social work, law, child development, psychology, and other fields have given considerable attention to the HCIA and its implications (Ballard et al., 2015; Fong & McRoy, 2015; Gibbons & Rotabi, 2012; Freundlich, 2000; Roby, 2007; Selman, 2000;

Smolin, 2006, 2010). Although criticism has been lodged about the Convention and the significant changes that have occurred since 1993 (e.g. see Bartholet, 2015), the vast majority of experts agree that international regulation was necessary to address illicit adoption practices while recognizing both the strengths and weaknesses of ICA (Ballard et al., 2015; Briggs & Marre, 2009; Gibbons & Rotabi, 2012; Selman, 2000).

The vision of those who developed the Hague Convention on Intercountry Adoption

Duncan (2000), one of the lawyers involved in some of the earliest work related to the development of the HCIA, points out that there were "four hopes" in the inception of the international private law. The Convention would:

1. Contribute to the elimination of various abuses that have been associated with ICA, such as profiteering and bribery, the falsification of birth documents, coercion of biological parents, the intervention of unqualified intermediaries, and the sale and abduction of children.
2. Bring about a more "child-centered" approach within ICA, so that the process would focus less on finding a suitable child for a childless couple and more on finding a suitable family for a child.
3. Improve the situation from the point of view of the prospective adopters, for whom lack of regulation and the absence of clear procedures were leading to delays, complications, and often considerable costs.
4. Bring about the automatic recognition in all Contracting nations of adoptions made in accordance with the Convention and thus avoid the legal limbo of non-recognition in which many children who are subjects of ICA have found themselves in the past.

(Duncan, 2000, pp. 46–7)

Moving forward, we will consider these issues identified by Duncan in case examples, including systems of care to support children and families and other issues relevant to the best interests of the child while underscoring practical application of the HCIA.

A closer look at key elements for implementation of the Hague Convention on Intercountry Adoption

The HCIA requires member countries to adhere to the principle of the best interests of the child. Social protections must include the right of a child to remain within his or her birth family, and when that is not possible, kinship care and other forms of alternative care are to be explored with a commitment to domestic adoption in cases that are logical for an adoption plan (Cantwell, 2014; Richards, 2014a; Hague Conference on Private International Law, 2008). Then, when these options have been diligently explored, a child may be deemed appropriate for intercountry adoption and listed as available by their nation's central authority overseeing child welfare and adoption policy and practice. This continuum of care is called the *principle of subsidiarity* and the Hague Convention specifically states that measures should be taken "to enable the child to remain in the care of his family of origin" when possible

(Preamble, Paragraph 2; Hague Conference on Private International Law, 2008). The necessary steps to meet this end begin with family preservation as described above and then, as necessary, transitioning over to other appropriate childcare practices in the community prior to determining that intercountry adoption is the best plan for a particular child—in other words, only when ICA is in the best interests of the child.

In order to carry out an assessment of each child's best interests, a thorough social history assessment must be carried out by competent authorities/social workers who are unbiased and their salaries *cannot* be contingent on the completion of an intercountry adoption (Hague Conference on Private International Law, 2008). Adequate field investigation in the assessment process includes looking for the family of origin and exploring the nuclear and extended family's ability to and interest in intervening (Rotabi, Pennell, Roby, & Bunkers, 2012). Then, expanding the circle, the greater community should be looked to as a resource for childcare solutions, including the kinship group identified through interviews in the casework process. This kinship aspect of care planning is particularly important in collectivist and tribal societies with various traditions of informal care and child guardianship (Pennell & Anderson, 2005).

Such a process prevents fast tracking a child into intercountry adoption without due diligence to meeting the child's needs within her own family, community, and country (Rotabi et al., 2012). This continuum of care is called the principle of subsidiarity in the HCIA. The process is safeguarded with oversight by each country's central authority, including requirements for financial transparency in which only reasonable and professional fees may be charged for adoption services (Hague Conference on Private International Law, 2008). When there is evidence of illicit adoption practices (child sales and/or abduction), member nations are expected to intervene appropriately with adequate administrative and legal responses, including international collaboration in case resolution in a manner that is supportive of the best interests of the child (Hague Conference on Private International Law, 2008). Such collaboration is an example of harmonizing practices between two signatory countries—acting in unison and within compatible legal systems on behalf of the best interests of the child (Boéchat, 2013).

Fundamentally, the idea is that the HCIA provides a framework by which ratifying countries may align their laws for cooperation and collaboration (Boéchat, 2013). Each country institutes domestic law and policy to ensure HCIA compliance, such as the US Intercountry Adoption Act of 2000, and this particular level of policy implementation is oriented to the autonomy of the state. Guidance from the HCIA is used to construct congruent laws, policies, and procedures which are reflective of contextual realities (Rotabi & Mónico, 2015). Aligning policy and practices across countries has been tremendously important and one can point to the imperfections in various countries—we explore some of these problems in the coming chapters.

Overall, the HCIA is paradigm changing in a way that allows for a universal and more rigorous response to illicit adoption practices that are now defined and new dialogues about adoption ethics and best practices have emerged (Fong & McRoy, 2015; Ballard et al., 2015; Briggs & Marre, 2009; Gibbons & Rotabi, 2012; Roby, 2007; Selman, 2000). Global adoption systems have been developing, aligning with international expectations to improve practices and cease illicit practices to prevent child trafficking into intercountry adoption. All of this must be carried out in a manner that advances the best interests of the child (Cantwell, 2014).

Hague Convention intersections with the Convention on the Rights of the Child

The HCIA used a foundation principle of the Convention on the Rights of the Child (CRC), sharing the core value of the best interests of the child principle (Cantwell, 2014; UNICEF, n.d.). Specifically, Article 3 of the CRC states that "The best interests of children must be the primary concern in making decisions that may affect them. All adults should do what is best for children. When adults make decisions, they should think about how their decisions will affect children. This particularly applies to budget, policy and law makers" (UNICEF, n.d.).

The CRC was developed as intercountry adoption problems in Latin America were becoming pronounced in the 1980s (Altstein & Simon, 1991; Herrmann & Kasper, 1992). Drawing upon the concerns that were being identified at this time, specific articles of the CRC, beyond the best interests of the child principle and directly related to intercountry adoptions are in Table 3.1 (UNICEF, n.d.).

There is also an Optional Protocol for the Sale of Children, Child Prostitution, and Child Pornography that gives further consideration to the ways in which children are trafficked (Roby & Maskew, 2012) and that particular instrument is discussed as we conclude in Chapter 10.

As we consider obligations to protect the vulnerable, particularly the rights of the child to enjoy protection in her community with respect for family life, the obligations of the HCIA will be further discussed in the following chapters in which practical implementation is considered and illustrated in country examples. The case of birth mothers and their rights to counseling and informed consent is found in the next chapter about Guatemala and system reform. Then, in Africa we look at other dimensions related to countries that have not signed the convention and the exponential rise in adoptions from the continent in recent years.

TABLE 3.1 Convention on the Rights of the Child: Articles most directly related to intercountry adoption

Article 7: Every child has the right to a name, a nationality, and to know and be cared for by her or his parents.

Article 8: Every child has a right to preserve her or his identity, including nationality, name, and family relations.

Article 9: Children cannot be separated from their parents against their will, except when competent authorities determine it to be in the child's best interests.

Article 11: Governments have a responsibility to protect children against illegal separations or adoptions.

Article 20: Children who are deprived of their family must receive alternative care with due regard to the child's ethnic, religious, cultural, and linguistic background.

Article 21: Governments have a responsibility to make sure that all rules and processes involving adoption are respected, and to make sure that there are protections against selling or kidnapping children.

Article 35: Parties shall take all appropriate national, bilateral, and multilateral measures to prevent the abduction of, the sale of, or traffic in children for any purpose or in any form.

Source: Author's own research

Note

1 These authors present similar dynamics that took place, in parallel, in Australia.

References

Altstein H. & Simon R. J. (1991). *Intercountry adoption: A multinational perspective*. New York: Praeger.

Babb, L. A. (1999). *Ethics in American adoption*. New York: Praeger.

Ballard, R. L., Goodno, N., Cochran, R., & Milbrandt, J. (Eds), (2015). *The intercountry adoption debate: Dialogues across disciplines*. Newcastle upon Tyne: Cambridge Scholars Publishing.

Bartholet, E. (2015). The Hague Convention: Pros, cons and potential. In R. L. Ballard, N. Goodno, R. Cochran, & J. Milbrandt (Eds), *The intercountry adoption debate: Dialogues across disciplines* (pp. 239–44). Newcastle upon Tyne: Cambridge Scholars Publishing.

Bartholet, E. & Smolin, D. M. (2012). The debate. In J. L. Gibbons & K. S. Rotabi (Eds), *Intercountry adoption: Policies, practices, and outcomes* (pp. 233–51). Farnham: Ashgate Press.

Boéchat, H. (2013, July). The grey zones of intercountry adoption: Where adoptability rules are circumvented. Paper presentation at the Fourth Intercountry Adoption Research Conference, Bilbao, Spain.

Bos, P. (2007). Once a mother: Relinquishment and adoption from the perspective of unmarried mothers in south India. Doctoral dissertation, Nijmegen University. Retrieved from http://dare.ubn.kun.nl/bitstream/2066/73643/1/73643.pdf

Briggs, L. & Marre, D. (2009). *International adoption: Global inequalities and the circulation of children*. New York: New York University Press.

Cantwell, N. (2014). The best interests of the child in intercountry adoption. Florence: UNICEF Office of Research. Retrieved from www-prod.unicef-irc.org/publications/pdf/unicef%20best%20interest%20document_web_re-supply.pdf

Coles, G. (2011). *Invisible men of adoption*. Melbourne: Book Pod.

Day, P. (1994). *A new history of social welfare*. Englewood Cliffs, NJ: Perdue University.

De Simone, M. (1996). Birth mother loss: Contributing factors to unresolved grief. *Clinical Social Work Journal*, 24(1), 65–76. doi:10.1007/BF02189942

Duncan, W. (2000). The Hague Convention on Protection of Children and Co-operation in Respect to Intercountry Adoption: Its birth and prospects. In P. F. Selman (Ed.), *Intercountry adoption: Developments, trends and perspectives* (pp. 40–52). London: British Association for Adoption and Fostering.

Fessler, A. (2006). *The girls who went away: The hidden history of women who surrendered children for adoption in the decades before Roe v. Wade*. New York: Penguin.

Fong, R. & McRoy, R. (2015). *Transracial and intercountry adoptions: Cultural guidance for professionals*. New York: Columbia University Press.

Freundlich, M. (2000). Market forces: The issues in international adoption. In M. Freundlich (Ed.), *Adoption and ethics* (pp. 37–66). Washington, DC: Child Welfare League of America.

Fronek, P., Cuthbert, D., & Willing, I. (2015). Intercountry adoption: Privilege, rights and social justice. In R. L. Ballard, N. Goodno, R. Cochran, & J. Milbrandt (Eds), *The intercountry adoption debate: Dialogues across disciplines* (pp. 348–65). Newcastle upon Tyne: Cambridge Scholars Publishing.

Gailey, C. W. (2010). *Blue-ribbon babies and labors of love*. Austin: University of Texas Press.

Gibbons, J. L. & Rotabi, K. S. (Eds). (2012). *Intercountry adoption: Policies, practices, and outcomes*. Farnham: Ashgate Press.

Goodno, N. L. (2015). The Hague: An endless balancing act on preventing intercountry adoption abuses and finding permanent homes for orphans. In R. L. Ballard, N. Goodno, R. Cochran, & J. Milbrandt (Eds), *The intercountry adoption debate: Dialogues across disciplines* (pp. 207–29). Newcastle upon Tyne: Cambridge Scholars Publishing.

Hague Conference on Private International Law. (1993). Convention of 29 May 1993 on Protection of Children and Co-Operation in Respect of Intercountry Adoption. Retrieved from www.hcch.net/index_en.php?act=conventions.text&cid=69

Hague Conference on Private International Law. (2008). The implementation and operation of the 1993 Hague Intercountry Adoption Convention: Guide to good practice. Retrieved from www.hcch.net/upload/wop/ado_pd02e.pdf

Herrmann K. J. & Kasper B. (1992). International adoption: The exploitation of women and children. *Affilia*, 7, 45–58.

Högbacka, R. (2012). Maternal thinking in the context of stratified reproduction: Perspectives of birth mothers from South Africa. In J. L. Gibbons & K. S. Rotabi (Eds), *Intercountry adoption: Policies, practices, and outcomes* (pp. 143–59). Farnham: Ashgate Press.

Högbacka, R. (2014, December). Intercountry adoption, countries of origin and biological families. ISS Working Paper Series/General Series, 598, 1–23. Retrieved from http://repub.eur.nl/pub/77406

Hollingsworth, L. D. (2003). International adoption among families in the United States: Considerations of social justice. *Social Work*, 48(2), 209–17.

Landes, E. M. & Posner, R. A. (1978). The economics of the baby shortage. *Journal of Legal Studies*, 7, 323–48.

Mónico, C. (2013). Implications of child abduction for human rights and child welfare systems: A constructivist inquiry of the lived experience of Guatemalan mothers publically reporting child abduction for intercountry adoption. Doctoral dissertation. Retrieved from VCU Digital Archives, Electronic Theses and Dissertations, http://hdl.handle.net/10156/4373

Pennell, J. & Anderson, G. (2005). *Widening the circle: The practice and evaluation of family group conferencing with children, youths, and their families*. Washington, DC: NASW Press.

Quartly, M., Swain, S., & Cuthbert, D. (2013). *Market in babies: Stories of Australian adoption*. Melbourne, Australia: Monash University Publishing.

Riben, M. (2007). *The stork market: America's multi-billion dollar unregulated adoption industry*. Dayton, NJ: Advocate.

Richards, S. (2014a, December). HCIA implementation and the best interests of the child. ISS Working Paper Series/General Series, 597, 1–22. Retrieved from http://repub.eur.nl/pub/77407

Richards, S. (2014b). Stories of paper and blood: Narratives of belonging in families with daughters adopted from China. Unpublished PhD thesis, Institute of Education, University College London.

Roby, J. L. (2007). From rhetoric to best practice: Children's rights in intercountry adoption. *Children's Legal Rights Journal*, 27(3), 48–71.

Roby, J. L. & Maskew, T. (2012). Human rights considerations in intercountry adoption: The children and families of Cambodia and Marshall Islands. In J. L. Gibbons & K. S. Rotabi (Eds), *Intercountry adoption: Policies, practices, and outcomes* (pp. 55–66). Farnham: Ashgate Press.

Roby, J. L. & Matsumura, S. (2002). If I give you my child, aren't we family? A study of birthmothers participating in Marshall Islands–U.S. adoptions. *Adoption Quarterly*, 5(4), 7–31.

Roby, J. L., Rotabi, K. S., & Bunkers, K. M. (2013). Social justice and intercountry adoptions: The role of the U.S. social work community. *Social Work*, 58(4), 295–303. doi: 10.1093/sw/swt033

Rotabi, K. S. (2014, December). Force, fraud, and coercion: Bridging from knowledge of intercountry adoption to global surrogacy. ISS Working Paper Series/General Series, 600, 1–30. Retrieved from http://hdl.handle.net/1765/77403

Rotabi, K. S. & Mónico, C. (2015). Intercountry adoptions: Legal and policy issues affecting adoption practice. In R. Fong & R. McRoy (Eds), *Transracial and intercountry Adoptions: cultural guidance for professionals and educators*. New York: Columbia University Press.

Rotabi, K. S. & Bunkers, K. M. (2011). In the era of reform: A review of social work literature on intercountry adoption. *Sage Open*. doi: 0.1177/2158244011428160. Retrieved from http://sgo.sagepub.com/content/early/2011/11/14/2158244011428160.full#aff-1

Rotabi, K. S. & Gibbons, J. L. (2012). Does the Hague Convention on Intercountry Adoption adequately protect orphaned and vulnerable children and their families? *Journal of Child and Family Studies*, 21(1), 106–19. doi: 10.1007/s10826-011-9508-6

Rotabi, K. S., Pennell, J., Roby, J. L., & Bunkers, K. M. (2012). Family group conferencing as a culturally adaptable intervention: Reforming intercountry adoption in Guatemala. *International Social Work*, 55(3), 402–16. doi: 10.1177/0020872812437229

Selman, P. F. (Ed.). (2000). *Intercountry adoption: Developments, trends and perspectives*. London: British Association for Adoption and Fostering.

Smolin, D. M. (2006). Child laundering: How the intercountry adoption system legitimizes and incentivizes the practices of buying, trafficking, kidnapping, and stealing children. *Wayne Law Review*, 52, 113–200.

Smolin, D. M. (2010). Child laundering and the Hague Convention on Intercountry Adoption: The future and past of intercountry adoption. *Louisville Law Review*, 48, 441–98.

UNICEF. (n.d.). Convention on the Rights of the Child. Retrieved from www.unicef.org/crc/

Wiley, M. O. & Baden, A. L. (2005). Birth parents in adoption: Research, practice, and counseling psychology. *Counseling Psychologist*, 33(1), 13–50.

4

GUATEMALA

Violence against women and force, fraud, and coercion, including child abduction into adoption and a new system emerging

FIGURE 4.1   Indigenous mother and her baby in Guatemala
Source: Photo credit Karen S. Rotabi

At the turn of the Millennium, the small Central American country of Guatemala sent more children, on a per capita basis, into intercountry adoption than any other country in the world. At that time ICA was not new, as it came into practice during the 36-year Civil War; however, in the post-conflict environment ICAs began to soar in record numbers.

There were 427 ICAs to US families during the year of the Peace Accords in 1996 (Bartholet, 2010). By the year 2000 that number more than tripled, rising to 1,518 children. By the year 2007, when Guatemala entered an ICA moratorium, Guatemala reached its peak of 4,726 children being adopted by US citizen families (US Department of State, n.d.b; see Figure 4.2).

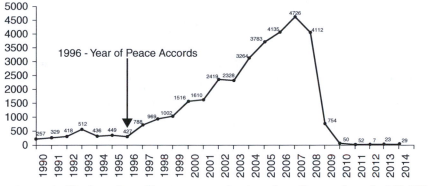

FIGURE 4.2 Total number of intercountry adoptions from Guatemala to the US, 1990–2014
Source: Author's own research

TABLE 4.1 Chinese, Guatemalan, and Russian adoptions to United States in 2006

Country	Population aged 0–14 in 2006*	Number of children adopted into the US in 2006**	Number of children adopted into the US per million
China (mainland)	273 million	6,493	24
Guatemala	5 million	4,135	827
Russia	20 million	3,706	185

* Data source: Central Intelligence Agency (2006)
** Data source: United States Department of State (n.d.b)

At its peak, Guatemala was estimated to be sending one child in every hundred live births abroad as an adoptee, most of them adopted by US citizens (Selman, 2012). The sheer number of children departing the country was so obvious that the morning flights departing the Guatemala City airport were often referred to as the "baby flight" by adoptive families and the flight crews making the daily journey. As many as 15–17 recently adopted infants and toddlers were boarded as outbound passengers daily during the peak years of Guatemala's ICA baby boom. Flight attendants were known to be celebratory of the infants—viewing them as rescued—and this was, to some degree, reminiscent of the Vietnam Babylift albeit on a larger scale over many years.

By 2006, Guatemala was the second most significant source of internationally adopted children in the world (Selman, 2012). This was startling, as Guatemala is approximately the size of the state of Tennessee in the United States and had a population of only 12–13 million people at the time (Central Intelligence Agency, 2006). China and Russia were the two other main sources for adopted children that year; those populations are massive compared with Guatemala. Table 4.1 compares each country's total of children adopted by US citizens in 2006 with that of its total child population (aged 0–14 years). It reveals that, of the children adopted into the US in 2006, Guatemala sent 34 times more children than China, and 4.5 times more children than Russia (Central Intelligence Agency, 2006; US Department of State, n.d.b).

By the end of 2007, when Guatemala had reached that all-time high of 4,726 children being adopted by US citizens, Guatemala entered into a child adoption moratorium as a result of new international standards related to the HCIA and international pressure to reform a system that had been marred by allegations of child sales and abduction. In December 2007 Guatemala passed a new child adoption law (Bunkers, Groza, & Lauer, 2009; Rotabi, Morris, & Weil, 2008).

International pressure in the popular press for women and children's rights

Just prior to the moratorium, in 2006, it was reported in the *New York Times* that the director of the Guatemalan government department that granted final official approval of ICAs said, "Babies are being sold, and we have to stop it" (Lacey, 2006, p. 3). The international media headlines were stunning, dating back to at least the year 2000 when the *New Internationalist* (2000) ran the headline "Baby Snatcher's Boom," while that same year the *Los Angeles Times* ran a story titled "Guatemala's Baby Business" (Goldsmith, 2000), with an account of a mother who reportedly was living in the streets with her children and was held at gunpoint as her baby was abducted. As would be expected, numerous reports appeared in Guatemalan newspapers, including phrases such as "*robo de niños*" ("stolen children"; Mónico, 2013; Dubinsky, 2010).

In 2006, a peak year for Guatemalan adoptions overseas, the BBC also ran a documentary film entitled *Killer's Paradise* that focused on the alarming killings of women that were occurring at astounding rates and receiving little or no law-enforcement response (Portenier, 2006). While the case of large-scale adoptions of infants and toddlers was never directly connected to violence against women in terms of Guatemalan government response, human rights defenders started to recognize that the violent context in which women were attempting to survive was not just a complicating factor in the adoption phenomena, but the context itself made a woman's self-determination to participate in an adoption plan nearly impossible. In the worst cases, violence against women was used to forcibly remove children as an act of child abduction. Sadly, there were some cases of women's bodies being found, most frequently documented as "Jane Doe," in which a cesarean section had been carried out on the victim prior to her death (Cruz, Martin, & Rotabi, 2010).

Context of violence against women: impunity and femicide defined

Lawlessness in Guatemala has been recognized as an environment of impunity, defined by Guatemalan human rights defenders as a "systematic absence of punishment, a violation of human rights in and of itself (distinct from the violent act [child abduction] that is under investigation); as a context that in turn becomes a causal factor; as a culture, social system or cultural régime; and as a means of social control" (Myrna Mack Foundation, 2009, p. 8). The concept of impunity and the lack of law-enforcement response has been applied by the Guatemala Human Rights Commission to the killing of women simply because they were women (Guatemala Human Rights Commission, 2009). The crime is called femicide, or *femicidio* in Spanish, and it is a tool of terror striking fear in communities throughout the small Central American country (Amnesty International, 2006; Costantino, 2006; Sanford, 2008). During the peak intercountry adoption years, it was estimated that two women died every day as a result of the crime of femicide, with their bodies typically being left in public places to send a message of fear. Only 2 percent of all cases were ever prosecuted, leaving the entire nation suspicious, controlling the movement of women and girls in their own neighborhoods and the greater community (Guatemala Human Rights Commission, 2009).

Confronting this reality is complicated, and achieving rule of law is a significant challenge in a nation known for hidden structures of organized criminal networks that traffic in a number of commodities, including human beings for sex, servitude, and adoption. In this context, it was essentially impossible to guarantee that any single Guatemalan adoption had been carried out ethically because organized crime was so pervasive and all forms of child sales and abduction into ICA were present in the country, according to multiple human rights reports (Casa Alianza et al., 2007; Estrada Zepeda, 2009).

Confronting illicit adoptions: pressure from human rights organizations

The earliest human rights report focused on ICA dates back to the year 2000 and was written by UN Special Rapporteur Calcetas-Santos. The report detailed the problems present as identified during interviews with key informants. Among the findings were that circumstances of extreme poverty and desperation entrapped birth mothers and families into an ICA system that was largely driven by a network of child sales. Various case examples were given; most were alarming, including stories of women being told by nurses and/or medical doctors that their child died during labor or delivery.

This report also told of a sex worker who was forcibly taken to the house of a midwife and was "kept there under lock and key with other pregnant prostitutes until she gave birth. She did not see her baby again" (United Nations, 2000, p. 8). Even in these early years of Guatemala's adoption boom, the belief that these children were being sold into ICA through networks of organized crime was already a grave concern.

This 2000 report sent shock waves throughout the human rights community, spurring concerted efforts to bring attention to the problem and start an adoption-reform process. An important NGO that was celebrated for its advocacy efforts for mistreated and "disappeared" street children took on the cause (Dubinsky, 2010). Casa Alianza was known for their human rights defense related to disappeared street children as well as the residential care facilities that they provided, at that time, for hundreds of Guatemala's orphaned and vulnerable children. Casa Alianza had a strong legal team in Guatemala and, as human rights defenders, they set forth to expose the fraud and reform the system.

One of those lawyers, Claudia Rivera, described a whole variety of ways in which Guatemalan women and their children were being sold into human trafficking; some of the methods were quite creative. For example, in the case of "Byron," a young boy was sold into "adoption" in Spain when both he and his then pregnant mother were brought there on a tourist visa (Rivera, Bromfield, & Rotabi, 2009). The Spanish family scripting the adoption fraud arranged for travel with the intent of adopting both children—Byron and his unborn sibling. In this case, Guatemalan and Spanish authorities intervened and Byron's mother was sent to prison in Guatemala while those orchestrating the crime went free. Byron and his infant sister were sent to a residential care home in Guatemala and were later adopted by a Guatemalan family (Rivera et al., 2009; personal communication, Steve Osborn, September 2010).

In Casa Alianza's (Casa Alianza et al., 2007) intensive advocacy effort to end ICAs from Guatemala, a variety of human rights defense tactics were used; their most controversial was the "barcode baby" social marketing campaign (Dubinsky, 2010). Using an exceptionally clever image of a healthy and smiling infant with a computer barcode on her forehead to indicate a merchandise sale, the image was provocative. Of course, the campaign was offensive to families adopting from Guatemala while attention to the issue of child sales and the baby market was gaining in the US, Canada, and elsewhere.

Casa Alianza also began issuing reports not only on the data on the alarming number of young children leaving the country as adoptees, but also highlighting stories of human rights abuses. Between the 2000 UN human rights report and Casa Alianza's advocacy work it was hard to ignore the point that was being made about illicit adoptions (Dubinsky, 2010). Not only did the international media join in with aggressive investigative reporting, but thousands of prospective adoptive parents in the process of adoption were deeply concerned—many of them worried that their own adoptions would not be completed because of the negative press reports and rumors of system reform, which could include a system shut down or moratorium. By the year 2004, several countries had suspended adoptions from Guatemala, including Canada.

As a result, prospective adoptive parent groups in the United States began to act beyond discussion forums that had been oriented to share information and advice about Guatemala. Members of the most influential internet-based adoption forum, *Guatadopt*, began to use their arsenal of highly educated prospective and adoptive parents and their articulate ability to refute claims. In 2003, calling themselves "Families without Borders," they went on the attack to question and undermine the UN report. Among their assertions was that the 2000 report was based on hearsay and lacked a sound research method. To human rights defenders, this group was acting with willful blindness as there was a failure to recognize that investigating illicit adoptions was very difficult when there was ample evidence of deep and dangerous problems—this fact was underscored when a Guatemalan university professor disappeared and is now presumed murdered as a result of her own research investigation into women's issues, including intercountry adoption fraud (US Department of State, 2001).

As various advocacy groups were forming, including both those who believed Guatemalan adoptions to be good and noble (adoptive families) and those who documented gross abuses (human rights defenders), the bad news continued to emerge in public discourse. Personal accounts continued to be reported, including Dr. James White's (2006, p. 5) reflection on his own experience during a medical mission to Guatemala.

> Last week a thirteen-year-old pregnant girl named Marta [last name withheld] came into my office. Her father works on a coffee plantation not far away, and she grew up on the verge of starvation in a cardboard house, with eleven siblings, six of whom are still alive. A man came in a car a year ago, and offered her family three hundred dollars—a year's wages for her father—for each baby she can make and give to him. She now lives and works in his house, tends his garden, washes clothes, was impregnated by men unknown to her, and only wants from me a checkup, perhaps some prenatal vitamins, so the baby she will soon give away will be as healthy as possible. This visit to see me is to be a secret; such things are not allowed by the man and his wife. The babies are delivered by the owners in the house. No hospital. No doctors. There are six other girls, ages twelve to fifteen, in the same house, same situation. One recently died in child birth, but the baby was saved, to be sold for three thousand dollars in Guatemala City, she tells me.

As a result of White's informal inquiry into the matter seeking advice from a Guatemalan friend, he was cautioned about speaking out against Marta's captors as he was told that "these people not only deal in selling lives; they launder money, sell narcotics, and trade in arms and explosives" (p. 5). He persisted and reported the alleged crime against Marta and the other young women to the local police in Guatemala as well as human rights organizations. In his account, he reports no satisfying investigation into the matter. There is no further information about Marta or her infant child who is believed to have been sold, as intended, into ICA.

White's reporting of the matter to human rights organizations makes an important point about human rights defense and how an organization like the Guatemalan Human Rights Commission (GHRC) can intervene. This particular NGO is an important one to consider because they have been exceptional in their advocacy efforts since the organization's founding during the war years. And, as already pointed out, they had an initiative specifically aimed at combating violence against women. Marta seems like the perfect candidate for human rights protection within this violence-against-women initiative.

However, at that time the organization was based totally in Washington, DC and they were not able to intervene in any one case at a law enforcement level—that simply was not in their mission or within their power. They did, however, have influence, and the human rights abuses related to intercountry adoption were being reported to the organization more and more frequently. However, commonly reports were from prospective families who were panicking that their cases would be stalled in an intercountry adoption moratorium. Prospective families considered any child left behind to be the victim of a human rights abuse—being deprived of a "better" life with a middle- to upper-class family in the United States.

GHRC did not take a public position on illicit adoptions from Guatemala. Looking back, it is understandable that responding to political pressures related to taking a position on inter-country adoption would have detracted from the bigger picture to which GHRC was deeply committed—confronting violence against women broadly, supporting union organizing, and documenting grave human rights atrocities, advocating for the protection of journalists, and occasionally funding the relocation of human rights defenders who were under threat of death in Guatemala. They were also helping individual Guatemalans in their bid for amnesty in the United States as well as carrying out other important work during this period.

One example of GHRC's quiet advocacy was their inclusion of several individuals con-cerned about ICA fraud into their 2009 delegation to Guatemala to investigate violence against women. While touring Guatemala and documenting testimony of human rights abuse, delegation members asked a variety of questions about adoption fraud and other related symp-toms of violence against women, such as sex work. Among the participants on this delegation was Mirah Riben, a highly vocal birth-mother advocate who wrote *The Stork Market: America's Multi-Billion Dollar Unregulated Adoption Industry* in 2007. Riben asked some pointed questions during visits to various organizations throughout Guatemala. The story of adoption fraud and human trafficking was, at this point, told as a retrospective because the ICA system had closed for reform by this time. One story in particular stood out as a stunning damnation of human trafficking into adoption.

While visiting a small NGO in Chimaltenango serving sex workers and their health and social support needs, delegates learned about advocacy efforts, including hearing the stories of women who were desperate to escape prostitution. Upon questioning about the rumored connection between sex work and ICA, the director recounted a story of an adolescent girl sold into prostitution by her stepfather. The 16 year old was trafficked into sex work by the stepfather who reportedly used the profit to build another room onto the family home. Not only was the adolescent girl sold into prostitution, but when she became pregnant the child was then reportedly also sold into intercountry adoption. This sort of double trafficking was one of many problems that emerged during the worst years of adoption fraud in Guatemala.

How such abuses persist: a corrupt system of intercountry adoption

The 2000 UN report written by Calcetas–Santos best describes a very loose "system" of ICA, prior to the adoption reforms. During this time as well as in the war years, there was no central adoption authority in Guatemala. The vast majority of international adoptions were carried out in an extrajudiciary process, based on a notary system in which adoption was executed by an attorney as the lead professional. Calcetas–Santos wrote, "This [notary] process, which apparently only takes place in Guatemala, is performed before a Notary, based on Regulatory Law of Notary Procedures in Matters of Voluntary Jurisdiction" (UN, 2000). This means the adoption process was most frequently carried out in a private attorney's office without meaningful oversight by a family court judge or social welfare agency. It is termed a notarial adoption because a notary and an adoption agent must participate, both of whom must be attorneys at law. According to Calcetas–Santos, in the majority of cases, the same attorney acts in both roles as notary and agent, resulting in a dual relationship.

Furthermore:

> the only other professional who may safeguard the process is a social worker who officially verifies the circumstances of abandonment or makes a socioeconomic assessment of the birth family for relinquishment purposes…Adoption through this route needs no resolution from a competent judge. The Family Court's only action is that of soliciting the social worker, under oath, to execute the respective socioeconomic investigation of the family.
>
> *(UN, 2000, p. 5)*

This means that an impartial judge had no means to directly question the grounds on which a parent relinquished a child. The process was further complicated because the recruitment of birth mothers was commonly carried out by a *buscadora* or *jaladora*[1] in collusion with the attorney. This recruiter was an entrepreneur, working without any judicial or social agency oversight to recruit pregnant women and mothers of young children for relinquishment. In some cases, medical providers, hospitals, social workers, and midwives were also involved in this criminal activity.

In the 2000 UN report, Calcetas–Santos also found that the scale of crime around intercountry adoption reached such alarming proportions that she wrote, "It would seem that in the majority of cases, international adoption involves a variety of criminal offences including the buying and selling of children, the falsifying of documents, the kidnapping of children, and the housing of babies awaiting private adoption in homes and nurseries set up for that purpose." The report also detailed the ways the attorneys orchestrated and financially benefited from international adoptions of Guatemalan infants. Infants were housed in homes or hogars called "'*casas cunas*' (cot or crib houses) but [these houses] are often derisively referred to as '*casas de engordeza*' (fattening houses)" (UN, 2000, p. 8). Calcetas–Santos also noted that this criminal activity supported the unregulated housing of birth mothers during pregnancy.

While other reports were also released after the 2000 UN report (e.g. Casa Alianza et al., 2007), the next report to gain considerable attention was the result of an extensive study carried out by the Comisión Internacional contra la Impunidad (the International Commission against Impunity in Guatemala, commonly called the CICIG). This UN-sponsored organization, established to confront the conditions of impunity in Guatemala, found evidence of illicit adoptions. This particular report came after the adoption boom years and had a strong focus on the transitional period as the new law of 2007 was being implemented. CICIG found that "illegal networks were engaged in trafficking for purposes of irregular adoption. These networks are made up, among others, of snatchers (*jaladoras*) who kidnap or 'buy' children from their birth mothers. In some cases, they threaten, coerce, or deceive the mothers into giving their children up for adoption" (CICIG, 2010, p. 7). According to this provocative report, these networks were composed of public officials, lawyers, adoption agencies, health personnel, and other public- and private-service entities and individuals who were forging identity documents and producing false DNA results. This report summarized the child-laundering activities that were common in Guatemala.

A human rights catastrophe

The obvious question, then and now, was, how did such a human rights catastrophe come to be? The answer is complicated, but most would agree that the daily experience of most Guatemalans during the post-conflict ICA era can be said to be unstable even though many citizens were going about their lives as usual. Sadly, an unstable economic and social environment is the norm for Guatemalans.

During the war years and since, the conditions of the Guatemalan people have been difficult—characterized by extreme poverty. The resulting manner in which fraud and coercion were carried out varies, but money and desperation were the entrapments. The unscrupulous capitalized on poverty, a coercive life experience that results in a kind of vulnerability that made Guatemala ripe for illicit intercountry adoptions.

Understanding Guatemala's historical context: extreme human rights abuses and genocide during the Civil War

Turning back to the question of how such a human rights scenario came to be, the social and health indicators during the peak of Guatemala's adoption boom are most telling. But before we begin exploring these indicators, understanding the history of Guatemala's Civil War is an essential precursor to the social environment and eventually the human rights catastrophe that became Guatemala's post-conflict ICA system.

Genocide of indigenous persons, the Mayan Indians, was the main outcome of the 36-year Civil War (1960–96) that resulted in the death of at least 200,000 Indigenous peoples (REMHI, 1999). Also, it is estimated that over 400 villages were destroyed when the government burned the corn and meager homes of the agricultural people and dumped countless bodies into mass graves, which are still being identified and exhumed (REMHI, 1999). Fear of such massive killings led to displacement of many Mayans internally; thousands more fled from Guatemala to Mexico or other Central American countries (Rodman, 2009).

As is typical in war, many children were orphaned and left to die in the countryside. The Truth and Reconciliation Commission (sponsored by the Catholic Archdiocese of Guatemala) noted that when families fled their villages as the death squads approached, it was not uncom-mon for the young to be abandoned, infants sometimes left sleeping in make-shift hammocks hanging from the village trees (REMHI, 1999). An escaping family with little time may have had to make the most difficult decision to leave their infant or toddlers in order to gather up the other children and run for their lives. Infants were a liability to families who were hiding in the forests because their cries of hunger would often give away the family's location to the military (REMHI, 1999). If the family was massacred, sometimes the youngest children were spared. These children were subsequently called the children of the "disappeared" or *desapareci-dos* (REMHI, 1999). It has been reported that in some cases military officers rescued children. In such cases, they would take the infants from the rural areas and place them in residential care institutions or alternatively place them with families who were willing and able to care for and informally or formally adopt the children.

A particular example of this practice was documented during the truth and reconcilia-tion process. General Hector Alejandro Gramajo stated in a newspaper report that "the fam-ilies of many army officers have grown with the adoption of victims of the violence since, at certain times, it was popular among army soldiers to take responsibility for little three- or four-year-olds found wandering in the mountains" (REMHI, 1999, p. 38). On the other hand, there are examples of children who were forcefully abducted from their Indigenous families in an effort to resocialize and assimilate them into the dominant culture—another form of cultural oppression. For example, during the truth and reconciliation process it was documented that:

> In 1984, the mayor of Rabinal ordered the auxiliary mayors to take children between the ages of five and ten from the Pacux settlement to the Children's Home of the Church of the Nazarene in San Miguel Chicaj. They took twenty boys and girls against their parents' wishes…Later, in 1988, the families complained to the parish priest that their children had been turned into evangelical Christians; they wanted their children returned to them. They were returned that same year.
>
> *(REMHI, 1999, p. 38)*

This type of forcible abduction is considered to be another aspect of genocidal practice accord-ing to the definition of genocide in Article 2 of the 1948 Convention on the Prevention and Punishment of Genocide that includes "forcibly transferring children from one group to another group."

While some children were spared, the majority killed were Mayan Indians who were called "Communists" at that time; history is now told in a much more balanced manner, and the fact is that Mayan peasants were fighting to keep their land, resisting slavery in the big coffee and other agricultural plantations as well as other injustices. History today has been informed by the truth and reconciliation process (REMHI, 1999), and it is clear that the Indigenous people of Guatemala were simply trying to survive in an environment where they were targets of a genocidal strategy scripted by the government. Called the "scorched earth policy," some of the worst abuses took place during the mid- to late 1980s.

During the war years, although impossible to prove, it was rumored that children were being abducted into adoption. In 1994 *Time* magazine reported on the illegal trafficking or sale of babies for adoption abroad, entitled "Dangerous Rumors" (Lopez & O'Kane, 1994). At that time, Guatemala had come under scrutiny for violent attacks on tourists who had been rumored to be "baby stealing." In two separate incidents in different locations within Guatemala, foreign citizens became the victims of vigilante mob attacks, including an American tourist attacked in the Spring of 1993 as a result of a child-abduction rumor which spread through the town square on market day (Honeyman, 1999).

The implications of child-abduction rumors during conflict reverberated during the post-conflict adoption boom. As infants and young children were leaving their communities and the country, there was a great deal of confusion as to why foreigners would want these children. Organ-theft rumors again surfaced and once a population living in a village begins to focus on allegations of child disappearances, the consequences of unbridled fear are often severe. For example, in 2006 an incident in the Mayan village of Sumpago illustrates an act of vigilante justice being carried out at the hands of angry citizens (Associated Press, 2006). A witness said that the church bells were rung to alert people that a man and woman suspected in abductions had been found. "When the alarm sounded today, the people went mad…the police captured them (and then) the people started screaming that they had stolen a boy and the mob went to get them where they were held" (p. 1). In the end, reportedly a mob of approximately 800 people beat and burned to death the man and woman accused of child abduction.

Vigilante violence related to ICA rose to the attention of the US Embassy, and the country's human rights report of 2007 reported the following:

> There were also reports of community lynchings of individuals suspected of kidnapping or attempting to kidnap children to sell for adoption. On June 14, nine-year-old Alba Mishel Espana Diaz disappeared from her village, Camotan, Chiquimula, and was found dead the next day. On June 15, mobs lynched a woman suspected of kidnapping the girl. Two days later, residents of neighboring Jocotan attempted to lynch two women suspected of kidnapping another child and burned patrol vehicles of police officers who intervened to prevent the lynchings.
>
> *(US Department of State, 2007)*

The problems were so extreme that doubt about foreigners' intentions and the kidnapping of children spread fear as Guatemalan families attempted to safeguard their children from abduction. Some families were clearly afraid of outsiders. This fear coincided with some high-profile and formal allegations of child abduction into adoption, thereby moving the rumor to public discourse that reached a peak when hunger protests began to demand justice.

At the end of July 2009 a hunger strike ended in Guatemala City after 15 days of protest over the alleged abductions of three daughters who are believed to be living in the United States with their adoptive families (Rotabi, 2009). The protest was organized to demand a determination from Guatemala's Supreme Court as to a legal route in which to present the facts of the cases. The court's subsequent decision that the cases should be heard in a civil hearing indicated early signs of hope that the cases would move forward with the potential to eventually nullify all three of the adoptions.

Research on illegal adoptions from Guatemala

Scholarship on the subject of child trafficking for adoption is difficult, to say the least. Inquiry into organized crime is obviously dangerous in a country known for endemic rates of violence and homicide. However, Mónico defined child abduction more broadly than most, capturing the various dimensions of the crime when she interviewed Guatemalan mothers who had publicly reported their children abducted into adoption:

- Child theft:[2] Use of force to remove a child unlawfully, kidnapping, or stealing, and subsequent commodification or selling of children that occurs openly against the will of the birth mother, birth parents, family, and community of origin.
- Deception: Lack of fully informed consent on the part of the birth mother throughout the relinquishment process, up to and including the time at which parental rights are legally terminated.
- Coercion: Intra- and extra-family coercion exerted on birth mothers and families of origin to induce relinquishment of the child for any reason.
- Fraud: Any legal, judicial, administrative, political, cultural, or socioeconomic fraud or deception of birth mothers, such as offering of payment or compensation, that leads to the forced separation or relinquishment of their children.

The aforementioned CICIG report, based on a large sample of final cases prior to moratorium, confirmed fears about child sales and abduction and indicated involvement of hidden structures/organized crime with many of the dimensions identified by Mónico. The CICIG traced the immense network necessary to orchestrate fraud on such a large scale, including corrupt actors from multiple sectors within society. The number of children and their families who were impacted are unknown and according to the commissioner of the CICIG, the three cases of child abduction are considered to be symbolic of an unknown number of cases in which women experienced force, fraud, and coercion for child trafficking into international adoption (Commissioner Francisco Dall'Anese Ruiz, personal communication, June 2, 2011).

Organized crime and international human-trafficking law

Illegal activities of organized crime that draw individuals into human trafficking are identified in international private law focused on human trafficking for sex and servitude. The UN Human Trafficking Protocol defines the crime as (with italics added for emphasis):

> (a) Trafficking in persons shall mean the recruitment, transportation, transfer, harbouring or receipt of persons, by means of the threat or use of *force* or other forms of *coercion*, of abduction, of *fraud*, of deception, of the abuse of power or of a position of vulnerability or the giving or receiving of payments or benefits to achieve the consent of a person having control over another person, for the purpose of exploitation. Exploitation shall include, *at a minimum*, the exploitation of the prostitution of others or other forms of sexual exploitation, forced labour or services, slavery or practices similar to slavery, servitude or the removal of organs.

Because abduction for adoption does not result in debt bondage or sexual exploitation of children, it is viewed as a victimless crime (Smolin, 2007), and it is further misunderstood because children join middle- to upper-class families with resources (Bromfield & Rotabi, 2012). In other words, the endpoint is not exploitive for the child (Roby & Brown, 2015). However, force, fraud, and coercion were necessary to carry out child trafficking for adoption.

The exploitation must be viewed in the context of the family system and at least the child's right to remain in his or her family group regardless of poverty (United Nations, 2009).

Human-trafficking dynamics found in child abduction for adoption: force, fraud, and coercion

The three elements of force, fraud, and coercion existed in an unknown number of Guatemalan adoptions. A review of these human-trafficking dynamics underscores these dynamics as they play out specifically in child trafficking into adoption. While the story of fraud is clear in Guatemalan adoptions thus far, a closer look at coercion and force as well as the concept of abduction into adoption is important.

Force: abduction for child trafficking into adoption

The kidnapping evidence put forth by the women protesting for their daughters' return includes the abduction case of Ester, daughter of Ana Escobar. As a young mother, Ana previously joined the three mothers in earlier protests and her story, like those of all the women, was treated with skepticism; however, in 2008 Escobar's allegations of abduction were validated with undisputable evidence (Parents for Ethical Adoption Reform, 2009). Her story begins when she was working in a Guatemala City shoe store. At gunpoint, her infant daughter Ester was abducted as Escobar pleaded with the kidnappers under threat of death. Immediately after the crime, the young mother began her search for baby Ester, including making a police report. Escobar states that the police treated her as the criminal when they accused her of child sales (A. Escobar, personal communication, August 9, 2009). Because many birth mothers were believed to have routinely received payment during the adoption era in child-sales schemes (Bunkers et al., 2009), Escobar was viewed by law-enforcement officials as just another birth mother who had changed her mind.

Escobar was not to be deterred and began a personal campaign to find her daughter (Rotabi, 2014). Escobar frequented offices for meetings with various authorities, including government adoption officials, to report her case and seek any known information about her daughter. While sitting in the waiting room of the national adoption authority offices, Escobar had a chance sighting of Ester as the young girl was being carried through the office by an unknown individual. Escobar was overtaken with emotion and was able to convince officials to DNA test the young girl for confirmation (A. Escobar, personal communication, August 9, 2009). With a positive match between Escobar and the young girl, Ester's impending adoption was ceased and she was eventually returned to her biological mother after two long years of searching. To this date, the kidnappers have not been apprehended or brought to justice for abduction or any other child-sales activities (Estrada Zepeda, 2009; Parents for Ethical Adoption Reform, 2009). Escobar's case illustrates impunity in both the initial stages of abduction with the failure of the police to act on the actual report of a crime and the long-term failure to prosecute.

Another example of impunity is the case of Raquel Par Socop, one of the three mothers who continue to protest for the return of their daughters believed to be living in the United States as an adoptee (Estrada Zepeda, 2009). Raquel, an Indigenous woman, also has a story of force but with different tactics. Reportedly, while awaiting a bus in Guatemala City with her infant daughter, Raquel was befriended by a woman accompanied by a young man who offered her a job doing daily work laundering clothes. Accepting the offer for one day of work, Raquel followed the pair across the city. During travel, the woman offered Raquel water which immediately made her feel dizzy and she eventually fainted. Reportedly, Raquel ingested a sedative-laced beverage and she reports awaking on a roadside bewildered, unable even to talk at first. Her infant daughter was missing. Asking for help from nearby neighbors, a witness reported to Raquel that the woman and young man had abducted her daughter. This particular witness actually gave Raquel the name of the woman in question and an address where she could be found. The very next day, Raquel and her husband went to the Public Ministry and the Public Prosecutor's Office to file a complaint and inform the authorities of the abduction. However, it was approximately ten weeks later that the authorities searched the house of the woman who allegedly abducted the child. The woman in question was no longer resident and she has never been apprehended. Realistically, even with concerted efforts, Raquel was unable to protect her daughter from abduction as she was incapacitated and entrapped in a chain of events constructed for child abduction and trafficking into intercountry adoption (Estrada Zepeda, 2009).

Like Ana Escobar, Raquel went to authorities alleging child abduction and she received no assistance in searching for her daughter. Unlike Escobar, Raquel has not been reunited with her daughter. This particular case illustrates the fact that once a child leaves Guatemalan jurisdiction, as is believed to be the case in this particular abduction, the chance of legal intervention diminishes even further. It is fair to argue that Raquel never really had a fair chance at justice as Indigenous people bear the greatest burden of impunity, violence against women, and underlying racism every day in Guatemala (Costantino, 2006; Sanford, 2008).

Fraud and the context of poverty and inequality: women face so-called "professionals"

The sad reality is that women living in poverty, often with circumstances complicated by the shame of illegitimacy and fear, are easy targets for force, fraud, and coercion. Their vulnerable position may be violated in a number of ways, ranging from the crude abduction techniques identified in Ana Escobar's and Raquel Par's cases and/or by unethical and illegal child adoption practices at the hands of unscrupulous entrepreneurs with titles like lawyer, counselor, social worker, judge, or other disciplines that imply trust, competence, and a commitment to self-determination (Bromfield & Rotabi, 2012). However, some people take on these professional titles as a cover for illegal activities, especially as a counselor or social worker, given the limited controls over title use (due to credential requirements, to call oneself a nurse or a lawyer is far more difficult in order to carry out fraud). Others such as judges may be corrupted with graft, as has been asserted in the case of a number of family court judges in Guatemala (CICIG, 2010). Coercion includes people in positions of power, using their status, to urge a child's parent(s) to give the child "a better life" in a country like the United States for it is the only thing to do given circumstances of poverty.

Regardless of the professional title, often the coercive tactics cross the line into child trafficking into adoption when excessive fees are earned for the transaction (US$20,000 and more for the Guatemalan lawyers alone). Unfortunately, an unknown number of birth mothers of Guatemala faced powerful people—so-called "professionals"—without a chance of a fair and informed consent for child relinquishment. Some of these mothers experienced outright and classic child abduction while others had more complicated experiences of fraud and coercion, some more subtle than others. Regardless of the mode, the outcome was the same. Illegal transfer of child custody from a poor family to another relatively wealthy family for intercountry adoption was the end result.

Consent and entrapment of birth mothers in Guatemalan adoptions

Informed consent issues are a recognized adoption ethics problem and a challenge in adoption practice (Babb, 1999). This was true in Guatemalan adoptions under the pre-reform system, which allowed for a thumbprint to suffice for a relinquishment signature and minimal investigation of birth-parent history and limited judicial oversight (Bunkers et al., 2009; Bunkers & Groza, 2012; Rotabi et al., 2008). Birth-mother illiteracy further complicated the issue, and given the traditional society, there was likely a lack of understanding of the permanent nature of intercountry adoption to individuals and couples in other countries—a complete and total legal break of family relations.

The money trap

The way fraud and coercion were carried out varies, but money and desperation were the entrapments capitalizing on poverty, a coercive life experience that results in vulnerability endemic in Guatemala. Bunkers et al. (2009) assert that some birth mothers were paid on each of the three required signature points for child relinquishment. The theory is that women would receive a sum for the first signature and then return for the second and third signatures at later dates. The fraud of child sales is obvious in this scheme, but coercion occurred when some mothers/birth families decided against going forward with the adoption. At that point, it is believed that the attorney or intermediary would inform the mothers that they must repay the initial sum, estimated to be as much as $500 for the first payment, plus expenses such as childcare, food, and supplies (Bunkers et al., 2009). The attorney or intermediary would then offer the second payment, and this entrapment left desperately poor women with little choice but to sign away their parental rights due to their inability to make repayment, combined with the inducement of a second and third payment (Rotabi et al., 2008). It is estimated that the payments totaled approximately $1,500 (Bunkers et al., 2009). Obviously this was a poverty and desperation trap, a violation of informed consent, and serious human rights abuse suffered by the mother, the child, and the greater biological family system. Ultimately this scheme capitalizes on poverty and vulnerability endemic in Guatemala—a ripe environment for illegal adoptions given the nation's poverty rate, second only to Haiti's in the Western Hemisphere (United Nations Development Program, 2015).

Advocacy in Guatemala: an outspoken and famous human rights defender and others weigh in

Survivors Foundation is a Guatemalan non-governmental organization whose mission focuses on violence against women, providing advocacy, legal representation, and psychological support for survivors of violence (Estrada Zepeda, 2009). The organization spearheaded the July 2009 and earlier hunger protests in Guatemala to demand justice for the three mothers and their abducted daughters. Director of Survivors Foundation Norma Cruz is an important figure in

Guatemala as a recognized human rights defender—a heroine to many—who was awarded the 2009 International Woman of Courage award from US President Obama's administration (US Department of State, 2009) and also nominated for a Nobel Prize. This status aided Cruz as an outspoken advocate for the mothers who have lost their children to illegal adoptions. Cruz recognized that violence against women is the context in which the abduction for adoption crimes took place (Cruz, Smolin, Dilworth, Rotabi, & DiFilipo, 2011), and impunity was the permissive environment necessary to allow for the crimes on such a large scale.

Cruz views child abduction and human trafficking for adoption as bringing about "eternal suffering" for the mothers and the cruelest form of violence against women (Cruz et al., 2011). The US Department of Justice's determination that the court order will not be honored was made on the grounds of insufficient evidence as well as the fact that the alleged crimes took place prior to Guatemala's ratification of the Hague Convention (Cruz et al., 2011). The government of Guatemala's request for collaboration in responding to the court order has all but fallen on deaf ears, a clear case of willful blindness as the United States and the adoptive family in question simply refuses to acknowledge the legal nullification of this particular child's adoption in Guatemala—and the recognition that she is a child abducted into adoption according to her country of birth's court system. This child is now living in Missouri and her case will be discussed next when we take a closer look at her mother, Loyda Rodriguez, and her fight for justice.

In solidarity: a US citizen joins in protest

In her outrage as a US citizen, Shyrel Osborn, living in Guatemala and directing a private and faith-based residential children's home, joined the 2009 hunger protest in support of the mothers. Reflecting on the protest experience, Osborn said that she never received a visit from the US Embassy during her 15 days of demonstration in 2009 (S. Osborn, personal communication, August 9, 2009). This is telling because US Embassy counsel officials are required to periodically visit US citizens imprisoned overseas to verify their health and other facts (US Department of State, n.d.a); however, they seemed unconcerned about a citizen engaged in non-violent and legal demonstration in a city infamous for crime and violence. While the press covered the protest, the lack of concern demonstrated by the US Embassy was a disappointment for Osborn because the three girls in question are now US citizens. If the allegations are true, the girls' identities were "laundered" or changed in order to secure their US citizenship (Smolin, 2004, 2006), passing the fraudulent paperwork through multiple hands of bureaucrats to include those within the US Embassy system.

Ironically, ambassadors from several other nations, including Spain, personally visited the women on hunger protest, indicating a symbolic support for justice (S. Osborn, personal communication, May 10, 2011). Of course, this is consistent with the fact that many of these countries, including Spain (Dubinsky, 2010), suspended adoptions from Guatemala a number of years before the system closed to the United States (Dubinsky, 2010).

The United States remained open as a receiving country even with evidence of deep and persistent fraud problems dating back to the 1990s (Bunkers et al., 2009) due to significant political pressure from agencies and prospective families. The lack of US diplomatic appearance at the site of protests further illustrates the political nature of adoption (Briggs, 2012; Goodwin, 2010; Yemm, 2010)—especially with the vehement denial of systemic problems by US prospective and adoptive families who were known to bring considerable political pressure as they pushed forward their own adoption cases during the early reform stages in Guatemala (see Families without Borders, 2003).

Application of the best interests of the child to the child-abduction cases

Intercountry adoptions in general and particularly from Guatemala have been the source of debate, sometimes quite contentious, especially when considering the best interests of the child (Ballard, Goodno, Cochran, & Milbrandt, 2015; Bartholet & Smolin, 2012; McKinney, 2007; Yemm, 2010). Fundamentally, the best interests of the child related to custody are to be determined on a case-by-case basis, taking into account a variety of considerations, including capacity to parent and other relevant factors when child custody comes into question. Applying the best-interests definition to cases of abduction is, in and of itself, a distortion of the purpose of the "best interests" principle and a further injustice to the mothers/families that allege abduction. The families who have lost their children to abduction were never under any scrutiny regarding their capacity to parent or any other problem. To question the best interests of these children, based on any perceived deficits of these families, is not only irresponsible but inhumane. Furthermore, the commitment of these women to searching for their daughters underscores that they are anything but neglectful in their role as mothers.

The case of Loyda Rodriguez and a failure to return an abducted daughter

This is the case of Loyda Rodriguez, a mother who finally received the court order for which she had protested and prayed for years. Loyda's daughter has been living with a family in Missouri for a number of years as she left Guatemala as an adoptee. Unfortunately, according to human rights defenders and court documents in Guatemala, the young child was abducted into nefarious child adoption networks and "placed" with the US family. In Loyda's case, she turned her back to her daughter only briefly—as she was unlocking the front gate of her home—and an unfamiliar car quickly stopped and the child was snatched from the roadside (Estrada Zepeda, 2009). Loyda never saw her daughter again, with the exception of photographs that were used to identify the child in the legal process. To date in 2016, Loyda still has not seen her daughter. The family that "adopted" the child refuses to return to Guatemala or even communicate with Loyda and her family while the United States Department of Justice refuses to intervene in the legal matter, even with a binding Guatemalan court order of child abduction (Cruz et al., 2011). The US family has retained a high-profile lawyer who claims to be a human rights lawyer, and they also paid a public relations firm to help them communicate a message about their position. The adoptive family has remained largely silent (Kirpalani & Ng, 2011). However, in the fall of 2011, the two American parents appeared on the popular morning news show Good Morning America and announced that they did not believe it to be in their daughter's best interests to send *their* daughter back to Guatemala.

From Loyda's point of view, as a mother, she has her own opinion about the scenario without a sophisticated public-relations firm advising her on how to frame her position. Her position and statements are powerful. Loyda told one reporter:

> All I want to tell them is to return my girl. I don't have anything against them because perhaps they took my daughter without knowing that she had been stolen from me. That's why I want to ask them to return her to me because I have been suffering for five years.
>
> *(Romo, 2011, p. 1)*

This story is tragic for all involved. Loyda has not been given the same platform of news broadcasts in the United States. While she has support in Guatemala, at this point, she is simply caught in a David versus Goliath scenario. While there was an attempt to secure pro bono legal aid from at least one high-profile member organization of lawyers in the child's current state of residence, even with a compelling request for help and the legal profession's ethical obligation to represent the poor and marginalized, the professional association did not step up with legal aid (personal communication, Norma Cruz, August 14, 2014). Ultimately, trying to fight within the legal structures of the United States will inevitably hold the case in limbo for years—and now one must wonder if the case will be resolved only when the child in question confronts her own past and the actions of those who made decisions on her behalf. As for the other two girls living with families in the US, their adoption nullifications have not moved as successfully through the courts although the evidence of abduction into adoption is credible (Estrada Zepeda, 2009).

US adoption agencies and their role in the adoption marketplace

For many years, as these stories unfolded, US-based adoption agencies pushed ahead with adoptions, even after repeated cautions from the US Department of State and the United Nations along with many dramatic international press stories. Many agency personnel saw themselves justified in their rescue of children from poverty and some engaged in outrageous actions, including gross abuses.

For example, one "agency" in Michigan called itself "Waiting Angels" and its website included imagery of angels along with a photo listing of children available for adoption from Guatemala. Such a bold use of images of children—used to market the work of the organization in an open internet forum—is largely criticized as a practice for ICA today. However, the photo listing was more than 80 percent of that particular agency website's content. In the end, the reason became clear—there was little more "service" than identifying readily available children and arranging for their immigration to the United States as adoptees.

When the agency was finally exposed for fraud, several alarming facts emerged. One was law enforcement's seizure of US$500,000 in cash found in the house of the agency director. Then, as the press followed the case, it was learned that this executive director had no social services work history. In fact, when she was sentenced to house arrest and ordered to wear an ankle bracelet the defendant asked the judge to allow her to remove the device so that she could return to her former profession of dancing.[3] This case illustrates how self-proclaimed adoption "professionals" set up shop with Guatemalan adoptions. This particular woman had previously adopted from Guatemala and apparently decided to jump into the system by establishing an adoption agency. In time she had a lucrative business, and the money laundering commenced as evidenced by half a million dollars in cash being hidden in a suitcase in her home.

The state of Michigan, where this agency was located, took a bold step and prosecuted the executive director and her boyfriend. "Unlike investigations in other states, the Michigan Attorney General did not just make an announcement, allow the agency to close its door and walk away. Michigan is the only state thus far who has prosecuted agency directors for this activity" (Fixel Law Offices, n.d.). Civil lawsuits against the agency have been lodged and families who lost large sums of money do not appear to have reached any satisfactory end to their claims (Fixel Law Offices, n.d.).

Waiting Angels, a small and relatively unknown agency amongst at least 200 agencies that were arranging Guatemalan adoptions, is only one example of poor practices. Other agencies with a notorious past include one in Florida in which the evidence is damning about their role in adoption fraud (Siegal, 2011). That particular agency has been documented in televised investigative journalism, including questionable practices in Africa (Boedeker, 2015). The organization has vehemently denied any wrongdoing (Celebrate Children International, n.d.); however, the agency was eventually denied accreditation for adoption services under the HCIA, and while they persisted for a while with their Africa programs and especially Ethiopia, the organization today is essentially defunct in terms of child adoption-placement services. We will look closer at the agency in Chapter 6.

As adoptions ended in Guatemala: one loss was to same-sex couples and single individuals

A lesser known part of the Guatemalan adoption-boom story is the fact the system was permissive of adoptions by gay and lesbian couples and single individuals. This is not an indicator of Guatemala being a tolerant society in terms of gay and lesbians building their families through adoption. In fact, Guatemala is known to have a problem with homophobia and extreme violence against gay and lesbian individuals (e.g. beatings and even homicide in the streets, etc.). However, in the adoption-boom era, amongst the gay and lesbian community in the United States, Guatemala became a well-known country for adoptions by same-sex couples. It should be said that the adoptions were carried out under the name of one person within the couple—in other words a single person was noted as the adopting parent on the necessary paperwork. Of course, the fact that single individuals (including heterosexuals) could adopt was also attractive to people who were not married.

Guatemalan adoptions today: reform and a new adoption system

Today, Guatemala's social service system is challenged by limited resources given extreme poverty and the resulting array of serious social problems experienced by children and families. However, the actual laws related to protecting vulnerable people are largely in place, including laws related to child protection such as the 2007 legislation that resulted from the ratification of the Hague Convention on Intercountry Adoption (Bunkers & Groza, 2012). This is a story of both a legal framework and practical implementation that truly safeguards the rights of vulnerable children and their families. The question becomes how a law is actually implemented in order to ensure social protection broadly and inclusive of the principle of subsidiarity.

Prior to the intercountry adoption moratorium, multiple systems gaps left impoverished families vulnerable to illicit adoptions (Rotabi & Bunkers, 2008; Rotabi & Morris, 2007). In response to reform and under obligations of the HCIA, a central adoption authority was established, called the Consejo Nacional (CNA). This organization, with main offices in Guatemala City, operates at the central government level and serves all 22 departments/states in the country. The organization was constituted as a national body and policies and procedures have been formed to safeguard child adoption processes. Table 4.2 provides a side-by-side comparison of the old versus new adoption system that emerged as a result of HCIA reform (Rotabi, 2014).

Systems changes, as indicated in Table 4.2, are based upon the adoption-service sector that now operates without profit and within the government structure. Those working with

TABLE 4.2 The old Guatemala system of ICA versus the reformed system

Old system	New and reformed system
Voluntary relinquishment by notary (intervention of private professionals/attorneys)	Initiation of declaration of adoptability by the government central authority (intervention of government professionals)
Selection of the child on behalf of prospective parent(s)	Government social workers/psychologists select a suitable child in systematic child–family matching process informed by social assessment
The will of the prospective family prevails	The best interests of the child prevail
High cost of adoption	No cost to adoption
Guatemalan families were excluded as they simply could not afford to participate in this expensive system	Guatemalan families are now the priority as per subsidiarity principle—services completely free to the family
No socioeconomic studies of prospective parents	Psychological, legal, and socioeconomic assessment of prospective parents
No post-adoption monitoring required	Post-adoption monitoring is required
No database of children adopted	Central authority now has a unit dedicated to collecting and managing this data
No possibility of locating the family of origin of the child with formal information	Adopted children will have the possibility of knowing the family of origin through appropriate record keeping

Note: This table is an adaptation of a similar table presented at the 2014 Forum on Intercountry Adoption and Global Surrogacy by Noe Erazo of the Guatemalan Central Authority and Carmen Mónico and reported by Rotabi (2014).

children in the adoption process are government employees, most frequently trained social workers and psychologists who have an orientation to domestic adoption as a first priority when an adoption plan is determined to be in the best interests of the child. A biological family adoption placement is the first step, and when that is not possible—this determination being made after a thorough assessment—then the particular child's unique issues and greater network of social resources are identified. A social resource may include an involved adult, like a family friend or neighbor, who may be willing to step in and take on child guardianship or domestic adoption. Once these avenues have been considered and there is no resolution, then other Guatemalan nationals are considered for adoption placement. Many Guatemalan families have registered and are waiting to be considered for such an adoption with the CNA while other families have now completed a domestic adoption.

It is important to underscore that such adoptions of young children were, in the old system, simply outside of the grasp of ordinary Guatemalans because young children were sent to individuals and couples who were essentially higher-paying customers in the United States and elsewhere. Now, the no-cost system is based on the best interests of the child, and Guatemalan families have a fair chance to adopt without interference from outside entities such as aggressive adoption agencies operating from countries like the US.

Today, throughout the adoption process, the government tracks cases and keeps appropriate documentation of each child to ensure there are identity records and other key information unique to each case. This is a great improvement over the previous system, which not only was lax in documentation, but allowed the absence of solid record keeping that was intentional, as honest documentation of identities and tracking of families was not in the interest of those engaged in wrongdoing.

Now, as one would expect from a child adoption system, post-adoption monitoring is required with specific steps to include follow-up assessments. Clear policy and procedures have been developed for this aspect of care, provided within a case-management framework and executed by trained Guatemalan professionals. Those working with children and families in the adoption system today are most likely either trained psychologists or social workers. In the pre-reform system, in the worst cases of adoption fraud, many of the unscrupulous entrepreneurs represented themselves as "adoption professionals" by self-proclaiming their status as social workers. They worked independently, and their claims of professionalism were a farce; under the new system this activity has ceased and child adoptions are based on child welfare practices that are consistent with international standards.

According to Noe Erazo of the CNA, when a Guatemalan woman with an unplanned/crisis pregnancy self-identifies as considering adoption for her child, she is categorized as a "woman in conflict with her pregnancy." She then receives unbiased counseling from an adoption professional as one service of the CNA system, an assessment is carried out, and a service plan is developed based on the individual case with a clear commitment to the self-determination of the pregnant mother. Rather than being counseled towards adoption as the plan, all possibilities are explored, including the immediate and extended family's interest in and ability to take on parenting the child. Policies and procedures that safeguard this particularly sensitive time are based on the following HCIA obligations for the mother:

- To receive unbiased counseling prior to legal adoption consent, particularly being informed of the legal impact of a full adoption decree, or clean break adoption, on the parent–child relationship (Art. 4c(1)).
- To give informed consent in writing with appropriate witnesses (Art. 4c(2)) and without financial incentives (Art. 4c(3)).
- To consent only after childbirth rather than making a firm adoption plan before labor and delivery (Art. 4c(4)).

Today, it is not uncommon for a Guatemalan woman to decide against an adoption plan with the CNA (Rotabi, 2014). When that is the case, there is no dilemma as the CNA has no obligation to identify children for adoption in a system pressured by waiting prospective families, as was the case in the old/pre-reform system. That is, there are no expectations for the number of babies entering into the system annually as there is no financial gain nor promises made; a woman choosing an alternative to adoption is seen as one of a number of potential CNA service outcomes (personal communication, Noe Erazo, August 2014). In the previous system, those orchestrating adoption financially benefited from each adoption and many worked entrepreneurially; compensation was based on the number of adoptions completed and individuals relied on and pushed for child adoption as the outcome in order to secure their incomes.

With this new, non-profit system, Guatemala has not re-opened its doors to intercountry adoption at the time of this writing. Politically speaking, Guatemala has been undergoing a time of great stress related to a new wave of truth and reconciliation in which one of their most notorious war criminal/former dictators has been brought to trial (Malkin, 2015). Also in 2015, President Otto Pérez Molina was removed from office on grounds of wide-scale corruption; although his removal from office was not directly related to his military service during the war years, his questionable involvement in the Civil War was always under scrutiny. Fundamentally, this is a dramatic time in Guatemala's push to address impunity, which was made perfectly clear when the congress voted to strip Molina of his immunity (Malkin & Azam, 2015). In parallel, a Guatemalan adoptee and now Belgian citizen who left her home country as an adoptee during the war years has recently opened a legal case to challenge her adoption as fraudulent—she is the first such adoptee to take legal action (personal communication, Norma Cruz, August 16, 2014; Rotabi, 2014). Consequently, reopening ICA after serious and persistent fraud and during this transition stage in a social justice movement is unlikely. Strides to fully reopen Guatemala's ICA system are untimely given the human rights abuses of the past and the need to heal and forge new trust.

However, there has been some discussion and speculation about Guatemala's willingness to begin a special-needs program for intercountry adoption. For example, Noe Erazo of the CNA shared the story of a young child, Sophia (Rotabi, 2014). A humanitarian visa for travel was granted so that the young girl could seek medical treatment in the United States for a life-threatening health condition. The US foster family who helped care for Sophia during her recovery applied to adopt Sophia in 2014. This unique case was managed such that the adoption process could take place in Guatemalan courts without the presence of the child. The two central authorities—Guatemala and the United States—agreed to this process for Sophia's case. This is an example of Guatemala and the United States acting in collaborative partnership between two central authorities for the best interests of the child, as is the intent of the HCIA (Rotabi, 2014). While Sophia's case is unusual, it is indicative of the humanitarian grounds on which children have entered the United States from Guatemala for medical treatment and some flexibility for child adoption in recent times (Rotabi, 2014). Of course, in this case, the best interests of the child are clear as Sophia must have life-saving treatment and follow-up care that is simply not available in Guatemala.

Sophia's case may be seen by some to be an indicator of hope for the opening of a special-needs program such as that currently in operation for Chinese adoptions. However, such a formal and systematic step is uncertain at this point. There certainly are many special-needs children with conditions such as spinal bifida and other seriously debilitating and life-threatening medical conditions in Guatemala. Like Sophia, such children can be treated in the United States, Canada, and Western Europe and then placed for adoption with families in those countries where ongoing follow-up care can be guaranteed. However, this is not currently the norm; rather, a case like Sophia and her adoption is an exception at this point in post-adoption system-reform history.

Conclusion

Guatemala serves as a reminder that "the best predictor of the future is the past," dating back to at least the Civil War and into contemporary post-conflict times—quite simply, children were disappeared into ICA—they may be considered to be the living disappeared (Rotabi, 2012). Although not all cases were characterized by fraud and organized criminal networks orchestrating the laundering of children, the situation was grave. That said, not *all* adoptions from Guatemala were illicit and sadly a gray cloud of uncertainty hangs over many adoptees from Guatemala as some are now searching for their origins (see Larsen, 2007).

We are now left with a question of how a broad system of care can be built to meet the obligations of the subsidiarity principle of the HCIA. At present, Guatemala has built one level of the system of care, the central adoption authority. However, a holistic approach to family support throughout the country is still lacking even with concerted efforts to build systems of care. We now turn to the question of building systems for children and families and their support needs as we look at progress being made in India as well as the United States.

Notes

1 In Spanish, the verb *jalar* means to pull or haul. The use of the word *jaladora* means here a worker who pulls or carries children from their families and community.
2 Women in Guatemala most frequently refer to child abduction as theft using terms such as *robo de niño*. See Mónico (2013) for an expanded discussion of the phenomena.
3 Presumably in the adult entertainment industry.

References

Amnesty International. (2006). Guatemala: No protection, no justice: Killings of women in Guatemala. Retrieved from http://web.amnesty.org/library/index/ENGAMR340172005

Associated Press. (2006, April 20). Guatemala mob burns kidnap suspects alive. Retrieved from www.foxnews.com/printer_friendly_story/0,3566,192408,00.html

Babb, L. A. (1999). *Ethics in American adoption*. New York: Praeger.

Ballard, R. L., Goodno, N., Cochran, R., & Milbrandt, J. (Eds). (2015). *The intercountry adoption debate: Dialogues across disciplines*. Newcastle upon Tyne: Cambridge Scholars Publishing.

Bartholet, E. (2010). International adoption: The human rights issues. In Goodwin, M. B. (Ed.), *Baby markets: Money and the new politics of creating families* (pp. 94–117). New York: Cambridge University Press.

Bartholet, E. & Smolin, D. M. (2012). The debate. In J. L. Gibbons & K. S. Rotabi (Eds), *Intercountry adoption: Policies, practices, and outcomes* (pp. 233–51). Farnham: Ashgate Press.

Boedeker, H. (2015, September 4). "48 hours" repeats Oviedo adoption story. Retrieved from www.orlandosentinel.com/entertainment/tv/tv-guy/os-48-hours-cbs-oviedo-adoption-agency-20150904-post.html

Briggs, L. (2012). *Somebody's children: The politics of transracial and transnational adoption*. Durham, NC: Duke University Press.

Bromfield, N. F. & Rotabi, K. S. (2012). The Haitian child abduction attempt: Policy analysis of human trafficking laws and implications for social workers. *Journal of Social Work Values and Ethics*, 9(1). Retrieved from www.socialworker.com/jswve/spring12/spr123.pdf

Bunkers, K. M. & Groza, V. (2012). Intercountry adoption and child welfare in Guatemala: Lessons learned pre and post ratification of the 1993 Hague Convention on the Protection of Children and Cooperation in Respect of Intercountry Adoption. In J. L. Gibbons & K. S. Rotabi (Eds), *Intercountry adoption: Policies, practices, and outcomes* (pp. 119–31). Farnham: Ashgate Press.

Bunkers, K. M., Groza, V., & Lauer, D. P. (2009). International adoption and child protection in Guatemala: A case of the tail wagging the dog. *International Social Work*, 52(5), 649–60.

Casa Alianza, Myrna Mack Foundation, Survivors Foundation, Social Movement for the Rights of Children and Adolescents, Human Rights Office of the Archbishop of Guatemala, & Social Welfare Secretariat. (2007). Adoptions in Guatemala: Protection or business? Retrieved from www.brandeis.edu/investigate/gender/adoption/docs/InformedeAdopcionesFundacionMyrnaMack.pdf

Celebrate Children International. (n.d.). Statement by CCI in response to the January 18 broadcast of 48 Hours. Retrieved from www.celebratechildren.org/2014/01/20/statement-by-cci-in-response-to-the-january-18-broadcast-of-48-hours/

Central Intelligence Agency. (2006). World fact book: Guatemala. Retrieved from www.cia.gov/cia/publications/factbook/index.html

CICIG (Comisión Internacional contra la Impunidad). (2010). Report on players involved in the illegal adoption process in Guatemala since the entry into force of the Adoption Law (Decree 77–2007).

Retrieved from http://cicig.org/uploads/documents/informes/INFOR-TEMA_DOC05_20101201_EN.pdf

Costantino, R. (2006). Femicide, impunity, and citizenship: The old and new in the struggle for justice in Guatemala. *Journal of Mujeres Activistas en Letras y Cambio Social*, 6(1), 107–21.

Cruz, N., Martin, A., & Rotabi, K. S. (2010, March). *Violence against women in Guatemala: Global connections and action in the US*. Orlando: University of Central Florida. Portions retrieved from www.youtube.com/watch?v=xPtJadrhZzk

Cruz, N., Smolin, D., Dilworth, A., Rotabi, K. S., & DiFilipo, T. (2011, April). Stolen children: Illegal practices in intercountry adoption and the need for reform. Invited presentation for the Human Rights Impact Litigation Clinic of the American University Washington College of Law, Washington, DC.

Dubinsky, K. (2010). *Babies without borders: Adoption and migration across the Americas*. Toronto: University of Toronto Press.

Estrada Zepeda, B. E. (2009). *Estudio Jurídico-social sobre trata de personas en Guatemala* [Socio-judicial study on human trafficking in Guatemala]. Guatemala City: Fundación Sobrevivientes [Survivors Foundation].

Families without Borders. (2003). UNICEF, Guatemalan adoptions, and the best interest of the child: An informative study. Retrieved from www.geocities.com/familieswithoutborders/FWBstudyGuatemala.pdf

Fixel Law Offices. (n.d.). Waiting Angels facts. Retrieved from www.fixellawoffices.com/waiting-angels-faq.html

Goldsmith, R. (2000, September 1). Guatemala's baby business. *BBC Crossing Continents*. Retrieved from http://news.bbc.co.uk/1/hi/programmes/crossing_continents/879859.stm

Goodwin, M. B. (2010). *Baby markets: Money and the new politics of creating families*. New York: Cambridge University Press.

Guatemala Human Rights Commission. (2009). Fact sheet: Femicide and feminicide. Retrieved from www.GHRC-USA.org/Publications/FemicideFactSheet2009.pdf

Honeyman, D. (1999). Lynch mobs and child theft rumors in the Guatemalan highlands. Unpublished doctoral dissertation. University of Alberta, Canada.

Kirpalani R. & Ng, C. (2011, August 5). Missouri couple silent on order to return adopted daughter to Guatemala. *ABC News*. Retrieved from http://abcnews.go.com/US/missouri-couple-silent-order-return-adopted-daughter-guatemala/story?id=14234379

Lacey, M. (2006, November 5). Guatemala system is scrutinized as Americans rush to adopt. New York Times. Retrieved from www.nytimes.com/2006/11/05/world/americas/05guatemala.html?_r=1&adxnll=1

Larsen, E. (2007, November/December). Did I steal my child? Mother Jones. Retrieved from http://motherjones.com/politics/2007/10/did-i-steal-my-daughter-tribulations-global-adoption

Lopez, L. & O'Kane, T. (1994). Dangerous rumors. *Time*, 143(16), 48.

Malkin, E. (2015, August 25). Genocide retrial is set for Guatemalan former dictator. New York Times. Retrieved from www.nytimes.com/2015/08/26/world/americas/genocide-retrial-is-set-for-guatemalan-former-dictator.html?_r=0

Malkin, E. & Azam, A. (2015, September 1). President Otto Pérez Molina is stripped of immunity in Guatemala. New York Times. Retrieved from www.nytimes.com/2015/09/02/world/americas/guatemala-votes-to-strip-its-president-of-immunity.html?_r=0

McKinney, L. (2007). International adoption and the Hague Convention: Does implementation of the Convention protect the best interests of children? *Whittier Journal of Child and Family Advocacy*, 6, 361–75.

Mónico, C. (2013). Implications of child abduction for human rights and child welfare systems: A constructivist inquiry of the lived experience of Guatemalan mothers publicly reporting child abduction for intercountry adoption. Doctoral dissertation. Retrieved from VCU Digital Archives, Electronic Theses and Dissertations, http://hdl.handle.net/10156/4373

Myrna Mack Foundation. (2009). Impunity, stigma and gender: Study of criminal case files related to violent deaths in the Department of Guatemala (2005–2007). Retrieved from http://mediaresearch-hub.ssrc.org/impunity-stigma-and-gender/attachment

New Internationalist. (2000, July). Baby snatchers boom. Retrieved from http://web23.epnet.com/citation.asp?tb=1&_ug=dbs+f5h+sid+8E1A00BF%2D412A%2D923B%2

Parents for Ethical Adoption Reform. (2009). Mothers in Guatemala demand justice. Retrieved from http://pear-now.blogspot.com/2009/04/mothers-in-guatemala-demand-justice.html

Portenier, G. (2006, May 4). Killer's paradise. *BBC*. Retrieved from http://news.bbc.co.uk/2/hi/programmes/this_world/4965786.stm

REMHI (Recuperación de la Memoria Histórica). (1999). *Guatemala never again!* Maryknoll, NY: Orbis.

Riben, M. (2007). *The stork market: America's multi-million dollar unregulated industry*. Dayton, NJ: Advocate Press.

Rivera, C., Bromfield, N. F., & Rotabi, K. S. (2009, April). *Sold into sex, servitude, and adoption*. Richmond, VA: Guatemalan Interest Group.

Roby, J. L. & Brown, T. (2015). Exploitation of intercountry adoption: Toward common understanding and action. *Adoption Quarterly*, 19(2), 63–80.

Rodman, D. H. (2009). Forgotten Guatemala: Genocide, truth and denial in Guatemala's Oriente (pp. 192–215). In A. L. Hinton & Y. K. O'Neill (Eds), *Genocide: Truth, memory, and representation*. Durham, NC: Duke University Press.

Romo, R. (2011, August 17). Guatemalan mother says daughter kidnapped, adopted in U.S. Retrieved from http://edition.cnn.com/2011/WORLD/americas/08/15/guatemala.kidnapping.adoption/index.html

Rotabi, K. S. (2009, August). Guatemala City: Hunger protests amid allegations of child kidnapping and adoption fraud. *Social Work & Society News Magazine*. Retrieved from www.socmag.net/?p=540

Rotabi, K. S. (2012). Child adoption and war: "Living disappeared" children and the social worker's post-conflict role in El Salvador and Argentina. *International Social Work*, 57(2), 169–80. doi: 10.1177/0020872812454314

Rotabi, K. S. (2014, December). Force, fraud, and coercion: Bridging from knowledge of intercountry adoption to global surrogacy. ISS Working Paper Series/General Series, 600, 1–30. Retrieved from http://hdl.handle.net/1765/77403

Rotabi, K. S. & Bunkers, K. M. (2008, November). Intercountry adoption reform based on the Hague Convention on Intercountry Adoption: An update on Guatemala in 2008. *Social Work and Society News Magazine*. Retrieved from www.socmag.net/?tag=adoption

Rotabi, K. S. & Mónico, C. (2015). Intercountry adoptions: Legal and policy issues affecting adoption practice. In R. Fong & R. McRoy (Eds), *Transracial and intercountry adoptions: Cultural guidance for professionals and educators*. New York: Columbia University Press.

Rotabi, K. S. & Morris, A. W. (2007, July). Adoption of Guatemalan children: Impending changes under the Hague Convention for Intercountry Adoption. *Social Work and Society News Magazine*. Retrieved from www.socmag.net/?p=171

Rotabi, K. S., Morris, A. W., & Weil, M. O. (2008). International child adoption in a post-conflict society: A multi-systemic assessment of Guatemala. *Journal of Intergroup Relations*, 34(2), 9–41.

Rotabi, K. S., Pennell, J., Roby, J. L., & Bunkers, K. M. (in press). Family group conferencing as a culturally adaptable intervention: Reforming intercountry adoption in Guatemala. *International Social Work*.

Sanford, V. (2008). From genocide to feminicide: Impunity and human rights in twenty-first century Guatemala. *Journal of Human Rights*, 7, 104–22. doi: 10.1080/14754830802070192

Selman, P. (2012). The rise and fall of intercountry adoption in the 21st century: Global trends from 2001 to 2010. In J. L. Gibbons & K. S. Rotabi (Eds), *Intercountry adoption: Policies, practices, and outcomes* (pp. 7–28). Farnham: Ashgate Press.

Siegal, E. (2011). *Finding Fernanda: Two mothers, one child, and a cross-border search for truth*. Boston, MA: Beacon.

Smolin, D. M. (2004). Intercountry adoption as child trafficking. *Valparaiso University Law Review*, 39, 281–325.

Smolin, D. M. (2006). Child laundering: How the intercountry adoption system legitimizes and incentivizes the practices of buying, trafficking, kidnapping, and stealing children. *Wayne Law Review*, 52, 113–200.

Smolin, D. M. (2007). Intercountry adoption and poverty: A human rights analysis. *Capital University Law Review*, 36, 413–53.

United Nations. (2000). Rights of the child: Report of the Special Rapporteur on the sale of children, child prostitution and child pornography, Ms Ofelia Calcetas-Santos. Retrieved from http://pound-puplegacy.org/node/30853

United Nations. (2009). Child adoption: Trends and policies. Retrieved from www.un.org/esa/population/publications/adoption2010/child_adoption.pdf

United Nations Development Program. (2015). Human development report 2015. Available from http://hdr.undp.org/en/2015-report

US Department of State. (n.d.a). Arrests or detention of an American citizen abroad. Retrieved from http://travel.state.gov/travel/tips/emergencies/arrest/arrest_3879.html

US Department of State. (n.d.b). Intercountry adoption: Statistics. Retrieved from http://adoption.state.gov/about_us/statistics.phpUnited States

US Department of State. (2001). Guatemala country report on human rights practices. Retrieved from www.state.gov/j/drl/rls/hrrpt/2000/wha/775.htm

US Department of State. (2007). Guatemala country report on human rights practices. Retrieved from www.state.gov/j/drl/rls/hrrpt/2007/index.htm

US Department of State. (2009). Dip note: Norma Cruz: Seeking justice and dignity for Guatemalan women. Retrieved from http://blogs.state.gov/index.php/entries/norma_cruz/

White, J. (2006, March). Journal entry: February 26, 2006, Coban, Guatemala. GSSG Newsletter, IV(1), 5.

Yemm, L. M. (2010). International adoption and the "best interests" of the child: Reality and reactionism in Romania and Guatemala. *Washington University Global Studies Law Review*, 9, 555–74.

5

CHILD-PROTECTION SYSTEMS OF CARE TO ENSURE CHILD RIGHTS IN FAMILY SUPPORT AND ADOPTION

India and the United States

Effective implementation of the Hague Convention on Intercountry Adoption must be tailored to the social, cultural, and economic context while adhering to the expectations set forth in the Convention, specifically the principle of subsidiarity and safeguards. Fundamentally, a ratifying country is expected to have congruent domestic laws, policies, and procedures that integrate a continuum of care supportive of families to parent the child in question. To reach this goal, governments must have at least a basic welfare and child-protection system oriented to supporting family life; as the term *welfare* means "well-being," the idea is that supportive family policy, programs, and community life are essential to meeting this end. From a child-rights perspective, the Convention on the Rights of the Child states in Article 19 to ensure:

> the establishment of social programmes to provide necessary support for the child and for those who have the care of the child, as well as for other forms of prevention and for identification, reporting, referral, investigation, treatment and follow-up of instances of child maltreatment described heretofore, and, as appropriate, for judicial involvement.
>
> *(UNICEF, n.d.)*

Practically speaking, International Social Services captures this idea in terms of family support, as follows:

> Governments and civil society should do everything possible to ensure that families have the chance and are motivated to take care of their child (CRC, art. 18, par. 2 and 3). This means formulating policies and programmes that translate, among other means, into psychosocial support and/or economic assistance for mothers or families in difficult circumstances; reaching out to the extended family, particularly the grandparents, to enlist their help in avoiding abandonment; raising awareness of the importance of the father's role; training for parental duties; and strengthening the child's ties with his family.
>
> *(International Social Services, 2005, p. 1)*

A family-support continuum of care requires that first the family of origin/biological family should receive social support to care for their child. When parenting by biological parent(s) or other relatives is not possible, care options in the child's community should be explored beyond the nuclear family and inclusive of a broad extended family and kinship group. Once the local options appear to be unavailable or inappropriate (including guardianship and domestic adoptions), then a country may determine that the child is appropriate for a financially transparent intercountry adoption. All of these steps are carried out with the best interests of the child as a fundamental principle, inclusive of the child's readiness for adoption and other factors, such as special needs and age. In the case of older children, their opinion in the matter of their long-term care, especially when considering intercountry adoption, is essential (Hague Conference on Private International Law, 2008).

All of these steps should be carried out in a manner that is not oriented to expedite inter-country adoption as the goal, but rather a careful exercise of the steps necessary to ensure an ethical adoption is critical. It is especially important to note that a large and/or impersonal residential care facility is not considered to be in the best interests of the child when other options are available and appropriate, including intercountry adoption (Hague Conference on Private International Law, 2008).

Different countries: different contexts and constraints in care systems

Social service systems are variable in each country, due to different contextual realities, and some of these systems are more aligned to the HCIA than others. Obvious limitations for many intercountry adoption countries of origin are extreme poverty and limited government infrastructure to carry out anything more than rudimentary services. This is especially true when the country is in a conflict or post-conflict scenario or there are other demanding problems like drought, floods, hunger, and the array of resulting health and social problems. In these resource-poor environments with a limited social service workforce, those working in social services are most frequently drawn into scenarios in which they typically focus on the bigger picture—social planning and large-scale intervention—rather than focusing on one child at a time. In the crisis situation, when a social worker or other social service professional focuses on one child at a time, she may serve a relatively small number of children and families. However, when the focus is the larger or macro picture, social planning to aid and assist families has the greatest impact broadly and in the long term. Furthermore, the removal of children from disaster zones across borders during crisis is counter to the United Nations Guidelines for the Alternative Care of Children (United Nations, 2009).

India and the United States as two case examples

Because each country has its unique underlying dynamics, we will focus on two countries, India and the United States. Both are very different in their intercountry adoption issues. Each country has ratified the Hague Convention on Intercountry Adoption, and they each illustrate different local needs, service orientation, and pressing issues in child protection and adoption ethics. To clarify, these two countries are not presented as points of comparison. Rather they are illustrative of some unique issues in adoption practices based on different contextual realities. For intercountry adoption, India is typically a country of origin while the United States is most frequently a destination country. However, in the case of the United States, there are a small number of "outgoing" cases and the problems surrounding these adoptions will also be considered.

As a starting point, it is critical to recognize that India has an estimated population of 1.29 billion people, and like the United States, it is a geographically large country, with multiple states and a central government framework for legislation (UNdata, n.d.). Some of the basic ideas in each system are similar, but the reality is that each country is carrying out its mandate to provide support to their children and families based on different social forces, much of which is related to central/federal and state government budgets and the inherent limitations.

The United States, with a fraction of India's population, has a well-established child-protection system whereas India has an emerging child-protection system. Neither system is perfect—in fact, one can find many aspects to criticize as child-protection systems are frequently blamed for the failure to adequately support children and their families (Harris & DiFilipo, 2015). When considering the problems, we do not look at these two systems in their entirety. Rather, we are looking at some system components, as greater exploration would require a far more expansive discourse that is outside the scope of this book.

Riddled with scandals: India's intercountry adoption system

In a 2013 India media article entitled "Overseas adoption racket: How children are sneaked out by the hundreds," it was asserted that a child goes missing in India once every eight minutes (Raza, 2013).[1] Government statistics indicate that between 2010 and 2011, the number of abducted children increased by 43 percent (Ministry of Statistics and Programme Implementation, 2012). In 2013 it was reported that families who believed their children to have been abducted into adoption networks staged protests to bring attention to the crime. Activists have asserted that gangs have organized in the abducting and selling of children for adoption (Raza, 2013). These allegations have come after a series of adoption scandals that have been well documented for many years (Bhargava, 2005; Smolin, 2005).

Bhargava (2005) and Smolin (2005) have documented the illicit activities and techniques that have led to wide-scale adoption fraud, including child abduction and sales into intercountry adoption. Bos (2007) has interviewed birth mothers and found an array of problems in the system in the Tamil region of India. Not unlike the previous case examples in the other countries that have been presented thus far, the modes of fraud in India are broad and diverse (Bhargava, 2005).

Bhargava (2005) points out that there are children who have simply been lost—on train platforms or in large crowds—and too often in the past there has been no meaningful search for or tracing of families. Rather, in many instances the children are sent to residential child-care institutions where they typically languish in these settings that are notoriously bad for child health, safety, growth, and development. Some are placed for adoption while others fall into the juvenile justice system as they come to law-enforcement attention as "delinquent" children; this is particularly true for adolescents who come into conflict with the law.

While it is hard to believe that a child can simply be "lost," the sheer population size of India makes this particular scenario a reality for poor families with little resources to search for a missing child. The law-enforcement environment has been such that marginalized people have been disregarded—often simply ignored—when seeking help. Furthermore, social services and law enforcement should collaborate and exercise due diligence in family tracing. Fundamentally, many lost children have been treated as social orphans, and inadequate responses to their needs has resulted in a failure to protect the child and family rights—especially when the child is placed in a residential childcare facility when a simple family-tracing exercise could prevent such an inhumane response (United Nations, 2009).

Missing and abducted children: recent improvements in India

In response to the thousands of children who go missing in India every year, the creation of a centralized database of missing children for family tracing was a major priority by order of the Supreme Court of India. The new system, called the National Tracking System for Missing and Vulnerable Children (http://trackthemissingchild.gov.in/) was in the early stages of being rolled out in 2015, and while the system is not yet fully functional in every state and every locality, the intervention is promising as a missing child's data input takes place at the local level (police, etc.) with information such as name, age, height, weight, and other key characteristics of the missing child. Tracking can then take place across the country. A family that has a missing child can seek information and potentially be reunified through a matching process based on this data system.

This database approach is found elsewhere, but it is different from those found in other countries with far smaller populations. For example, Guatemala and every state in the United States have an alert system, called the Amber alert in the United States.[2] In this first response, a child's description is broadcast through local networks immediately following a report of abduction, including announcements on major highways. However, in a country the size and scale of India, with reports of lost and abducted children taking place hundreds of times a day, a system such as Amber alert is simply not feasible. There are far too many children and families affected, and the alert would lose meaning if it were sounded every day. Rather, with the data-information system, tracking missing children with digital technology within an aggressive networking system has been the logical strategy in India, given contextual realities and the demands for family tracing.

Practically speaking, once data are entered into the system effectively, a child's whereabouts may now be traced across India's 28 states by linking a missing child's profile with a found child in another location. Also, children who may be helped include those who are living in institutions. Once a child is located in the child-protection system, local social services are charged with assisting in the reintegration of the child (India Ministry of Women and Child Development, n.d.). This may include the identification of children who have been trafficked within India, who will inevitably need support or rehabilitation in their community reintegration, including support to prevent any further trafficking when they are returned to the community in which their traffickers are still present (including family members, in some cases). As each case is different with unique circumstances and vulnerabilities, social-care plans are developed to meet the best interests of the child on a case-by-case basis as per the Juvenile Justice Act in India (International Social Services, 2005; India Ministry of Women and Child Development, n.d.; Supreme Court Committee on Juvenile Justice, 2015).

Other important initiatives in child protection to support families

Systems transformation is taking place under India's integrated child-protection scheme, and care systems are improving gradually, including the provision for cash transfers/assistance for some families in poverty to help prevent the institutionalization of their children. This strategy, which is one of the preventive approaches in family support, has been developed to meet the needs of children nationwide (India Ministry of Women and Child Development, n.d.). Social service providers, including social workers, at the district level may assess the need for cash transfers or other assistance. Additionally, relative foster care is now being developed in some parts of India. In the case of relative foster care, relatives who foster a child may also receive a small financial stipend to maintain the child's basic needs.

In this system, which is quite broad with a wide array of services and sectors including volunteer child welfare committees, healthcare providers, the police and judiciary converge to support children and their families at the local level (India Ministry of Women and Child Development, n.d.). At the federal government level, there is the Central Adoption Resource Authority that operates within the Ministry of Women and Child Development framework, with a network of State Adoption Resource Authorities carrying out work in each state (Chakrabarty, 2016; Bhargava, 2005; India Ministry of Women and Child Development, n.d.). Theoretically, these organizations interface with government child-protection officials as well as non-government organizations/charities/private residential care facilities working collaboratively in the spirit of the best interests of the child. In reality, orchestrating this system effectively in such a large country has considerable challenges and some actors have a profit motive. Furthermore, today there remain serious and persistent challenges in the child-protection system (Supreme Court Committee on Juvenile Justice, 2015). Concerns continue to be raised about adoption fraud in India, as evidenced by the March 2016 Supreme Court of India ruling that there "should be a 'credible mechanism' for intra and inter-country adoption of children" and the necessity to frame "rules" for ethical procedures were among the details of the court order (Hindustan Times, 2016).

The priority for domestic adoption is one of the concerns. Inevitably, this movement in the Supreme Court is a response to changes in 2015, catalyzed by the highest levels of the India Ministry of Women and Child Development, to set relatively expedient timelines for meeting adoption targets (Stays, 2015). There are many Indian couples hopeful to adopt,[3] thereby meeting the principle of subsidiarity when a domestic adoption is appropriate for a child. However, expediting processes may actually move the child along and around other care options to include domestic adoption—this could result in a gateway to intercountry adoption without giving meaningful time and energy to in-country domestic solutions (especially a concerted effort to keep the child in his/her family and kinship system). Fundamentally, there are worries that the emergent timeline is too fast to really operationalize a social service continuum for the child when it comes to the critical determination that a child is truly appropriate for intercountry adoption. Time will only tell if pressures, new rules, and involvement of the Supreme Court helps or hurts the children and families of concern as rules, policies, and procedures continue to be defined and the question is always in the execution of rules/procedures and how they support the best interests of children.

These are just a handful of the features of the emergent child-protection system in India. Inevitably, with the size, poverty, and major challenges of India, the child-protection system as a whole has an overwhelming implementation task. Even with planning for cash transfers and other social services, inevitably there will be children and families who are in such a crisis situation that meeting their needs will be very difficult, if not impossible. These realities pose obvious problems in India's capacity to meet the principle of subsidiarity and safeguards under the Hague Convention on Intercountry Adoption and the best interests of the child, more broadly.

The United States and its unique country dynamics as a country of origin

The United States is mainly a receiving country or destination country for ICA. However, some children—mainly infants and toddlers—are sent to other countries such as the Netherlands, Canada, and Ireland (Selman, 2015). In the case of the Netherlands, the very low birth rate and the existence of comprehensive social services (including cash and other assistance) for vulnerable families has been reason for prospective adoptive parents to look elsewhere for child adoption. Many Dutch prospective parents who seek adoption services in the United States are gay men (Naughton, 2012). This is a well-known practice amongst adoption professionals, a few of whom see themselves as engaged in a social justice cause of helping same-sex couples build a family.

Turning to Belgium, one adoption service provider has an HCIA-congruent agreement to send US children to that country though his accredited organization.[4] The agreed-upon cost for infant adoptions, within a collaborative agreement as per the HCIA intent, is reportedly approximately US$5,500 for the Belgium agency fees, US$33,000 for the US accredited service provider, and the birth mother can receive US$1,500–8,000 for her "expenses" (see Against Child Trafficking, 2016). In other words, the adoption of an infant can range upwards to US$45,000. Such a fee structure certainly challenges the notion of reasonable professional compensation as per the HCIA. However, it should be noted that guidance for limits on fees has never been set by the United States, a gray area here allowing for ambiguity that crosses the line, at some point. There is a cost of professional services—the question is what is appropriate or not. That has yet to be defined concretely by regulatory standards and the above example certainly raises the need to consider setting limits.

Another adoption lawyer has historically sent very young biracial children and infants to Canada. This particular lawyer is known to justify his work on the grounds that biracial children are better off in Canada rather than in the area of the United States in which he works—an area of the country that has historically struggled with race relations. This is a distorted "best interests of the child" position that is outdated at this juncture in US history; not because racism is no longer a problem, but because there are many American families in racially diverse and tolerant communities who stand ready to adopt these children as in domestic adoptions. Furthermore, as Dubinsky (2010) documents, Canada is not a race-relations utopia, and the practice of moving biracial children from Canada is complicated and ethically loaded (Balcom & Dubinsky, 2005).

In the case of infants leaving the United States, those adoptions are like other private US infant adoptions—they are typically very expensive, and lawyers are frequently engaged (Freundlich, 1998). Also notably, the United States is exceptional as an HCIA country as it allows for-profit adoption-service providers (Duncan, 2000). At the time of writing there were only a few such providers—and they are lawyers.[5] This allowance for for-profit lawyers' involvement in ICA has been a somewhat thorny issue in the US implementation of the HCIA, as ethical questions have arisen (Groza & Bunkers, 2014).

Looking at what is known about children leaving the United States since 2008, there is one obvious fact. Many of these children were processed by adoption agencies in Florida. Figure 5.1 illustrates this point. We may ask, why Florida? Bluntly, Florida is known as a state with an outdated adoption law, and as a result, weak state child-placement agency licensing standards make the location attractive for agencies looking for an easy pathway in terms of state oversight.

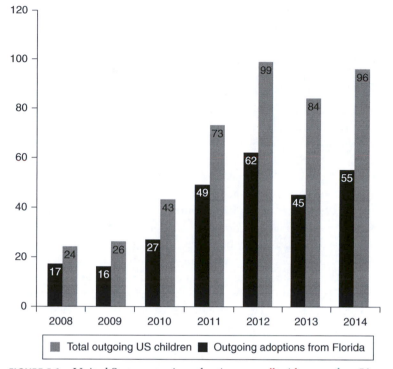

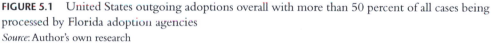

FIGURE 5.1 United States outgoing adoptions overall with more than 50 percent of all cases being processed by Florida adoption agencies

Source: Author's own research

The United States and for-profit intercountry adoption activities

Fundamentally, the problem of for-profit activities dates back to agreements made in the development of the Hague Convention on Intercountry Adoption when the United States insisted on the right to allow for-profit adoption providers (Duncan, 2000). This particular exception to the HCIA's intent is unique; some may call it a loophole for a small service sector of private infant adoptions that is notorious for high fees for service (Freundlich, 1998; Harris & DiFilipo, 2015).

However, almost all US providers are actually non-profit agencies that do not have the necessary accreditation to send children to another country; rather, the vast majority of agencies only receive children for adoption (O'Connor & Rotabi, 2012). The small group of organizations that send children out of the United States are unusual and not all of them specialize in infants and very young children. For example, VIDA, a non-profit adoption agency of Hudson, New York, has the HCIA status necessary to send children overseas (outgoing cases), but they are not known for infant adoptions. As a small agency, most frequently they handle unique cases of children who are matched to families living outside of the United States. One example of service that they provide is cases in which one of the prospective parents is a US citizen and living overseas with a foreign spouse.

Regarding profit and the structure of US adoption agencies, it is important to understand that the idea of a non-profit agency should not be judged on the category of title alone. The question is, how much are their staff paid and how high are the adoption fees? In the post-HCIA environment, some agencies have continued to pay their staff extraordinary

salaries of *well over* US$100,000.[6] At some point, six-figure salaries arguably come into con-
flict with the HCIA. Professional compensation is to be regulated within a set of reasonable
professional-fees framework by countries enforcing the Convention. Again, there are no
concrete regulatory standards for this area of agency functioning in terms of US government oversight and agency-accreditation standards (Council on Accreditation, 2007).

During the adoption boom, prior to the dramatic decline in intercountry adoptions, many
US-based agencies paid multiple family members' salaries. For example, an executive director
of an agency with a handsome salary might then pay her husband and other family members
as employees. This well-known activity does not always cloud financial transparency, as sometimes these employees really are working, but it certainly is questionable. This dynamic has
persisted to some degree in the post-HCIA environment, although it is far less frequent with
the dramatic downturn in ICA and agency-accreditation requirements.

Finally, many adoption-agency professionals in the United States would point out that
operating expenses for ICA are extraordinarily high, and they must develop a financial model
that keeps them sustainable, even in times of an unexpected downturn such as a country
closure/moratorium. Admittedly, these are some important points to be understood about
agency solvency and functioning. In some European countries,[7] the government provides
modest financial support for agencies and thereby a baseline of cash flow may buffer financial
stress for some adoption organizations in Europe during times of downturn and crisis.

However, in the United States, well over 100 agencies have essentially closed their doors to
ICA since the implementation of the Hague Convention in the United States. Tracy Blustein,
executive director of Adoption Alliance, said upon the closure of the agency, "We have been
hit really hard with the change in economic climate and international and domestic adoption…In previous years, we would be able to place 60 kids per year—now we are down to 25.
Our financial resources have diminished" (Illescas, 2011, p. 1). This was just one agency, closing
after 22 years, that had to shutter their doors due to the dramatic shift in the availability of
children and adoption practices, in general.

Fundamentally, ICA as a practice has become too difficult to manage, given a variety of
dynamics, including the expense of services, legal liability, and risk due to fraudulent practices
(especially overseas activity that is difficult to supervise and control). Financial solvency problems were especially true for agencies that were dependent on a single country for their base
of functioning (e. g. China, Russia, or Guatemala). As a result, extraordinary salaries are far
less frequent today in the downturn of ICA. In fact, some agency directors have taken deep
cuts in salaries and lay-offs of multiple employees to stabilize the organization are a common
occurrence in a new and difficult financial environment.

Differences in the US system after Hague Convention on Intercountry Adoption implementation

As the United States has implemented the HCIA with an emphasis on agency functioning within an adoptee-destination framework, significant changes have occurred as adoption agencies are now reviewed and evaluated to ensure that they meet regulatory standards
(Council on Accreditation, 2007). Although the standards are not perfect, especially when
looking critically at problematic practices that still exist, a number of changes have strengthened the system considerably (Rotabi & Gibbons, 2012). Table 5.1 identifies some of these
changes in the old versus the new and reformed system. The Council on Accreditation (2007)
standards set the requirements for HCIA compliance and anchor the changes.

TABLE 5.1 The old US system of ICA versus the reformed system

Old system	New system after HCIA implementation
ICA agencies, based in the US, worked in overseas locations without oversight by US child welfare or other authorities on a national level. Rather, state-by-state licensing regulations governed the process for child-placement agencies and some states had minimal standards when it came to intercountry adoption.	ICA agencies in the US now must be accredited to work in an overseas country, and this includes countries that have not ratified the HCIA. Accreditation is carried out on a national basis, and oversight is now linked to the 2007 Intercountry Adoption Act, which is a federal law.
US agencies were often involved in the determination that a child, in another country, was adoptable.	Now, in the case of HCIA-compliant countries, the foreign government determines the child's readiness for ICA weighing in a variety of factors related to the Principle of Subsidiarity. A US adoption agency does not ethically involve itself in this part of the process, especially related to putting undue pressure on the central authority of another country to determine a child as adoptable.
US adoption agencies charged families fees without any oversight or financial transparency requirements.	US adoption agencies now must follow requirements of financial transparency, including providing the family with a set fee schedule from the earliest family/agency contact. Then a contract is signed with stages of payment that are considered reasonable fees.
US adoption agencies operated with little financial security, leaving those agencies and the families they served vulnerable in times of crisis.	US adoption agencies must now be bonded to carry out the work of adoption, they must have several months of cash reserves for operating expenses in times of crisis, and they must have a clear policy and procedures related to legal liability including appropriate contracts with prospective parents. If and when an agency is closing, they must have a viable plan to transfer unfinished cases to another HCIA-accredited agency that stands ready to carry on the case management. It should be noted that some agency plans could be called flimsy as the viability/feasibility of transfer is not looked at very closely in most cases.
US adoption agencies used varying pre-adoption training for families—some material was simply not based on evidence and was poor quality if it existed at all.	US adoption agencies now must verify that families have received at least ten hours of pre-adoption training, which is expected to include content on the HCIA obligations, child-development issues such as attachment disorder and disabilities related to institutional care of children, and transracial/cross-cultural issues, etc. It should be noted that training quality varies, although more and more agencies are using video resources that have become somewhat standardized in recent years.

(*continued*)

TABLE 5.1 *(cont.)*

Old system	New system after HCIA implementation
Many adoption agencies operated without a clear service plan developed specifically for each placement family, identifying unique issues and areas for family support to ensure a successful adoptive placement.	US adoption agencies are expected to have a personalized service plan, on record, for each family they serve. However, it should be noted that there are no significant criteria for service-plan quality and many organizations are lacking in this area.
No data tracking of children, especially when there was an adoption disruption/dissolution.	US adoption agencies must now report to the US central authority/Department of State when there has been an adoption dissolution. Then, the country of origin is informed of the case in a manner that encourages collaboration as per the HCIA. It should be noted that there are failures to report dissolutions and this reality has come to bear in the rehoming scandals.
Non-profit adoption agencies operated with boards of directors as per requirements related to their non-profit tax status. However, many agencies had largely inactive boards in terms of being in oversight of agency practices.	US adoption agency board of director meetings are reviewed to ensure that they are meeting and overseeing the agency budget as well as risk-management issues appropriately. Evidence includes meeting minutes and verification that board members are participating in oversight, including interviews with board members when the agency is undergoing accreditation evaluation. It should be noted that still many agency boards of directors meet only a few times a year and often they engage in a "rubber stamp process" based on trust of their executive director rather than a firm oversight of finances and operations as per legal obligations.
Adoption agencies operated in virtual secrecy with little oversight other than state child-placement licensing standards. Those requirements were often scant (especially in some states) as they were generally not written to regulate ICA. The qualifications of those working in the agency and other issues of accountability reflected this reality in some states.	Organization records are now reviewed by the US Council on Accreditation. This oversight body verifies state licensing and complaints made at the state level in addition to an intensive review of bank statements, insurance and bonding documentation, as well as reviewing employee files including verification of their employee education and training as appropriate, etc. Also, prospective parent case files are reviewed across a range of documentation.

Source: Author's own research

Fair and impartial judicial processes mindful of the principle of subsidiarity

Thus far, the focal point has been on adoption agencies; however, the judicial processes in countries of origin affect ethical adoption processes. This was found to be true in Guatemala where today a handful of attorneys and judges as well as residential childcare-facility employees (including an American citizen[8]) have been imprisoned for their involvement in illicit adoptions (CICIG, 2010). Those involved in corruption were fundamentally unethical "professionals." When these corrupt individuals interfaced with adoption agencies in the pre-reform era, they presented case files that appeared to be in order and populated with relevant documents such as the social histories of birth families. However, at closer look, it was clear that in the case of adoption fraud many of these records in Guatemala were manufactured or falsified to make the child appear to be an "orphan" as is necessary for child laundering and travel visa application (Bunkers & Groza, 2012). These supposed records contained multiple falsehoods necessary to process the case within a court setting. Some judges accepted questionable paperwork and turned a blind eye and/or were enriched through bribery (CICIG, 2010; Rivera, Bromfield, & Rotabi, 2009).

Now, even with greater transparency and international child welfare standards for adoption practice, inevitably some judges still act with impunity when they engage in bribery in countries in which there are deep-seated problems related to corruption and a weak judiciary. Also, other judges are simply not trained to consider issues of the principle of subsidiarity when making important child welfare decisions in family-court deliberations. Either way, the judgments made in the court system have a significant impact on the best interests of the child.

Conclusion

In this era of reform, each HCIA member country is charged with improving adoption practices in child-protection services. Developmental steps necessary to meet HCIA obligations are most often gradual improvements. Some countries like Guatemala have instituted a self-imposed ICA moratorium in order to work through the developmental process without outside interference. Other countries, like India, have remained open to ICA, and their scheme for improving child-protection services is broad and ambitious—the scheme itself has emerged not as a result of the HCIA, but as a result of the call to action to protect children across India including the need to strengthen the domestic- and intercountry adoption system.

In the United States there are unique country dynamics, including the small but surprising practice of sending very young children abroad as adoptees.[9] The issues presented illustrate varying implementation strategies of the HCIA and areas of flexibility and the problems that arise. Nonetheless, the United States has made considerable strides in regulating adoption agencies on the whole. This step forward is substantial in terms of requiring financial transparency and professionalism for safeguarding the intercountry adoption process although problems do persist.

Issues of professionalism cannot be overlooked. Adoption agencies rely on a chain of professionals in other countries, and frequently most of what occurs in another country is largely out of an adoption agency's control. It is true that HCIA standards require supervision of providers operating on their behalf in another country (Council on Accreditation, 2007), however, that is a difficult task. This is especially true when a country has severe problems, such as persistent practices of adoption fraud in a context of a weak judiciary and impunity.

Even the most committed and ethical agency may find itself faced with difficult circumstances when other unethical agencies are engaging in corruption—they often find that they

are "scooped" by the unscrupulous who are willing to pay a bribe to secure a child. And, well-intentioned adoption professionals and/or adoptive families may find themselves in difficult scenarios such as an immigration officer (in a foreign country) who threatens the departure visa disposition to leverage a bribe. That is just one example of the kinds of ethical dilemmas and scenarios that can arise for even the best and most diligent of adoption professionals trying to finish an adoption to which they have invested many hours of hard work.

Fundamentally, the HCIA system requires everyone acting with integrity, like an honor system that respects the boundaries of ethics rather than looking for loopholes and opportunities to stretch definitions of HCIA standards. This has been the case in Africa, a region we look at next.

Notes

1   The fears are that children fall into a number of different nefarious trafficking scenarios.
2   The Amber alert was named after a child who was abducted, sexually assaulted, and murdered in California. Guatemala now has the Kenneth-Alba system, also named after two children who were abducted and killed.
3   An issue that is important to consider, when it comes to domestic adoptions, is the fact that many families in India are interested in very young children. As such, there are thousands of children who will likely never be considered seriously by an Indian family for adoption. In those cases, the timeline for such children should be managed appropriately. Some advocate for "concurrent" planning in which domestic solutions are explored while intercountry adoption processes are initiated as a back up that can be executed as needed in the best interests of the child.
4   In the case of the US, adoption agencies are accredited by the Council on Accreditation (2007) as per HCIA standards developed for financial transparency, quality adoption services, and ethics, etc. These standards were developed by the US Federal government and for US agencies. Many of the standards are quite good. However, agencies are only required to meet the minimum threshold of the standard.
5   See http://travel.state.gov/content/adoptionsabroad/en/hague-convention/agency-accreditation/adoption-service-provider-search.html
6   High salaries were not uncommon during the adoption boom, but with the slowdown and closure of countries, most US-based agencies simply cannot persist in paying extraordinary wages. The size of the agency, etc. must be weighed in when one begins to make a salary critique. HCIA standards require that employees cannot be paid based on contingency fees—wages cannot be set on the number of children secured for adoption.
7   Norway is one such country.
8   Nancy Bailey is a US citizen who was arrested for her role in illicit adoptions in Guatemala. After well over 15 years of running her own "children's home" in Antigua, Guatemala Bailey was finally arrested in 2014. Her imprisonment came after Bailey fled to the United States to avoid legal proceedings as an arrest warrant was actually issued in 2008. Bailey was detained when she traveled to neighboring El Salvador; arrested on the border of Guatemala. This was a somewhat shocking turn of events as American citizens may have been heavily involved in the adoption boom of Guatemala, but holding them legally accountable for fraud was a new development. And, Bailey was highly regarded by many of those who adopted through her organization as a child rescuer who had saved many children's lives. Arguably, she ran a high-quality residential childcare facility (Semillas de Amor/Seeds of Love), but the means in which some of the children entered the care of Bailey's organization was the problem. Furthermore, over the years Bailey amassed a fortune as she owned several exceptionally expensive real-estate properties in Guatemala in which she ran her organization, charging families upwards to $40,000 for an adoption (see Associated Press, 2014). While some see Bailey sympathetically, she has become the symbol of how an organization can look highly professional with happy customers from the US whereas local government authorities saw the scenario quite differently and ultimately moved to prosecute Bailey.

9   It is important to note that sending older foster children abroad is legitimate when the principle of subsidiarity is exercised. However, as we have discussed, sending infants abroad is highly suspect given the demand for infant adoption in the US.

References

Against Child Trafficking. (2016, January). Adoption lobby alert: American babies for 45,000$ and up. Retrieved from www.againstchildtrafficking.org/2016/01/adoption-lobby-alert-american-babies-for-45-000-and-up/

Associated Press. (2014, December 17). Guatemala arrests US fugitive in illegal adoptions. Retrieved from http://bigstory.ap.org/article/b663248fbad040b3a1bbf36f4b8660ca/guatemala-arrests-us-fugitive-illegal-adoptions

Balcom, K. & Dubinsky, K. B. (2005, October 13). Babies across borders; Canadians like to think that adopting Black U.S. infants is an act of rescue. Others call it "kidnap." Let's outgrow both terms. Globe and Mail, 21.

Bhargava, V. (2005). *Adoption in India: Polices and experiences*. New Delhi: Sage.

Bos, P. (2007). Once a mother. Relinquishment and adoption from the perspective of unmarried mothers in south India. Doctoral dissertation, Nijmegen University. Retrieved from http://dare.ubn.kun.nl/bitstream/2066/73643/1/73643.pdf

Bunkers, K. M. & Groza, V. (2012). Intercountry adoption and child welfare in Guatemala: Lessons learned pre and post ratification of the 1993 Hague Convention on the Protection of Children and Cooperation in Respect of Intercountry Adoption. In J. L. Gibbons & K. S. Rotabi (Eds), *Intercountry adoption: Policies, practices, and outcomes* (pp. 119–31). Farnham: Ashgate Press.

Chakrabarty, S. (2016, January 17). Adoption boost for future parents. Sunday Standard. Retrieved from www.newindianexpress.com/thesundaystandard/Adoption-Boost-for-Future-Parents/2016/01/17/article3230207.ece

CICIG (Comisión Internacional contra la Impunidad). (2010). Report on players involved in the illegal adoption process in Guatemala since the entry into force of the Adoption Law (Decree 77–2007). Retrieved from http://cicig.org/uploads/documents/informes/INFOR-TEMA_DOC05_20101201_EN.pdf

Council on Accreditation. (2007). *Hague accreditation and approval standards*. New York: Author. Retrieved from www.coanet.org/files/Hague_Accreditation_and_Approval_Standards.pdf

Dubinsky, K. (2010). *Babies without borders: Adoption and migration across the Americas*. Toronto: University of Toronto Press.

Duncan, W. (2000). The Hague Convention on the Protection of Children and Co-operation in Respect of Intercountry Adoption. In P. F. Selman (Ed.), *Intercountry adoption: Developments, trends, and perspectives* (pp. 40–52). London: British Agencies for Adoption & Fostering.

Freundlich, M. (1998). Supply and demand: The forces shaping the future of infant adoption. *Adoption Quarterly*, 2(1), 13–46.

Groza, V. K. & Bunkers, K. M. (2014). The USA as a sending country for intercountry adoption: Birth parents rights versus the 1993 Hague Convention on Intercountry Adoption. *Adoption Quarterly*, 17(1), 44–64.

Hague Conference on Private International Law. (2008). The implementation and operation of the 1993 Hague Intercountry Adoption Convention: Guide to good practice. Retrieved from www.hcch.net/upload/wop/ado_pd02e.pdf

Harris, R. & DiFilipo. T. (2015). Creating systems that protect children: Elements of success. In R. L. Ballard, N. Goodno, R. Cochran, & J. Milbrandt (Eds), *The intercountry adoption debate: Dialogues across disciplines* (pp. 708–29). Newcastle upon Tyne: Cambridge Scholars Publishing.

Hindustan Times. (2016, March 15). Supreme Court asks centre to frame rules for adoption. Retrieved from www.hindustantimes.com/india/supreme-court-asks-centre-to-frame-rules-for-child-adoption/story-wsk5d5JbRA0buBeUuzJJHI.html

Illescas, C. (2011, December 28). Denver adoption agency to close after 22 years. Denver Post. Retrieved from www.denverpost.com/ci_19628951

India Ministry of Women and Child Development. (n.d.). The integrated child protection scheme (ICPS): A centrally sponsored scheme of government-civil society partnership. Retrieved from http://wcd.nic.in/childprot/drafticps.pdf

International Social Services. (2005). *Fact sheet number one: A global policy for children and the family*. Geneva: International Reference Centre for the Rights of Children Deprived of Their Family.

Ministry of Statistics and Programme Implementation. (2012). *Children in India 2012: A statistical appraisal*. New Delhi: Author. Retrieved from http://mospi.nic.in/Mospi_New/upload/Children_in_India_2012.pdf

Naughton, D. (2012). Exiting or going forth? An overview of USA outgoing adoptions. In J. L. Gibbons & K. S. Rotabi (Eds), *Intercountry adoption: Policies, practices, and outcomes* (pp. 161–71). Farnham: Ashgate Press.

O'Connor, M. K. & Rotabi, K. S. (2012). Perspectives on child welfare: Ways of understanding roles and actions of current USA adoption agencies involved in intercountry adoptions. In J. L. Gibbons & K. S. Rotabi (Eds), *Intercountry adoption: Policies, practices, and outcomes* (pp. 77–88). Farnham: Ashgate Press.

Raza, D. (2013, February 20). Overseas adoption racket: How children are sneaked out by the hundreds. First Post. Retrieved from http://poundpuplegacy.org/node/54227

Rivera, C., Bromfield, N. F., & Rotabi, K. S. (2009, April). *Sold into sex, servitude, and adoption*. Richmond, VA: Guatemalan Interest Group.

Rotabi, K. S. & Gibbons, J. L. (2012). Does the Hague Convention on Intercountry Adoption adequately protect orphaned and vulnerable children and their families? *Journal of Child and Family Studies*, 21(1), 106–19. doi: 10.1007/s10826-011-9508-6

Selman, P. F. (2015). Global trends in intercountry adoption: 2003–2012. In R. L. Ballard, N. Goodno, R. Cochran, & J. Milbrandt (Eds), *The intercountry adoption debate: Dialogues across disciplines* (pp. 9–48). Newcastle upon Tyne: Cambridge Scholars Publishing.

Smolin, D. M. (2005). The two faces of intercountry adoption: The significance of the Indian adoption scandals. *Seton Hall Law Review*, 35, 403–93.

Stays, N. L. (2015, August 1). New guidelines of adoption of children become operational. Times of India. Retrieved from http://timesofindia.indiatimes.com/india/New-guidelines-for-adoption-of-children-become-operational/articleshow/48310526.cms

Supreme Court Committee on Juvenile Justice. (2015, April). *Effective implementation of the Juvenile Justice (Care and Protection of Children) Act 2000: Recommendations of Regional Round Table Conferences*. New Delhi: Author.

UNdata. (n.d.). Country profiles. Retrieved from http://data.un.org

UNICEF. (n.d.). Convention on the Rights of the Child. Retrieved from www.unicef.org/crc/

United Nations. (2009). Guidelines for the alternative care of children, Human Rights Council, Eleventh Session Resolution 11/7. Retrieved from http://ap.ohchr.org/documents/E/HRC/resolutions/A_HRC_RES_11_7.pdf

6

"SINS OF THE SAVIORS"

Africa as the final frontier

FIGURE 6.1   Children line up in a residential childcare institution
Source: Photo courtesy of Tony Bradley

In 2012, the African Child Policy Forum released a report entitled *Africa: The New Frontier for Intercountry Adoption* and identified that from 2003 to 2010 the practice of international adoptions of African children had increased "three fold" in that short time span (African Child Policy Forum, 2012, iii). The report was the result of a child-policy conference that convened in Ethiopia and deliberated on the topic of child adoption; guidelines for child adoption were drawn up to ensure that the best interests of the child were paramount in the continent's surge in intercountry adoption (Fifth International Policy Conference on the African Child, 2012). Because many African countries have not signed the Hague Convention on Intercountry

Adoption (Mezmur, 2010; Provost, 2013), the guidelines generated at this forum were an important step towards a unified stance on the adoption activities across the continent of 55 countries. Learning from the past, including a history of international adoption problems and illicit practices in the region (Mezmur, 2010), and with the commitment to the prevention of future illicit activities, the forum made recommendations for when states should *not* allow intercountry adoption, as follows:

- When a state does not provide the basic minimum substantive and institutional safeguards necessary to promote a child's best interests in the context of intercountry adoption.
- When systemic irregular activities are taking place in a state in the context of intercountry adoption, and efforts are underway to address the irregularities.
- When poverty, however defined, seems to be the sole reason why the child cannot grow up in his or her biological (including extended) family environment.
- When there is a possibility for successful tracing and family reunification in the child's best interests.
- If it is contrary to the expressed wishes of the child or the parents.
- Unless a reasonable time has passed during which all feasible steps to trace the parents or other surviving family members has been carried out. This period of time may vary with circumstances, in particular, those relating to the ability to conduct proper tracing. However, the process of tracing must be completed within a reasonable period of time.
- In haste at the height of an emergency, including in both natural and manmade disasters or situations.

(Fifth International Policy Conference on the African Child, 2012, p. 7)

Guidelines: a response to an exponential rise in intercountry adoption in the region

These guidelines were written in response to, in part, a critical turning point when the famed actress Angelina Jolie adopted a child from Ethiopia in 2005. This highly public adoption is now recognized to have been one of the catalysts for ICA in combination with the declining availability of young children in Guatemala and elsewhere.

As intercountry adoptions entered into a significant decline from 2004, African countries are the only ones in which there has been a significant and sustained rise in the practice (Selman, 2012, 2015). Stricter policies and practices as well as significant slowdowns (China) and moratoriums in a number of countries, especially Guatemala and Russia, combined with Jolie's very public adoption and other factors to include greater openness of White families to adopting children from Africa have led to an undeniable change in intercountry adoption patterns.

This was Jolie's second adoption, with her first son being adopted from Cambodia. Jolie's adoption from Ethiopia captured considerable media attention, much of which was focused on a storyline of child rescue and the "very lucky" child, not unlike the comic strip (and later musical play) *Orphan Annie* in which Oliver "Daddy" Warbucks rescues Annie from a miserable life in an orphanage. The millionaire's rescue of an orphan in the context of extreme poverty was a captivating storyline during the Great Depression, when the cartoon was originally published (Auster, 1954). Today, in the globalized reality of extreme poverty and privilege intersections, the story persists in the popular press as found in the gossip magazines. Modern-day celebrities are woven into the narrative of child rescue—now with transracial dimensions fitting into progressive notions of multiculturalism and race. Today's "orphan" child's departure from poverty to riches remains a captivating story for many.

However, the narrative has been shifting a bit. In 2007 a US-based gossip magazine ran a cover story reporting that a woman claiming to be Zahara's birth mother said that she never signed any papers legally relinquishing her daughter for adoption (In Touch Weekly, 2007). Although the circumstances of the child's background are unclear and unverifiable as the story is written (e.g. no DNA tests reported), this news story does indicate a shift in the narrative. The idea of "orphan" was being questioned as the child also had a maternal grandmother who was interviewed. That particular storyline of the complexities of family life and "orphanhood" was unusual at this point in 2007. Interestingly, the story missed a provocative parallel fact. Angelina Jolie's first adoption, from Cambodia, also came under scrutiny as it was reported that this particular adoption was handled by the notorious Seattle Adoptions International agency (World Entertainment News Network, 2004). As discussed previously (Chapter 1), that agency's facilitator was prosecuted and incarcerated for her role in illicit adoptions (and money laundering), and she was known to have boasted that she personally escorted the Cambodian child to Jolie while the star was working on a movie set in Africa. Even with bad press, the adoption of children from Africa was inevitably "marketed" to some degree by the fame of Jolie, although that was never her personal intention. In fact, Jolie has been relatively private about adoption. However, during the 2010 earthquake disaster emergency in Haiti, in a rare comment about child adoption on CNN News, Jolie cautioned against the practice of child removal in the haste of emergency (Rotabi & Bergquist, 2010).[1]

Ethiopia: the first aggressive push into Africa

Known to have one of the greatest concentrations of orphaned and vulnerable children in the world in part due to elevated rates of HIV/AIDS, extreme poverty, and consistent food insecurity, Ethiopia may have seemed a logical beginning in the surge of African adoptions (Bunkers, Rotabi, & Mezmur, 2012). This African country became the new "adoption destination," for the same reasons that Guatemala originally became the popular choice for hopeful families. The system was relatively expedient and the children were typically young, as was demonstrated in the numerous websites of United States agencies that highlighted the fact that "Children from 3 months to 15 years of age are available for adoption. Children will be at least five months old when they come home with their adoptive parents" (All God's Children International, 2009).

For prospective families the good news, on the surface, was that a majority of the children sent abroad as adoptees were fairly healthy, and national oversight of foreign adoption-agency practices was relatively lax thereby making the process user friendly for families willing to pay approximately US$20,000 for their adoption in 2010. This figure was relatively inexpensive within intercountry adoption programs; agencies even used this fact as a selling point for potential adoptive families. One US-based agency stated on their website that there are "lower costs as compared to other international adoption programs" (Adoption Associates, 2010). In the years since, the costs have been steadily rising, consistent with most countries—as the country becomes more popular the costs increase.

Just as the adoption boom began in Ethiopia, a number of problems quickly became apparent; some of the small agencies that previously focused solely on Guatemala moved to focus in on Ethiopia. For many of these agencies, a shift to Ethiopia was the only way for the agency to remain fiscally solvent—in other words, Ethiopia became the next big country for those agencies that previously only generated a consistent income from Guatemalan adoptions.

The problems that emerged were complicated because Ethiopia has not signed or ratified the Hague Convention on Intercountry Adoption. In addition, unfortunately, a loophole was capitalized upon by United States adoption agencies that had failed to meet agency-accreditation standards: the requirements in the United States at this point were crafted to focus *only* on adoptions that originated from Hague Convention countries. As a result, the activities that an adoption agency engaged with in another country that was *not* a Hague Convention country took place outside of Hague-related oversight. The loophole was significant; agencies that had failed to meet accreditation standards in the United States just looked for non-Hague Convention countries to continue their work.[2] In other words, agencies that were *not* Hague accredited could continue to operate in Ethiopia and elsewhere, most especially in Africa. This was a particularly alarming prospect as these agencies failed to meet international standards based on a variety of factors, including evidence of financial instability and a lack of transparency in the use of funds, poor case management, and a range of ethical violations.

One agency that was denied Hague accreditation because of their failure to demonstrate capacity to engage in Hague practices was the Florida-based agency called Celebrate Children International (now simply called Celebrate Children). Their agency evaluation for accreditation was based on their practices in countries like Guatemala where they once had a large program. One of the children allegedly abducted into adoption networks was processed by this particular organization (Siegal, 2011).

When one looks at the complaints about this agency's operations and practices during this period, the documentation of the child-placement licensing authority of the state of Florida (the Department of Family Services (DFS))[3] indicated serious concerns about ethics and general practices as voiced by their own consumers/placement families. When we requested the complaint files for our research, the Florida DFS responded that there were well over a thousand pages of documents related to complaints. The allegations include alarming accounts of dishonesty. For example, the following complaint was made to Florida DFS:

> The "relinquishment" videos we received have the mothers being interviewed by [the agency director], which according to other adoption service providers and sources is undeniably a conflict of interest and could easily be perceived as persuasive and unethical.
>
> [The agency director] told us that CCI has nothing to do with the relinquishment process, and yet, she is interviewing the birth mothers…Parents with their children appear to be waiting in the background and lined up to be interviewed, leading us to believe that there is some type of child harvesting or recruitment going on at the time these videos were taken.
>
> We have asked multiple times about the events leading up to the relinquishment, and the reasons the mothers were unable to care for the children. We have been referred by [the agency director] back to the videos over and over again. We asked [the agency director] to remove the music and after much persuasion through an outside source, she finally complied. Then we found four local Ethiopian Americans to translate the videos. All four who saw the video have advised us to be very cautious, as at least one mother

does not appear to understand about adoption. We have taken their advice. When the mother is shaking her head "no" when asked if she understands about adoption, and after four Ethiopians told us to be very cautious, how could we in good conscience proceed without asking questions? Why is CCI even talking to birth mothers about adoption anyway? Are these mothers truly unable to care for their children, or are they being told by adoption service providers that their children will have a better life in America? Or are they being told their children will be educated and returned to them?

When we could not get answers to the questions we went to another CCI adoptive mother to compare stories and ask questions. Without any explanation, we were removed from the [agency internet support group] and our client login was disabled.

(Department of Family Services, Florida (child-placement agency licensing))

This was one complaint of many and this particular agency has been the subject of high-profile investigative journalism that has been pretty damning of the organization as well as the actions of the executive director, a well-known and controversial figure who has long claimed to be on an evangelical Christian mission to rescue the orphans (Boedeker, 2015; Siegal, 2011).

Slowing down adoptions from Ethiopia because of fraud

Many adoption agencies quickly engaged in Ethiopia; some were better agencies than others in terms of qualified staff and ethical practices. Inevitable problems resulted such that five years after Jolie's adoption, in 2010, the United States embassy in Ethiopia placed a message on their website in the section on adoption. This message politely warns potential adopters that there have been "recent allegations of misconduct in Ethiopian adoptions" and reminds people that the US consulate is required to investigate whether the adoption is legal and if the child is eligible to immigrate under US immigration law. The embassy also posted the following, "The Department of State continues to be concerned about reports highlighting adoption related fraud, malfeasance, and abuse in Ethiopia, and acknowledges the concerns expressed by families over the integrity of the adoption process" (US Department of State, 2010). Meanwhile, the children of Ethiopia continued to be placed at risk as the US embassy continued to process the travel visas necessary for adoption. On the other hand, governments like Australia began to institute moratoriums (Department of Human Services, Victoria, 2009). It was in 2010 that the international media began to consistently report on the problems in Ethiopia in earnest, including "cleaning up the system" (Heinlein, 2010a, 2010b).

Problems in Ethiopian adoptions

Maru (2009) lamented that you can buy anything in Ethiopia's open-air market—including children, and intercountry adoption from the country was capitalizing on this sad reality of poverty. The problems in Ethiopia, which led to child sales and abduction, echo many of those already presented in other countries. Mezmur (2010) addressed the Hague Permanent Bureau describing the "Sins of the Saviors" throughout Africa, in which he outlines a number of concerns in Ethiopia including "one instance [in which] traffickers were allegedly caught transporting a group of children from one administrative locality (the authorities of which refused to issue a declaration of abandonment letters) to another administrative locality" (p. 12). This particular illicit activity takes place when one locality has a judge and/or government bureaucrats enforcing due process and standards and another locality has a judge or other authority figures whom are permissive—often engaged in accepting bribes for his or her signature to "expedient" processing of cases. Moving children from one judicial area for a court hearing in a different court is not an uncommon tactic of traffickers.[4] Other concerns raised by Mezmur include problematic legal declarations of child abandonment, including such documents originating from "one police officer (all written at the same time) raising concerns of child laundering" (p. 12). Free and informed consent for adoption have been a problem and, like in other countries we have discussed, many birth families have claimed after the adoption that they did not understand the permanent nature of adoption—they believed that the children would visit and that they were simply going to another country for the purpose of an education (Bunkers et al., 2012).

In the case of child-abandonment declarations, Mezmur points out that there have been instances in which there are claims that parents have died when they are very much alive. All of these activities underscore the concept of child laundering and the falsification of the child's origin to make him or her appear to be an "orphan." That is, "birth certificates, paternity declarations, passports, identity documents, letters of consent, and letters declaring abandonment of a child" (Mezmur, 2010, p. 12) and sometimes death certificates of parent(s) are falsified thereby making the child a "paper orphan," as discussed in Chapter 1. This process of document falsification, an essential element of child laundering, is especially challenging in many African countries given the weak structures and processes that exist in terms of birth registration and other legal documentation.

Malawi: the celebrity effect without growth in intercountry adoptions

The small Sub-Saharan African country of Malawi has some of the worst social and health indicators in the world (World Health Organization, 2015). Violence against children is endemic, including alarming rates of child marriage (Human Rights Watch, 2014; Ross, Rotabi, & Maksud, 2016). Although there are concerted attempts to develop laws, policies, and programs to address the underlying dynamics, serious social problems persist. Most of the population is vulnerable as a result of a high rate of extreme poverty as well as serious and persistent problems that include environmental catastrophes such as flooding and thus food insecurity (Ross et al., 2016).

In 2013, the "Cashgate" scandal came to light when the highest levels of the then president Joyce Banda's executive cabinet were implicated in the siphoning of millions of dollars from government funds (Masina, 2014). The lack of the international community's trust in Banda's government led to greater despair as some development organizations scaled back foreign aid to the country because of fears of corruption and general fiscal mismanagement (Ross et al., 2016).

Given internal problems and extreme poverty, funding of social-welfare programs is one of the core problems along with inadequate (and poorly trained) social service staffing to execute social programs (Anderson, 2013; Ross et al., 2016). Furthermore, stressors such as natural disasters and food insecurity are major distractions for child-protection social workers as they must leave their day-to-day posts and respond more broadly to crises such as flooding

(Ross et al., 2016). Concerted efforts to strengthen a very nascent child-protection system are underway including the implementation of an array of promising prevention approaches to the care and protection of children, but ultimately the system is simply not poised to deal with intercountry adoptions including an inadequate workforce of social workers (Ross et al., 2016) and weak implementation of policies and protocols that would ensure the protection of the best interests of the child.

Malawi is one of the African countries that requires residency for intercountry adoption. Because of the residency rule, which commonly included a time in the country in which the foreign family fostered the child for 18 months, Malawi was not expected to be a next possible country in Africa with the consistent exercise of this rule requiring a prolonged and official presence (US Department of State, n.d.). However, the famed singer Madonna adopted a child from Malawi and, in that process, a challenge to the residency rules became a test as the singer was clearly *only* present in the country to adopt a child. Her interests dated back to 2006 when her then husband, film director Guy Ritchie, visited multiple children's institutions to videotape children in order for his wife to choose a child (Mezmur, 2010). This practice was not only troubling but crossed ethical lines when the couple was seeking a child without adoption professionals assisting in determining adoptability and family–child match—in essence browsing for the child that one desires. Furthermore, in the process of building relationships Madonna reportedly made a donation of more 2 million dollars to the childcare institution along with other acts of charity (e.g. funding a scholarship for a government employee to study in the United Kingdom) (Mezmur, 2010). All of this coincided with concerns that the legal consent necessary for Madonna's adoption did not meet the criteria of due diligence for a fully informed and free consent (for analysis, see Mezmur, 2010). The first child that Madonna adopted had a biological father who reportedly was indecisive on the consent and the international media seized upon this fact (Mezmur, 2010). In the end, Madonna eventually adopted two children from Malawi, first a son and then later a daughter.[5] As in the case of Jolie's adoption, the press reported that biological family members were coming forward and making comments about their desires to have their children back (see Leach, 2009).

Madonna's story is not all that surprising and it underscores a number of troubling ethical dimensions of intercountry adoption and the interface with wealth, power, and privilege. However, what unfolded next is the interesting twist that no one expected. Like many adoptive parents, Madonna was personally affected by the poverty of Malawi and she looked for ways to help, including more donations. She attempted to start a massive humanitarian project as a personal commitment to making a meaningful difference in the daily lives of children—such a project would far surpass her initial financial donations. Setting up a foundation to manage the funds, Madonna hired a small team of individuals to establish a school with an ambitious vision. A substantial piece of land just outside of the capital Lilongwe was selected and plans were drawn up.

Although it is not entirely clear what occurred, rumors of financial mismanagement and corruption were rampant and it appears that Madonna eventually shut the project down. It is believed that the corruption was such that the project became impossible to complete. The sister of the country's then president, who had been employed by Madonna as part of the local team, was implicated in project-management problems. When this particular high-profile employee was terminated from her job, it was speculated that Madonna angered the President personally as her sister's character was called into question over financial mismanagement. Another speculation was that then President Banda had encouraged Madonna to embark on a clean-water project and this idea was rejected as the school project was of greater interest to the singer. Others wondered if Madonna's desire to include the teachings of Kabala, her Jewish faith, in the school curriculum was also a problem. Whatever occurred, the school project was plagued with problems and the construction of the school never fully came to fruition on a large scale despite a ground-breaking ceremony, attended by the country's president and other dignitaries, in 2010 (Ross, 2013).

As Madonna continued with her passionate interest in Malawi, including visits to residential childcare homes, what happened next was truly stunning. President Banda issued a press release in 2013 making it perfectly clear that the singer's presence in the country would not be treated with any "very important person" status as the singer apparently expected (Daily Telegraph, 2013). Supposedly angered by the singer's purported complaints about a lack of special treatment while visiting Malawi, the President's office made her position and general distaste for the singer's expectations clear, including a very pointed statement about child adoption and future expectations.

> Madonna has adopted two children from Malawi. According to the record, this gesture was humanitarian and of her accord. It, therefore, comes across as strange and depressing that for a humanitarian act, prompted only by her, Madonna wants Malawi to be forever chained to the obligation of gratitude. Kindness, as far as its ordinary meaning is concerned, is free and anonymous. If it can't be free and silent, it is not kindness; it is something else. Blackmail is the closest it becomes.

(For the statement in entirety with all eleven points, see Daily Telegraph, 2013).

Interestingly, in contrast to Jolie's influence on the increase of adoptions from Ethiopia, Madonna's presence may have had an opposite effect in Malawi. Intercountry adoptions from Malawi have not increased dramatically, and if anything, there appears to be a heightened awareness about the residency rule and a sensitive (and even agitated) government.[6] Also, the power dynamics in the adoption equation and "significant interest" in Malawi have had consequences.

Liberia and the Evangelical movement of children

While the adoptions of Angelina Jolie in Ethiopia and Madonna in Malawi captured the press' attention, Liberian adoptions were quietly building at the same time. The Christian adoption movement was a clear catalyst and was almost exclusively the only active group in Liberia (Joyce, 2013). Numerous Evangelical groups encouraged their members to pursue adoptions from poverty-stricken countries as part of their service to God (Joyce, 2013). At this point in the Christian call to adopt, an annual Orphan Sunday to "Defend the cause of the fatherless" (following Isaiah 1:17) was promoted by the Christian Alliance for Orphans. In their annual Orphan Sunday they promoted the rescue of the orphan as a personal act of faith and ministry (see Cheney & Rotabi, 2015; www.ChristianAllianceforOrphans.org).[7] Opportunities for families to raise funds within their faith communities were promoted (e.g. donations from others who were not adopting) and the calling was quite broad and compelling for many (Medefind, 2015). Adoption, at this point, was promoted as a one-size-fits-all approach for Christian families whose good intentions, values, and love for the child could overcome all obstacles.

In this call to faith, US-based Evangelical Christians became particularly interested in adoptions from Liberia after they were called "cheap, easy, and fast" by those touting adoptions from this nation known for tribal conflict and chaos (Joyce, 2013). The number of adoptions to the United States from Liberia rose from 27 in 2003 to a peak of 353 in 2006 (US Department of State, n.d.), after word spread within the Evangelical community about the ease with which couples could finalize an adoption from this country.

However, by 2009 Liberia imposed a moratorium on ICA because of adoption fraud and mismanagement largely on the part of the US-based Christian adoption agencies, some operating without oversight and unaccredited in the country. Numerous cases of adoption fraud were feared to have occurred, not unlike other African countries undergoing the pull into intercountry adoption (Bunkers et al., 2012; Joyce, 2013). Child buying was a clear dynamic as well as the general misunderstanding of adoption on the part of the families of origin.

What is particularly troubling about the intercountry adoption of Liberian children, in addition to the apparent adoption fraud that occurred in many of these cases, is that these children originated from an extremely poverty-stricken and war-torn country and many had significant behavioral and emotional issues that the adopting parents were not equipped to handle. On Liberian adoption forums, adoptive parents of Liberian children complained of their older adopted children lying, stealing, and acting out sexually (Joyce, 2013), and according to Joyce, the Evangelical community eventually began to cease touting Liberian adoptions, because of the ensuing problems faced by children and adoptive parents after the children went to the US.

This may be the result, in part, of the death of a Liberian child who was adopted by a fundamentalist Christian family in the United States. Seven-year-old Lydia Schatz was killed in 2010 at the hands of her adoptive parents as a result of extreme physical abuse. At the same time, her biological sister who was also adopted by the family suffered severe injuries and required hospitalization (Eckholm, 2010). There have been other cases of Liberian children being abused by their adoptive families, such as harsh corporal punishment due to beliefs about "spare the rod and spoil the child." Furthermore, cases of adopted Liberian children who were sent back to Liberia by their adoptive families have also been exposed (Joyce, 2013). Adoption dissolutions occurred in those cases, which is not only painful for those involved, but are embarrassing for the Evangelical Christian movement (Joyce, 2013). Lastly, there have been cases in which an adoption is not legally dissolved, but the original adoptive family arranges for a "rehoming" (see Chapter 2), in which the child is passed along to another family, often because the child is viewed by the adoptive family to be too difficult to manage, frequently due to mental health and other emotional issues (Testerman, 2015) or simply because the family loses interest in the child.

When the 2009 moratorium on intercountry adoption was put into place, President Ellen Johnson Sirleaf's annual message to the country's national legislature underscored that adoptions from Liberia had become so problematic that she had ceased the practice. She stated that the law in effect was obsolete, as it dated back to the 1950s. Included in the deficits that she cited were that "neither did the law contemplate calamities caused by nature or by humans that would separate children from their biological parents and other immediate family. The law also did not contemplate circumstances that would coerce biological parents to give their children to other persons to be reared in foreign lands" (Government of Liberia, 2015, p. 1), underscoring the fact that many Liberian families did not understand the permanent nature of intercountry adoption, and they simply "thought their children would be taken abroad for school and that the children would return periodically to visit their biological parents and these biological parents became heartbroken when they discovered otherwise" (Government of Liberia, 2015, p. 1). In addition:

> President Sirleaf further indicated that adoption agencies [previously] operating in the country were not carefully vetted or licensed. She said though orphanages were estab-lished to cater to the needs of children whose parent(s) died during the war or who were involuntarily separated from their parent(s), frequently, these orphanages were not governed by clear laws and regulations. Thus, some orphaned and adopted children were made vulnerable to abuse, neglect, human trafficking, exploitation, and other violations of human rights.
>
> *(Government of Liberia, 2015, p. 1)*

Addressing these issues through strengthened regulations and operating procedures, Liberia lifted the ban and reopened intercountry adoptions in the summer of 2015 (Government of Liberia, 2015). New requirements have been set forth to strengthen the process. Liberia has not moved forward to become a party to the Hague Convention on Intercountry Adoption, but they identified a "preference for [working with]…adoption agencies whose home country is a 'Hague Convention Country' because in those countries the govern-ments are under international obligation to monitor and provide protection for adopted persons" (Government of Liberia, 2015, p. 1).[8] These steps towards improved practices will inevitably be tested, and Liberia may once again rise as an intercountry adoption destina-tion in the years to come. However, there is expected to be only a select few number of agencies that will be approved for the work. This regulatory approach is becoming more and more common as countries seek to place controls on the practice by being careful about the agencies with which they engage. This is a wise step on the Government of Liberia's part, but bad news to adoption agencies that are looking for new country pro-grams. Their organizational viability continues to be threatened with this particular regula-tory approach to the practice of intercountry adoption.

Uganda: the rise of the residential care institution in parallel with intercountry adoption

Uganda became one of the next adoption destinations in Africa. Like many other adoption nations in the continent, Uganda has suffered the consequences of a protracted civil war along with the HIV/AIDS epidemic, placing extreme stress on families (Roby & Shaw, 2006; Cheney & Rotabi, 2015). Uganda, as a country, illustrates the problematic assumptions about unparented children and the concept of "orphan" that interfaces with the pull of children into institutions and ultimately intercountry adoption. The data underscore that families and communities have historically solved their own problems in Uganda when it comes to caring for children. Sending children into institutions and intercountry adoption was truly a foreign concept until very recently. Institutions have been opening rapidly in parallel with the demand for child adoptions from Uganda, many of which are unregistered and managed without standards of care (Cheney & Rotabi, 2015; Riley, 2015).

In 1992 only 2,900 children were in institutional care in Uganda (Williamson & Greenberg, 2010). According to the official government count, today 14 percent of Uganda's 17.1 million children (2.43 million) have lost at least one parent to death. This represents an increase from

11.5 percent in 2000. Just under half of these children have lost one or both parents to HIV/ AIDS (Uganda Ministry of Gender, Labor and Social Development, 2011, p. 4). Even with such staggering numbers of children in need of care, 90 percent of orphaned children are cared for in their families and communities (Joint Learning Initiative on Children and HIV/ AIDS, 2009, p. 2). However, by 2009 the number of children in residential care facilities had seen a dramatic rise to 40,000. By 2013, the number of children documented to be in institutional care was 50,000.[9] Fears are that the number of such children continues to rise, and the phenomenon raises the question: With these stark facts at hand in parallel with a rise of child-care institutions and intercountry adoptions, what else is true? The child-protection experts in Uganda see the institutional crisis as being fueled by intercountry adoption, with the advent of the practice from which fueled the opening of institutions that are frequently staging areas for the appearance of orphanhood (Cheney & Rotabi, 2015; Riley, 2015).

All of this was taking place against the backdrop of the Uganda Children Act of 1997 that required a three-year residency before foreign parents could adopt a child there. However, when the US embassy issued a visa for a Ugandan child under the legal guardianship of US citizens in 2007, a loophole was identified by intercountry adoption agencies allowing them to work around the law (Cheney & Rotabi, 2015). And, agencies looking for an adoption landscape of opportunities found Uganda; the next adoption destination country was quickly claimed.

The scenario was as follows. Legal guardianship was awarded to prospective adoptive parents and they were allowed to take the children out of the country. Then, an adoption finalization was carried out in the courts of the prospective parents' home country (e.g. the United States). To carry this out, technically legal guardianships were still under Ugandan courts' jurisdiction, but there were no real teeth or will in enforcement once a child left Uganda. In the Ugandan law at this point, guardianship was explicitly designated as a temporary agreement/ measure and it was *not* for the purpose of adoption. However, Ugandan courts were granting legal guardianship orders to foreigners and it was an open secret that this work around had a variety of actors, especially lawyers and unregulated children's home directors/owners, who were becoming exceptionally wealthy.

The abuses in Uganda were like other places, misunderstandings of the concept of a legal break in the biological family–child's relationship and, as Cheney (2014) points out, some of these families saw the child's departure to a wealthy country to be an act of "deploying adoptees as agents of the entire family's social mobility, particularly because their migration to richer countries as 'innocent children' and desirable adoptees is much less complicated than adults' migration from the same country" (p. 257). The misunderstandings and motivations in Uganda proved to be profound as children kept leaving Uganda in significant numbers against the persistent protest of human rights defenders trying to stop illicit adoptions. Reportedly, "62 children in 2010 to 207 children in 2011, with at least 95% of these adoptions finalised in the United States" courts (Agaba, 2012, p. 1). As the flow of children out of Uganda under the care of their "guardians" continued to grow, the Children's Act was amended to close this loophole in March 2016. Many prospective US adoptive families, who had been pushing through their guardianship orders, responded with outrage. Proclamations of unfairness inevitably emerge when countries close doors to adoption due to fraud.

The President of Uganda signed the amended act at the end of May 2016 as some adoption agencies were quickly processing as many cases as possible with even more hasty paperwork. The last adoptions from countries where fraud has been marked are often questionable.

However, the adoptive families come home to applause and even media stories that will chronicle their journey; the story narrative will be framed by a looming country shutdown and the joy in prevailing against the odds and building family through intercountry adoption.

Democratic Republic of Congo: is exit possible?

The Democratic Republic of Congo's (DRC) adoption history and problems with fraud have the all too familiar stories of cultural misunderstandings in the context of extreme poverty and civil conflict. Particularly notable, though, is the complete lack of a civil society in the DRC as it is recognized to be a failed state and the social context is a general environment of lawlessness (Messner & Lawrence, 2013).

Problems processing adoptions in the DRC became abundantly clear in 2006 when a number of Spanish families were refused the necessary travel visas to bring home the children they had adopted in Congolese courts. This particular incident is thought to be the first scandal in the African country that was widely covered by the national media in Spain (Trillas, 2006) and the crisis was a foreshadow of what was to come for other countries. According to published information, the Spanish embassy said they had repeatedly warned the central adoption authorities in Spain about their concerns regarding adoption processes in the DRC. The exact reasons— specifically, acts of fraud—for the embassy's refusal to grant travel visas remained unclear for a number of months while Spanish prospective parents were outraged, leaving the idea that a cold-hearted bureaucracy was prevailing and the lives of children were at stake. However, in time the media began to report that some birth parents had protested and alleged that their children had been taken for adoption without their legal consent; that is child abduction into adoption.

In recent years, the United States embassy has also found itself embroiled in problematic adoptions from the DRC. Prospective parents who were attempting to adopt children from the DRC found that they were unable to secure the exit permits (issued by the DRC) necessary for them to actually depart the country. In October 2015 the US Department of State posted a statement by the DRC government indicating that the suspension of exit permits would persist and cautioned US citizens from engaging in acts that "circumvent the exit permit suspension" (US Department of State, 2015a). Even so, it is widely known that hundreds of children have been transported across the border into a second country (with a DRC national being paid to literally move the child across the border so as to avoid the legal charge of abduction being lodged against a foreigner) and then the child departs for their new home/family life (in the US and elsewhere) from this second location. This "work around" has been lamented as smuggling, while the adoptive parents who pay for the illegal movement of the children across the border see themselves as saving "their child" from the misery of a country where hundreds of children die daily from preventable health conditions. By the end of 2015, with a concerted effort on the part of the US embassy, diplomacy was making headway in resolving the problems in favor of prospective adoptive families; many have now departed the DRC successfully with their adoptive child (US Department of State, 2015c).

From controversy of illicit activities on the continent of Africa to the rehoming controversy in the United States

Rehoming was touched upon in Chapter 2 with two Russian adoptees and a highly public case of adoption disruption. As a reminder, in that case the New York judge called the practice "child trafficking" (Chapter 2). The problem extends far beyond that particular case and the rehoming of African and other children has been particularly concerning. In an exposé series, Reuters published the highly provocative article entitled "The child exchange: Inside America's underground market for adopted children" (Twohey, 2013). In investigative journalistic style, the story begins with "Todd and Melissa Puchalla struggled for more than two years to raise Quita, the troubled teenager they'd adopted from Liberia. When they decided to give her up, they found new parents to take her in less than two days—by posting an ad on the Internet." Two days later after the Puchallas signed the child's guardianship (with a simple notarized document) over to an unvetted couple, Nicole and Calvin Eason, the child was "missing" (Twohey, 2013, p. 1). Today, this now young adult woman is known to have been forced to sleep naked with the couple, and the sexual and other abuse that ensued was unthinkable. The couple had a history of abuse as other children had been removed from their custody by the state authorities, one of which alleged sexual abuse (Twohey, 2013). In 2015 the couple was indicted on kidnapping charges (Twohey, 2015).

In the broad investigation of "private rehoming" Reuters found, on one internet forum alone, at least one child a week was being advertised as "available." Many were older children from an array of countries. Children from Africa seem to be increasingly common in the rehoming movement and the problem, overall, has been that since 2013 at least five states have "passed new restrictions on advertising the availability of children, transferring custody, or both. Lawmakers in those states noted that the absence of government safeguards can result in children ending up in the care of abusers" (Twohey, 2015, p. 1).

Sadly, the practice persists in many US states with various forums on the internet. Adoption agencies that originally place the child with the adoptive family are frequently unaware of the child's long-term well-being and dramatic change of circumstances. While the story of rehoming casts doubt on the children and their behavior—emotional and mental health problems— -the reality is they are the children under care of adults who have made a commitment to care for them in an adoption order, beginning with the adoption agency (facilitating the process and securing the order) and then extending to the adoptive family who were vetted with a formal home study. When the agreed-upon family scenario collapses the children suffer and the term "dissolution" is used, often in a manner that divorces the real issues and blames the children for being difficult or unmanageable.

In the case of HCIA-related adoptions, dissolution of an adoption is supposed to be reported to the central adoption authority in that country—in the United States documentation is frequently lacking due to limited adoption agency follow-up with families in the years after intercountry adoption as well as families taking matters into their own hands with practices like rehoming.

Minimal influence of the Hague Convention on Intercountry Adoption in Africa and the case of Kenya

By and large, very few African countries have signed and ratified the Hague Convention on Intercountry Adoption (Mezmur, 2010), and such a step towards international regulation is recognized to be essential. Kenya is one country that ratified the Convention. However, this does not mean that there are no longer challenges with adoption practices and processes in Kenya. In fact, in late 2014, an adoption moratorium was put in place by the Kenyan government as a result of pervasive fraud linked to a variety of problems, including issues with child guardianship (Njeru, 2011; Mezmur, 2010; US Department of State, 2015b), concerns about the eligibility of children being placed and accusations of unethical processes and interests of residential care facilities and adoption agencies. Furthermore, despite having ratified the Hague Convention on Intercountry Adoption, there are still significant challenges and barriers in terms of the subsidiarity principle and promotion of domestic adoption prior to intercountry adoption being considered (Stuckenbruck, 2013). Kenya has disbanded their central authority and the remaining cases that were caught in the pipeline are being processed very slowly. Like other countries that have entered a moratorium, prospective parents around the world are uncertain of the outcomes of the adoptions that they hoped to complete in Kenya. They too have moved into crisis mode as they push to have their own cases resolved in their favor with cries that such a resolution is in the best interests of the child.

Conclusion

With the extreme decline in intercountry adoptions globally, there has been a transition—most notably a shift from Guatemala, Russia and China to Ethiopia and other African countries (Rotabi, 2010). While the African Child Policy Forum (2012) declared the continent to the "next frontier" for intercountry adoption, we assert that the region is actually the "final frontier" as there are no obvious large regions left for expansion.

When considering this final frontier, it should be noted that in many regions in Africa the conception of *orphan* did not exist before Western humanitarian interventions began to seek children as subjects of "care" (Cheney, 2014, in press). However, in many communities this was an unnecessary and disrupting interference in natural processes in which children were frequently circulated within their extended family, kinship group, and larger community (in Ethiopia the practice is called "gudifecha"—see Bunkers et al., 2012). In essence, children have been typically absorbed within community networks with informal care agreements amongst families and kin, sometimes even with tribal group oversight in the spirit of "it takes a village to raise a child" (Bunkers, 2010; Cheney, 2014, in press; Riley, 2015).

Furthermore, when moving towards a more formal structure for adoption, fundamentally most countries of Africa simply do not have a complete legal and policy framework necessary for safeguarding structures and processes. Also, lacking in many cases is the necessary civil society to safeguard ethical intercountry adoptions based on the best interests of the child (Mezmur, 2010). The social services necessary to assist and strengthen the biological family before considering intercountry adoption are limited throughout Africa.

At the beginning of this chapter, we pointed out that this inadequate social service infrastructure was identified in 2012 forum recommendations. A multitude of issues persist even with concerted efforts by local government and the development sector to build systems of care that are oriented to local family-based care. Some of the problems stem from the fact that many countries have laws dating back to colonial occupation (e.g. Malawi—Adoption of Children Act of 1949) and outdated legislation across Africa requires refinement in the new intercountry adoption environment (Mezmur, 2010).

Child-protection and family-support systems improvement simply cannot happen soon enough as adoptions from the region continue with expansions into other countries. There is a clear need for African countries to become party to the Hague Convention on Intercountry Adoption. However, even with some country's attempts to take steps in moving forward to join the Convention (e.g. in Uganda, see Rotabi, 2014), change has been slow in adopting this global approach to regulation and social protection in Africa.

Notes

1 Jolie was interviewed on CNN news by acclaimed journalist Anderson Cooper and he himself was clearly moved by the plight of children when reporting from the ground in the days after the earthquake.
2 The loophole that allowed for unaccredited agencies (based in the United States) to continue operations in countries that had not ratified the HCIA, like Ethiopia, was closed in July 2014 when the Universal Accreditation Act was passed. The passage of this particular law required that adoption agencies cease their operations.
3 Adoption agencies in the United States are regulated by each state. Some states are more structured in their licensing standards than others. In the case of Florida, the laws in that state are outdated and known to be lax and written for the purpose of domestic adoptions rather than reflecting the complexity of intercountry adoption and ethical standards of care. A Hague-accredited agency in the United States must be licensed in a state and then also meet accreditation standards in a separate organizational evaluation (Council on Accreditation, 2007).
4 This problem was also identified by the United Nations International Commission against Impunity in Guatemala as certain judges were identified to be corrupt. Movement of children from one part of the country to another for these judicial processes was one problem in the chain of illicit adoptions.
5 In reality, the second girl child was the child that Madonna originally selected to adopt. However, the girl's grandmother refused. In time and reportedly after considerable pressure, the child's grandmother finally conceded and the second adoption was made possible (Mezmur, 2010).
6 In 2009 there was a court ruling further clarifying the rule which appears to create greater flexibility than the original long-term residency rule.
7 The group has since changed their campaign and begun to promote more family-centered and local care strategies. Some very important work has now begun, with leadership by some very high-profile Evangelical Christian leaders, including innovative work in Rwanda. For more about the Christian orphan-care movement see Medefind (2015) for historical analysis, as well as Joyce (2013) who captures many troubling dynamics in her investigative journalism.
8 Russia is another country that has not become a party to the HCIA. Prior to the moratorium with the United States, one added safeguard instituted by Russia was the requirement for US adoption agencies that are approved/accredited providers under the Convention.
9 These data were originally reported in Cheney & Rotabi (2015) and the reader is directed to this publication for more information.

References

Adoption Associates. (2010). International adoptions. Retrieved from www.adoptassoc.com/international/ethiopia/

African Child Policy Forum. (2012). Africa: The new frontier for intercountry adoption. Addis Ababa: African Child Policy Forum.

Agaba, M. (2012, October 1). This country urgently needs strict guidelines to regulate intercountry adoption. Saturday Monitor. Retrieved from www.monitor.co.ug/OpEd/Commentary/-/689364/1521464/-/115vwl0z/-/index.html

All God's Children International. (2009). Website information. Retrieved from www.allgodschildren.org/adoption/ethiopia/

Anderson, L. (2013). *Assessment of the capacity of the Ministry of Education, Science and Technology to identify, prevent and respond to violence, abuse, and exploitation and neglect and the development of specific frameworks for violence prevention for children attending primary and secondary schools in Malawi.* Colchester: CORAM Children's Legal Centre.

Auster, D. (1954). A content analysis of "Little Orphan Annie". *Social Problems*, 2(1), 26–33.

Boedeker, H. (2015, September 4). "48 hours" repeats Oviedo adoption story. Retrieved from www.orlandosentinel.com/entertainment/tv/tv-guy/os-48-hours-cbs-oviedo-adoption-agency-20150904-post.html

Bunkers, K. M. (2010). *Informal family-based care options: Protecting children's rights? A case study of gudifecha in Ethiopia.* Geneva: Institut Universitaire Kurt Bosh and Universite de Fribourg.

Bunkers, K. M., Rotabi, K. S., & Mezmur, B. (2012). Ethiopia: Intercountry adoption risks and considerations for informal care. In J. L. Gibbons & K. S. Rotabi (Eds), *Intercountry adoption: Policies, practices, and outcomes* (pp. 131–42). Farnham: Ashgate Press.

Cheney, K. (2014). Conflicting protectionist and participation models of children's rights: Their consequences for Uganda's orphans and vulnerable children. In A. Twum-Danso and N. Ansell (Eds), *Children's lives in an era of children's rights: The progress of the Convention on the Rights of the Child in Africa* (pp. 17–33). New York: Routledge.

Cheney, K. (in press). *Crying for our elders: African orphanhood in the age of HIV and AIDS.* Chicago, IL: University of Chicago Press.

Cheney, K. E. & Rotabi, K. S. (2015). "Addicted to orphans": How the global orphan industrial complex jeopardizes local child protection systems. In T. Skelton, C. Harker, & K. Horschelmann (Eds), *Geographies of children and young people: Conflict, violence and peace* (pp. 1–19). New York: Springer Reference.

Council on Accreditation. (2007). *Hague accreditation and approval standards.* New York: Author. Retrieved from www.coanet.org/files/Hague_Accreditation_and_Approval_Standards.pdf

Department of Human Services, Victoria. (2009, November). Interim suspension of Ethiopia-Australia program, November 2009. Retrieved from www.cyf.vic.gov.au/intercountry-adoption/library/news/interim-suspension-of-the-ethiopiaaustralia-program-november-2009

Eckholm, E. (2010, November 6). Preaching virtue of spanking, even as deaths fuel debate. New York Times. Retrieved from www.nytimes.com/2011/11/07/us/deaths-put-focus-on-pastors-advocacy-of-spanking.html?pagewanted=all&_r=0

Fifth International Policy Conference on the African Child. (2012, May 29–30). Guidelines for action on intercountry adoption of children in Africa. Retrieved from www.wereldkinderen.nl/websites/implementatie/mediadepot/8559606e8da.pdf

Government of Liberia. (2015, June 30). President Sirleaf lifts moratoriums on child adoptions in Liberia. Retrieved from www.emansion.gov.lr/2press.php?news_id=3336&related=7&pg=sp

Heinlein, P. (2010a, December 14). Under pressure, Ethiopia plans crackdown on baby business. Retrieved from *Voice of America*, www.voanews.com/content/under-pressure-ethiopia-plans-crackdown-on-baby-business-111848424/132261.html

Heinlein, P. (2010b, December 17). Ethiopia working with child advocacy groups to clean up adoptions. Retrieved from *Voice of America*, www.voanews.com/content/ethiopia-working-with-child-advocacy-groups-to-clean-up-adoptions-112078034/157071.html

Human Rights Watch. (2014). "I've never experienced happiness": Child marriage in Malawi. Retrieved from www.hrw.org/node/123427

In Touch Weekly. (2007, November 26). Zahara's family wants her back: It's Angelina's worst nightmare. Will she lose her child? In Touch Weekly. Retrieved from www.intouchweekly.com/posts/will-angelina-lose-zahara-24136

Joint Learning Initiative on Children and HIV/AIDS. (2009). *Home truths: Facing the facts on children, AIDS, and poverty.* Geneva: Association François-Xavier Bagnoud, FXB International.

Joyce, K. (2013). *The child catchers: Rescue, trafficking, and the new gospel of adoption.* New York: Public Affairs.

Leach, B. (2009, June 28). Madonna's adopted daughter Mercy was to be returned to family, grandmother claims. Telegraph. Retrieved from www.telegraph.co.uk/news/celebritynews/madonna/5663029/Madonnas-adopted-daughter-Mercy-was-to-be-returned-to-family-grandmother-claims.html

Maru, M. (2009). On international adoption of Ethiopian children. Reporter. Retrieved from http://en.ethiopianreporter.com/content/view/1282/1/

Masina, L. (2014, February 9). Malawians push for speedy Cashgate trial. Al Jazeera. Retrieved from www.aljazeera.com/indepth/features/2014/02/malawians-push-speedy-cashgate-trials-20142818328786397.html

Medefind, J. (2015). Ancient commitment, modern trend: The history, hazards and hope of today's orphan care movement. In R. L. Ballard, N. Goodno, R. Cochran, & J. Milbrandt (Eds), *The intercountry adoption debate: Dialogues across disciplines* (pp. 417–44). Newcastle upon Tyne: Cambridge Scholars Publishing.

Messner, J. J. & Lawrence, K. (2013, June 24). Failed states index: The troubled ten. Retrieved from http://library.fundforpeace.org/fsi13-troubled10

Mezmur, B. N. (2010, June). The sins of the saviors: Trafficking in the context of intercountry adoption from Africa. Paper presented at the Special Commission of the Hague Conference on Private International Law, The Hague. Retrieved from https://assets.hcch.net/upload/wop/adop2010id02e.pdf

Njeru, G. (2011, April 23). Corruption in Kenya drives rise in girl-child trafficking. Truthout. Retrieved from www.truth-out.org/news/item/700-corruption-in-kenya-drives-rise-in-girlchildtrafficking

Provost, C. (2013, November 18). Adoption from Africa: Children's rights group demands urgent crackdown. Retrieved from www.theguardian.com/global-development/2013/nov/18/adoption-africa-children-rights-crackdown

Riley, M. (2015). An imbalance of justice: Birth mothers in Uganda. In R. L. Ballard, N. Goodno, R. Cochran, & J. Milbrandt (Eds), *The intercountry adoption debate: Dialogues across disciplines* (pp. 618–25). Newcastle upon Tyne: Cambridge Scholars Publishing.

Roby, J. L. & Shaw, S. A. (2006). The African orphan crisis and international adoption. *Social Work*, 51(5), 199–210.

Ross, B., Rotabi, K. S., & Maksud, N. (2016). Violence against children in Malawi and social work. In M. Gray (Ed.), *Handbook of social work and social development in Africa*. Farnham: Ashgate Press.

Ross, E. (2013, April 11). Madonna earns the wrath of Joyce Banda—full statement. Guardian. Retrieved from www.theguardian.com/world/2013/apr/11/malawi-madonna

Rotabi, K. S. (2010, June). From Guatemala to Ethiopia: Shifts in intercountry adoption leave Ethiopia vulnerable for child sales and other unethical practices. *Social Work and Society News Magazine*. Retrieved from www.socmag.net/?p=615

Rotabi, K. S. (2014, December). Force, fraud, and coercion: Bridging from knowledge of intercountry adoption to global surrogacy. ISS Working Paper Series/General Series, 600, 1–30. Retrieved from http://hdl.handle.net/1765/77403

Rotabi, K. S. & Bergquist, K. J. S. (2010). Vulnerable children in the aftermath of Haiti's earthquake of 2010: A call for sound policy and processes to prevent international child sales and theft. *Journal of Global Social Work Practice*. Retrieved from www.globalsocialwork.org/vol3no1/Rotabi.html

Selman, P. (2012). The rise and fall of intercountry adoption in the 21st century: Global trends from 2001 to 2010. In J. L. Gibbons & K. S. Rotabi (Eds), *Intercountry adoption: Policies, practices, and outcomes* (pp. 7–28). Farnham: Ashgate Press.

Selman, P. F. (2015). Global trends in intercountry adoption, 2003–2012. In R. L. Ballard, N. Goodno, R. Cochran, & J. Milbrandt (Eds), *The intercountry adoption debate: Dialogues across disciplines* (pp. 9–48). Newcastle upon Tyne: Cambridge Scholars Publishing.

Siegal, E. (2011). *Finding Fernanda: Two mothers, one child, and a cross-border search for truth.* Boston, MA: Beacon.

Stuckenbruck, D. (2013). *The rights of the child deprived of a family environment: Domestic adoption of children in Kenya.* Bramois: University Institute Kurt Bosch.

Telegraph. (2013, April 8). Madonna stripped of VIP status in Malawi after spat with president. Telegraph. Retrieved from www.telegraph.co.uk/news/celebritynews/madonna/9980175/Madonna-stripped-of-VIP-status-in-Malawi-after-spat-with-president.html

Testerman, S. M. (2015). A world wide web of unwanted children: The practice, the problem, and solution for private re-homing. *Florida Law Review*, 67, 2103–47.

Trillas, A. (2006). Siete familias no pueden salir de Congo con sus niños adoptados [Seven families cannot leave Congo with their adopted children]. El País. Retrieved from http://elpais.com/diario/2006/08/20/sociedad/1156024802_850215.html

Twohey, M. (2013, September 9). The child exchange: Inside America's underground market for adopted children. Retrieved from www.reuters.com/investigates/adoption/#article/part1

Twohey, M. (2015, May 8). "Re-homing" couple exposed by Reuters is indicted on kidnap charges. Retrieved from www.reuters.com/article/us-usa-kidnapping-adoption-idUSKBN0NT2GK 20150508

Uganda Ministry of Gender, Labour and Social Development. (2011). National Strategic Programme Plan of Interventions for Orphans and Other Vulnerable Children 2011/12–2015/6. Kampala: MGLSD.

US Department of State. (n.d.). Intercountry adoption: Liberia. Retrieved from http://travel.state.gov/content/adoptionsabroad/en/country-information/learn-about-a-country/liberia.html

US Department of State. (2010). Notice: Adoption processing at the U.S. Embassy in Addis Ababa. Retrieved from http://adoption.state.gov/country_information/country_specific_alerts_notices.php?alert_notice_type=notices&alert_notice_file=ethiopia_4

US Department of State. (2015a, October 5). Alert: Update on the exit permit suspension in the Democratic Republic of Congo (DRC). Retrieved from http://travel.state.gov/content/adoptionsabroad/en/country-information/alerts-and-notices/DRC15-10-05.html

US Department of State. (2015b, April 30). Notice: Update on the details of moratorium on intercountry adoptions in Kenya. Retrieved from http://travel.state.gov/content/adoptionsabroad/en/country-information/alerts-and-notices/kenya15-04-24.html

US Department of State. (2015c). Statement of Ambassador Michele Thoren Bond, Assistant Secretary for Consular Affairs before the Senate Judiciary Committee on November 18, 2015. Retrieved from www.judiciary.senate.gov/imo/media/doc/11-18-15%20Bond%20Testimony3.pdf

Williamson, J. & Greenberg, A. (2010). *Families, not orphanages*. New York: Better Care Network.

World Entertainment News Network. (2004, June 25) Angelina Jolie's adoption agent admits fraud. Retrieved from www.contactmusic.com/angelina-jolie/news/angelina-jolie.s-adoption-agent-admits-fraud

World Health Organization. (2015). *Malawi: WHO statistical profile*. Geneva: World Health Organization.

7

FROM INTERCOUNTRY ADOPTION TO COMMERCIAL GLOBAL SURROGACY

It is impossible to say exactly how many individuals and couples have turned away from inter-country adoption and looked to commercial global surrogacy to build their families, how-ever, there has been a shift for some in the context of the ICA decline (Rotabi & Bromfield, 2012) and the trend has even been called "perfecting adoption" by Australian researchers, Cuthbert & Fronek (2014).

In 2009, the celebrity effect on intercountry adoption illustrated this dynamic and also highlighted the problem of discrimination and child adoption. When the famed singer, Elton John, and his same-sex partner (married in a civil union in the UK) attempted to adopt a young boy who was HIV-positive from the Ukraine they were treated with a swift negative response—the singer was deemed too old to adopt (62 years old) and furthermore same-sex couples are not allowed to adopt from the Ukraine because same-sex unions are not recog-nized as legitimate marriages (Associated Press, 2009).

By Christmas Day of 2010, Elton John and his partner welcomed a baby boy born via a surrogate pregnancy that was arranged with a surrogate mother living in California. The story of Elton John building a family through surrogacy highlights that gay and lesbian couples have systematically been excluded from intercountry adoption, with a few exceptions (Davis, 2011), and a shift to commercial global surrogacy arrangements has been one way to accom-modate such individuals and couples. Also, many heterosexual couples are choosing surrogacy as a result of infertility or other medical issues, such as a pregnancy being high risk for some women (e.g. diabetic women). And, there is a broad array of service providers throughout the United States poised to facilitate the arrangement; some surrogate mothers are circumventing facilitative assistance and directly negotiating with an individual or couple through the inter-net. In the case of Elton John and his partner, they used a high-profile service to arrange the transaction and, because money was not a barrier, this choice to engage an intermediary is not a surprise. Paying in the range of USD$75,000 or more for the surrogacy was easy enough for this mega-wealthy couple. They have since added a second son, via a surrogacy arrangement in California using the same surrogate mother and egg donor (People Magazine, 2013).

Elton John and his partner sought surrogacy services in the most popular destination coun-try and in one of the most surrogacy-friendly states, California. The surrogate received an embryo transfer, using the eggs of another woman fertilized by one of the two men/fathers (People Magazine, 2013). This form of surrogacy, called gestational surrogacy, is the most common today. The child is not genetically related to the surrogate mother (also commonly called gestational carrier), thereby establishing genetic parentage and excluding the surrogate from contesting the legal arrangement and any custody rights at a later date, in some states. This is different from traditional surrogacy where the child is the biological offspring of the surrogate mother because her eggs are used in the transaction; such surrogacy arrangements are not the norm today in this era of advanced fertility technology (Rotabi & Bromfield, 2012).

The turn away from traditional surrogacy is related to advanced reproductive technologies that are accessible today and also due to controversy related to the now infamous Baby M case (Suter, 2010). This particular case played out in the 1980s in the United States, raising a variety of biomedical ethical questions amongst the media, some groups of feminists, and the general public. In that case, which was followed rigorously by the press and others questioning women's rights and social ethics (Corea, 1985), the surrogate mother contested the surrogacy contract and reportedly abducted the child, known as "Baby M," for several months until she was located by law enforcement in another state (Goldberg, 2016). Because the child was her genetic offspring, eventually the state supreme court ordered the contract nullified and parental and child-visitation rights for the surrogate mother, Mary Beth Whitehead. Child custody hinged on a number of issues including Whitehead's emotional stability that was called into question during legal proceedings (Goldberg, 2016). Also important to note, the child adoption by the commissioning mother was also nullified in the Baby M case (Goldberg, 2016). In 2004, when Melissa Stern (Baby M) turned 18 years old, she formalized her parental relationship with Elizabeth Stern, the commissioning mother, through adoption and officially terminated Mary Beth Whitehead's parental rights and also any further contact with Whitehead (Kelly, 2012).

Another case, taking place during the same time period, played out in the United Kingdom with connections to Sweden and the United States. This particular case, also a traditional surrogacy arrangement, took place in 1985. It is referred to as the Baby Cotton case (Cotton & Winn, 1985). The global dimensions of the case are important as a British surrogate, Kim Cotton, gave birth to a baby for a Swedish couple living in the United States. Commercial surrogacy was not considered in British law at this point in history and it was not yet banned. When British authorities learned of the financial agreement, the infant was ruled to be a ward of the court. The public responded with great criticism of Cotton and the commissioning couple with a pervasive view that the activity was "baby selling" (Cotton & Winn, 1985). As a result, a new law was passed in the United Kingdom (Surrogacy Arrangements Act of 1985), banning the practice of commercial surrogacy. In this particular case, the custody of the child was eventually settled when the Swedish couple was allowed by the courts in the United Kingdom to take the child back to their home of habitual residence, the United States, with an agreement that the child would not have contact with the surrogate (Cotton & Winn, 1985).

A recent scandal and the intersection of surrogacy and adoption with global dimensions

Today, the business of surrogacy is incredibly lucrative for those who "arrange" the transaction (Goodwin, 2010) and the legal quagmire of the Baby M case is now avoided with gestational surrogacy arrangements in surrogacy-friendly jurisdictions (where such contracts are recognized as legal). As a result, there is a whole range of "service providers" that one can find with a simple internet search (Hawkins, 2012). This is not unlike intercountry adoption in which the internet has been a critical component in the marketing and coordinating of the service (Roby & White, 2010).

Internet discussion boards and forums are incredibly common for both intercountry adoption and surrogacy information sharing and advertising. When the following advertisement appeared on Baby Crowd in the "adoption" section (Darnovsky, 2011), at least one respondent on the discussion board said as a warning that the situation sounded like "baby selling." That comment was responding to the following advertisement and proved correct:

> Lawyer currently has a situation available…not an adoption, but will be treated as a surrogacy…baby conceived via IVF and donor embryos. Caucasian Infant…names of new parents will be put on the birth certificate, no adoption necessary, no homestudy needed!
>
> *(www.babycrowd.com/forums/adoption/Caucasian_baby_USA_Updated_Information_/)*

The lawyer also warned of "high expenses."

Once the United States Federal Bureau of Investigation opened the case and eventually prosecution commenced, they were blunt when they issued a press release entitled "Baby-Selling Ring Busted" (Federal Bureau of Investigation, 2011). While the story may seem complicated, it really was rather simple. Theresa Erickson advertised for women who agreed to be surrogates and the arrangement included a trip to the Ukraine for in vitro fertilization/embryo transfer. These women believed themselves to be gestational carriers for an individual or couple in the United States. That was a core and critical falsehood. Erickson and others in her organization would then advertise the healthy fetus as being available as a surrogacy arrangement—telling those interested in the unborn baby and transaction that a surrogacy arrangement had fallen apart and that the unborn baby was no longer wanted by the commission parent(s). As a result, the child was available *if* they could afford the expense which would be over USD$100,000 (Federal Bureau of Investigation, 2011). In this process, several laws were broken, and outrageously enough further fraud was committed when the surrogate mothers requested welfare benefits under California's Access for Infants and Mothers to cover their medical costs.

Erickson was just one attorney who pleaded guilty in the scheme which the Federal Bureau of Investigation (2011) considered to be an organization that created an "inventory of unborn babies" (p. 1). In order to carry out the fraud, false statements were made before California courts. How far the fraudulent scheme went is a question and to clarify, the child was conceived with donor egg and sperm—those donors apparently had no idea of the fraud. Also, none of the surrogates were charged with fraud in this case. The paying customers/ prospective parent(s) also were unaware of the fraudulent procedures—although one should question their willful blindness given the sheer expense of the transaction.

The individuals and couples who sought to build their families through this means trusted Erickson and others as internationally recognized members of the fertility "industry"; she appeared to be ethical and one of the organizations involved was highly polished with the title: *The National Adoption and Surrogacy Center, Adoption and Reproductive Law*. What appeared trustworthy as an organization had a dark truth, the organization engaged in a chain of events that are not unlike child laundering in intercountry adoption.

The children were sold as Erickson and her co-conspirators became multi-millionaires who capitalized on the marketplace for healthy infants and the capacity to move women across the globe for fertility treatments and then labor and delivery elsewhere. Reportedly Erickson told the press, after her prosecution, that her actions were the "tip of the iceberg" in the fertility-surrogacy industry (as reported by Darnovsky, 2011). However, it is critically important to acknowledge that there have been no similar prosecutions in the years since this case.

Ethically complicated practices lead to the practice of commercial surrogacy being banned in Canada and many European countries

The Baby Cotton case was a foreshadow of what was to come as today commercial surrogacy is illegal in many countries throughout Western Europe, as well as Canada. In many of these countries, including the UK, altruistic surrogacy is only possible as compensation for surrogacy is illegal (Crawshaw, Blythe, & van den Akker, 2012). For individuals and couples in these countries looking to build their family through surrogacy, the availability of women who are willing to engage in an altruistic endeavor (being reimbursed for expenses only) is limited. In fact, in a 2013 report on European altruistic and commercial surrogacy, the Policy Department for European Legal and Parliamentary Affairs found that "160 million European citizens have no full access to donor procedures in their own country" (Brunet et al., 2013, p. 26).

As a result, a global marketplace has grown to meet the demand. The most active commercial surrogacy country is the United States, where there is no federal regulation and surrogacy-friendly states have laws that are protective of commissioning parents (Goldberg, 2016). Additionally, all children born in the United States receive US citizenship upon birth. This added citizenship benefit is particularly attractive for various reasons, including that there is no chance of statelessness for these children, as has happened in global surrogacy arrangements in some other countries.

For those individuals and couples who are interested in the far less expensive but highly efficient surrogacy-arrangement option, India has been the second-choice destination country (Pande, 2014). Like the United States, India lacks a comprehensive national legal framework to regulate the practice. While that has been changing in recent times, with the banning of surrogacy for gay couples in 2011 and new regulations in the fall of 2015 regarding foreign nationals seeking surrogacy in India, the industry has largely been guided by fertility-surrogacy entrepreneurs. This is true around the globe.

It is a billion-dollar business today and a range of moral and social concerns have emerged in recent years as the human rights of the surrogate mother have now captured a great deal of attention by the media, human rights defenders and scholars (Cheney, 2014; Crawshaw et al., 2012; Darnovsky & Beeson, 2014; Fronek & Crawshaw, 2014; Karandikar, Gezinski, Carter, & Kaloga, 2014; Markens, 2007; Pande, 2014; Rotabi, 2014; SAMA, 2012; Trimmings & Beaumont, 2011). Ironically, the ban in many countries of Europe and elsewhere has led citizens of these countries to seek surrogacy services in a second country with limited regulation (although, India has begun to require commissioning parents seeking surrogacy arrangements to have documentation of permission from their countries of citizenship). This is not an insignificant issue when the second country has an industry poised to capitalize on the fact that there are few or no regulations—or those that exist which have been set in place to protect intended parents as the main framework—combined with women living in poverty.

The case of Thailand: regulation and country closure

By 2014, Thailand was a prominent global surrogacy destination, especially for Australian couples, although commercial surrogacy was officially banned in Thailand in 1997 (Head, 2015). In 2014, two high-profile surrogacy scandals eventually led to Thailand's military-dominated parliament to criminalize and ban surrogacy arrangements for non-Thai couples and same-sex couples in early 2015 (Head, 2015), bringing all new global surrogacy arrangements taking place in the country to an abrupt halt.

The first scandal, known as the "Baby Gammy" case, involved an Australian couple who contracted a surrogacy arrangement in Thailand. Boy/girl twins were born from the arrangement, but the Australian couple, Wendy and David Farnell, took only the girl back to Australia and abandoned the boy, who had Down's Syndrome, in Thailand. The boy, known as "Baby Gammy," remained with his surrogate mother, Pattharamon "Koy" Janbua. The Baby Gammy case quickly made international headlines with people worldwide condemning the Farnells. The scandal further intensified when it was revealed that David Farnell was a convicted child sex offender (Engle, 2014).

The second high-profile scandal occurring in Thailand broke shortly after the Baby Gammy case and involved a young, wealthy Japanese man, Mitsutoki Shigeta (purportedly the son of a Japanese billionaire), who fathered 16 children with at least 11 Thai surrogates. When police raided his flat in Thailand, they found nine babies and nine nannies inside. Although Shigeta has been investigated for human trafficking and child exploitation by Thai authorities, there has been no evidence of trafficking and Shigeta said that he simply wanted a large family and had the financial means to do so. According to Shigeta's lawyer, he had opened savings accounts and purchased investments for each of the children (Jabour, 2014).

Shortly after these two stories broke, ethical issues related to surrogacy dominated headlines worldwide. Thailand swiftly banned all new surrogacy arrangements for people who were not Thai citizens.

Risks of low-resource countries in commercial global surrogacy

When the massive 2015 earthquake struck Katmandu, Nepal the world learned of a quiet but thriving practice of commercial global surrogacy taking place there. The news story was particularly dramatic when the government of Israel sent in military aircraft to evacuate their adult citizens and babies born of surrogacy (Stoffel, 2015; Kamin, 2015). While there was an attempt to also evacuate the surrogates who had not yet given birth, that became problematic when it was ascertained that by and large they had inadequate travel documents (passports) necessary for Israeli immigration (Kamin, 2015). As a result, these women were left behind; not without great consternation on the part of the commissioning individuals and couples (Stoffel, 2015).

Without a doubt, the story was provocative for a number of reasons. First, many of the Israeli citizens engaged in surrogacy arrangements were gay men seeking services in the region— avoiding India, given new laws banning gay couples. Also, surprising was the fact that the surrogates themselves were not Nepal citizens. Rather, they were Indian women who had crossed the border, many from the neighboring and deeply impoverished state of Bihar, India. This particular area of India is known for high levels of illiteracy, large numbers of indigenous people, and significant levels of human trafficking, all adding up to vulnerability for poor women who transit to another country for a surrogacy arrangement (Singh, Meena, Singh, & Abhay, 2011).

The involvement of Indian women in Nepal was necessary as it was illegal to make such a contract with a Nepali woman as per the laws of Nepal. However, the loophole was that women from another country (India) could be contracted to carry out the surrogacy arrangement in Nepal. One clinic, opened with a strong commitment to gay men, had a thriving business that was quietly operating in Nepal until the massive earthquake disaster.

The evacuation efforts, carried out officially by the Israeli government, illustrate the vulnerabilities of arranging for commercial surrogacy in a low-resource country like Nepal. Rightfully so, those commissioning surrogacy were deeply concerned about the lack of health facilities and the general lawlessness in the days after the earthquake, in a time with aftershocks and fears about clean drinking water and other life-threatening issues that arise in the aftermath of disaster. Nepal provides just one example of potential risks for individuals and couples seeking surrogacy services in low-resource countries. Today, Nepal has banned any further surrogacy arrangements for foreigners (News.com.au, 2015).

Commercial surrogacy arrangements and multi-fetal pregnancy reductions

One area that has been problematic for US surrogacy arrangements is the periodic requirement for multi-fetal pregnancy reductions. This situation occurs because IVF is generally more successful when more than one embryo is transferred to a woman's uterus during an IVF procedure; one, some, or all of the embryos which were transferred may or may not implant into the uterine lining and begin to develop into fetuses. If there is a high-order gestation (three or more fetuses) then a multi-fetal pregnancy-reduction procedure usually would take place during the first or second trimester of the pregnancy, to reduce the number of fetuses to one or two.

There has more recently been a movement towards single embryo transfers in IVF to reduce the chances of a multiple birth and the need for multi-fetal pregnancy reductions in cases of dangerous high-order gestations. "Infants born as part of a multiple pregnancy are at increased risk of prematurity, cerebral palsy, learning disabilities, slow language development, behavioral difficulties, chronic lung disease, developmental delay, and death" (American College of Obstetricians and Gynecologists, 2013, p. 2). The risks of perinatal as well as maternal death increase with the presence of each additional fetus. In most northern European countries, multiple embryo transfers for all IVF procedures are banned, despite the fact that overall IVF success rates are reduced, especially among older women.

Problems related to multiple embryo transfer in surrogacy arrangements became quite marked with a recent 2015–16 case in the United States in which a commissioning (single) father requested that his surrogate abort a third fetus of triplets. When the surrogate decided to not honor this request, even though the contract clearly stated the father's rights to exercise this request, the case broke open into a media firestorm. With public scrutiny, it was learned that the commissioning father admitted that affording a second child (twin) was going to be difficult, and he felt a third child to be an impossible financial obligation (not to mention the risks of miscarriage, stillbirth, and lifelong disability which increase with each additional fetus). When the surrogate mother offered to adopt the third child, the father was adamantly opposed and was standing his ground based on his assertion that the child was not her genetic offspring due to gestational surrogacy. Both sides claimed the other was emotionally unstable. While this case was not a global surrogacy arrangement, it is mentioned to highlight the complexities of the technology at hand and moral dilemmas that may arise with multiple embryo transfers and births in a surrogacy arrangement.

In other countries, such as India, the commercial surrogacy arrangements are designed such that the above dilemma would not play out with the surrogate in this position of power. This case does illustrate the power that US women have in their surrogacy contracts and the importance of thorough screening of women for such an agreement, i.e. that surrogates understand the implications of multiple embryo transfer and the subsequent possibility of multi-fetal reductions in cases of high-order gestations. Indeed, this is also an issue that any woman seeking IVF treatment confronts, and doctors agreeing to transfer multiple embryos during IVF will usually ask the patient to consider the possibility of a multi-fetal reduction in the case of a high-order pregnancy.

Child rights and statelessness

There are no international treaties, conventions, or regulations regarding global surrogacy arrangements, and because surrogacy is banned in some countries and virtually unregulated in others, there have been cases where children born of global surrogacy arrangements have been subject to not having legal parents and/or have been left stateless for a period of time (Malhotra & Malhotra, 2013). This occurs due to conflicting national laws (or lack of laws) regarding anonymous gamete donors, surrogacy, parentage rights, and citizenship rights. This is a critical issue in global surrogacy cases, when considering the best interests of the child (Bromfield & Rotabi, 2014). One reason that the United States is a popular global surrogacy destination is that there is no chance for child statelessness, due to US federal citizenship regulations.[1]

As an example of how disagreements on parentage rights and the child's national identity can play out in a global surrogacy arrangement, we will discuss the Balaz case. In 2008, commissioning parents from Germany, where commercial surrogacy is banned, sought a surrogacy arrangement in India. In this well-known case, Mr. and Mrs. Balaz used Mr. Balaz's sperm and donated eggs for a surrogacy arrangement in India, with an Indian gestational surrogate (Henaghan, 2013). Twin boys were born of the arrangement. However, because Germany had banned commercial surrogacy, the German government refused to recognize the twins as German citizens and the German commissioning mother as a legal parent. India refused to issue Indian passports because neither of the registered parents on the birth certificate (the Balazes) were Indian.

The case ended up being a legal test as India's central adoption resource authority became involved. Eventually, the original birth certificates, which listed the Balazes as parents, were rescinded by India and new birth certificates were issued, listing the Indian surrogate mother as the mother, along with Jan Balaz, the commissioning and biological father of the children. Germany issued visas for the children to go to Germany, and the children were eventually adopted by the Balazes in Germany with involvement of the central adoption authority that normally serves in oversight of intercountry adoptions in Germany.[2] This conundrum, related to different country laws, took two years to overcome, with the Balazes being forced to stay in India with their children during that time (Henaghan, 2013).

There were other similar cases in India involving statelessness and parentage issues in surrogacy arrangements and as per the Convention on the Rights of the Child the right to nationality (Art. 8) is in conflict with statelessness—a critical human rights abuse. However, in 2014, India mandated that commissioning couples from countries and/or states in which commercial surrogacy is illegal would not be able to obtain a medical surrogacy visa for India, which is required in order to leave India with a child born of a surrogacy arrangement there. At that point, the Indian government required a medical/surrogacy visa application to be accompanied by a letter from the foreign commissioning couple's government, stating that the foreign nation recognizes surrogacy and that the child/ren born of the arrangement will be permitted entry into their country as a biological child of the couple commissioning surrogacy in India.

Similarities, differences, and parallels between intercountry adoption and commercial global surrogacy

It is far too simplistic to say that intercountry adoption and global surrogacy are similar given that most surrogacy arrangements today are gestational and thus there is no genetic link between the surrogate mother and the child, while there most often is a genetic link between at least one of the parents commissioning the surrogate arrangement and the child born of such an arrangement. While there are arguments about parentage and the many complexities involved (see the introduction in Goodwin, 2010), the genetic connection between the surrogate mother and child (or lack thereof) is established prior to the embryo transfer. That is, the lack of a genetic relationship is identified explicitly and the surrogate ostensibly fully understands this fact as it is outlined in the legal contract.

There are parallels between intercountry adoption and global surrogacy (Scherman, Misca, Rotabi, & Selman, 2016), particularly the demands of what is frequently called the "baby market" (Goodwin, 2010). However, there are stark differences beyond the obvious genetic relationship when the surrogacy is gestational and at least one of the commissioning parents has a direct genetic link to the child. The contractual and commercial arrangements in global surrogacy are different from intercountry adoptions that occur in most cases because of poverty and the array of related social problems that act as social forces leading to child abandonment or relinquishment, to include war and disaster. Among other points, in surrogacy the infant child is almost always immediately separated from the surrogate and received by the commissioning parent/s and the concept of the "orphan" in need of crisis care does not enter into a compelling equation. Furthermore, the pregnancy and contractual arrangements in surrogacy are planned with great care, while infant adoptions are more related to crisis/unplanned pregnancies and/or the social/environmental stressors, as previously explored.

Conclusion: research we have undertaken

With all of these considerations at hand, we aim in the next two chapters to look at global surrogacy arrangements in which contracts are clearly delineated and the surrogates were fully informed of their role in the arrangement, risks of the fertility procedures, the constraints in their actions and behaviors while pregnant, and so forth. The two studies that we have undertaken are focused on such women in the United States and India. Before we present each study, it is imperative to point out that we have not carried out research with women who claim fraud and malfeasance in their surrogacy cases. While such a study is important, evidence in this area is outside of our scope of research.

Notes

1   Some foreigners commissioning surrogacy in the US are actually attracted to their future child's rights to citizenship. For example, some Chinese intended parents have admitted that they have chosen the US as a surrogacy destination due to the rights to the birth of a US-citizen child and the related US residency rights as parents (Harney, 2013).
2   The Indian central adoption resource authority refused to process the case as an adoption because the child was not abandoned and there had been pre-birth contact with the surrogate mother. Both of these conditions were problematic in India's legislation governing child adoption.

References

American College of Obstetricians and Gynecologists. (2013). Committee opinion. Retrieved from www.acog.org/Resources-And-Publications/Committee-Opinions/Committee-on-Ethics/Multifetal-Pregnancy-Reduction

Associated Press. (2009, September 14). Elton John blocked from adopting HIV- positive Ukrainian child. Retrieved from www.theguardian.com/society/2009/sep/14/elton-john-adoption-ukraine

Bromfield, N. F. & Rotabi, K. S. (2014). Global surrogacy, exploitation, human rights and international private law: A pragmatic stance and policy recommendations. *Global Social Welfare*, 1(3), 123–35. doi: 10.1007/s40609-014-0019-4

Brunet, L., Carruthers, J., Davaki, K., King, D., Marzo, C., & McCandless, J. (2013). A comparative study of the regime of surrogacy in EU member states: Report submitted to European Parliament's Committee on Legal Affairs. Retrieved from www.europarl.europa.eu/RegData/etudes/etudes/join/2013/474403/IPOLJURI_ET(2013)474403_EN.pdf

Cheney, K. E. (2014). Executive summary of the International Forum on Intercountry Adoption and Global Surrogacy. ISS Working Paper Series/General Series, 596, 1–40. Retrieved from http://hdl.handle.net/1765/77408

Corea, G. (1985). *The mother machine: Reproductive technologies from artificial insemination to Artificial wombs.* New York: Harper & Row Publishers.

Cotton, K. & Winn, D. (1985). *Baby Cotton: For love and money.* London: Gollancz Publications.

Crawshaw, M., Blythe, E., & van den Akker, O. (2012). The changing profile of surrogacy in the UK: Implications of national and international policy and practice. *Journal of Social Welfare and Family Law*, 34(3), 265–75.

Cuthbert, D. & Fronek, P. (2014). Perfecting adoption? Reflections on the rise of commercial offshore surrogacy and family formation in Australia. In A. Hayes & D. Higgins (Eds), *Families, policy and the law: Selected essays on contemporary issues for Australia* (pp. 55–66). Melbourne: Australian Institute of Family Studies. Retrieved from https://aifs.gov.au/sites/default/files/publication-documents/fpl.pdf#page=73

Darnovsky, M. (2011). Surrogacy and baby selling: Another fertility industry scandal. Psychology Today. Retrieved from www.psychologytoday.com/blog/genetic-crossroads/201108/surrogacy-and-baby-selling-another-fertility-industry-scandal

Darnovsky, M. & Beeson, D. (2014). Global surrogacy practices. ISS Working Paper Series/General Series, 601, 1–54. Retrieved from http://hdl.handle.net/1765/77402

Davis, M. A. (2011). *Children for families or families for children: The demography of adoption behavior in the U. S.* Rotterdam: Springer.

Engle, M. (2014, August 11). Baby Gammy's father David Farnell defends himself on Australia's 60 Minutes. Daily News. Retrieved from www.nydailynews.com/life-style/health/gammy-father-david-farnell-defends-article-1.1899348

Federal Bureau of Investigation. (2011, August 9). Baby-selling ring busted. Retrieved from www.fbi.gov/sandiego/press-releases/2011/baby-selling-ring-busted

Fronek, P. & Crawshaw, M. (2014). The "new family" as an emerging norm: A commentary on the position of social work. *British Journal of Social Work*. doi: 10.1093/bjsw/bct198

Goldberg, M. (2016, February 15). Is a surrogate a mother? Slate. Retrieved from www.slate.com/articles/double_x/doublex/2016/02/custody_case_over_triplets_in_california_raises_questions_about_surrogacy.html

Goodwin, M. B. (2010). *Baby markets: Money and the new politics of creating families.* New York: Cambridge University Press.

Harney, A. (2013, September 22). Wealthy Chinese seek U.S. surrogate for second child, green card. *Reuters*. Retrieved from www.reuters.com/article/us-china-surrogates-idUSBRE98L0JD20130922

Hawkins J. (2012). Selling ART: An empirical assessment of advertising on fertility clinics' websites. *Indiana Law Journal*, 88: 1147–79.

Head, J. (2015, February 20). Thailand bans commercial surrogacy for foreigners. *BBC News*. Retrieved from www.bbc.com/news/world-asia-31546717

Henaghan, M. (2013). International surrogacy trends: How family law is coping. *Australian Journal of Adoption*, 7(3). Retrieved from www.nla.gov.au/openpublish/index.php/aja/article/view/3188

Jabour, B. (2014, August 4). Baby Gammy: conflicting reports about baby boy "abandoned" in Thailand. Guardian. Retrieved from www.theguardian.com/world/2014/aug/04/baby-gammy-conflicting-reports-about-baby-boy-abandoned-in-thailand

Kamin, D. (2015, April 28). Israel evacuates surrogate babies from Nepal but leaves the mothers behind. Time. Retrieved from http://time.com/3838319/israel-nepal-surrogates/

Karandikar, S., Gezinski, L. B., Carter, J. R., & Kaloga, M. (2014). Economic necessity or a noble cause? Exploring motivations for gestational surrogacy in Gujarat, India. *Affilia*, 29(2), 224–36.

Kelly, M. (2012, March 30). Kelly: 25 years after Baby M, surrogacy questions remain unanswered. Retrieved from www.northjersey.com/cm/2.1593/news/kelly- 25-years-after-baby-m-surrogacy-questions-remain-unanswered-1.745725

Malhotra, A. & Malhotra, R. (2013, August). Surrogacy: Imported from India—the need for a regulatory law. In International Social Services/International Reference Center Team (Eds), *ISS monthly review (special issue): The international resort to surrogacy: A new challenge to be addressed urgently* (pp. 8–9). Geneva: International Social Services.

Markens, S. (2007). *Surrogate motherhood and the politics of reproduction.* Oakland: University of California Press.

News.com.au. (2015, September 3). Australian families left in limbo as Nepal joins India and Thailand in banning commercial surrogacy. News.com.au. Retrieved from www.news.com.au/lifestyle/parenting/kids/australian-framilies-in-limbo-as-nepal-joins-india-and-thailand-in-banning-commerical-surrogacy/news- story/1135c51937c27545bdcf3e09ddd54c25

Pande, A. (2014). *Wombs in labor: Transnational commercial surrogacy in India.* New York: Columbia University Press.

People Magazine. (2013, January 27). Elton John introduces son Elijah Joseph Daniel. Retrieved from http://celebritybabies.people.com/2013/01/27/elton-john-introduces-son-elijah-first-photo/

Roby, J. L. & White, H. (2010). Adoption activities on the internet: A call for regulation. *Social Work*, 55(3), 203–12.

Rotabi, K. S. (December, 2014). Force, fraud, and coercion: Bridging from knowledge of intercountry adoption to global surrogacy. ISS Working Paper Series/General Series, 600, 1–30. Retrieved from http://hdl.handle.net/1765/77403

Rotabi, K. S. & Bromfield, N. F. (2012). Intercountry adoption declines lead to new practices of global surrogacy in Guatemala: Global human rights concerns in the context of violence and the era of advanced fertility technology. *Affilia*, 27(2), 129–41. doi: 10.1177/0886109912444102

SAMA. (2012). Birthing a market: A study on commercial surrogacy. Retrieved from www.samawomenshealth.org/downloads/Birthing%20A%20Market.pdf

Scherman, R., Misca, G., Rotabi, K. S., & Selman, P. F. (2016). Parallels between international adoption and global surrogacy: What the field of surrogacy can learn from adoption. *Adoption & Fostering*, 40(1), 20–35.

Singh, K. M., Meena, M. S., Singh, R. K. P., & Abhay, K. (2011, September). Dimensions of poverty in Bihar. Retrieved from http://dx.doi.org/10.2139/ssrn.2017506

Stoffel, D. (2015, May 2). Israeli airlift of Nepal babies fuels debate around surrogate mothers. *CBC News*. Retrieved from www.cbc.ca/news/world/israeli-airlift-of-nepal-babies-fuels-debate-around-surrogate-mothers-1.3055462

Suter, S. (2010). Giving in to baby markets. In M. B. Goodwin (Ed.), *Baby markets: Money and the new politics of creating families* (pp. 278–94). New York: Cambridge University Press.

Trimmings, K. & Beaumont, P. (2011). International surrogacy arrangements: An urgent need for legal regulation at the international level. *Journal of Private International Law*, 7(3), 627–47.

8

VOICES OF US SURROGATES

A content analysis of blogs by US gestational surrogates

As discussed in Chapter 7, with the rise of contemporary gestational-surrogacy arrangements, surrogacy has recently re-emerged as a hot-button issue. Surrogacy arrangements have increasingly received much attention from the media, academics, and organizations such as bioethics and feminist groups. Most of the focus is on surrogacy arrangements in lower-resource countries, such as India, although the United States is also a popular global surrogacy destination (Bromfield & Rotabi, 2014). Markens (2007) has noted that much of the media attention on surrogacy has been sensationalized and politicized. Numerous articles and reports have recently been published on surrogacy, with some activists calling for a ban on surrogacy worldwide (Damelio & Sorensen, 2008), the primary motivation being the protection of women who work as surrogates as well as a concern for child rights. For the full-length article on the study discussed in this chapter see Bromfield (2016).

Surrogacy in the United States

As we previously noted, throughout most European countries and in some other countries worldwide, commercial surrogacy, altruistic (non-commercial) surrogacy, or both forms have been banned and/or criminalized based on the grounds that surrogacy is exploitive, commodifies women and/or children, and violates their human rights (Storrow, 2013). These assertions are not well grounded in empirical data (Storrow, 2013) and rely mostly on feminist or other critiques about the practice (Teman, 2008) in which surrogates themselves were not consulted or given a voice (Berend, 2012).

In the United States, surrogacy regulations vary state to state, and although sociodemographic dimensions such as ethnicity and income levels of US surrogates are largely unknown (Gugucheva, 2010), it is often assumed and even asserted by some that mostly young, impoverished women of color work as surrogates. Surrogacy is portrayed as a form of severe reproductive injustice with the surrogacy market preying on vulnerable women (Fixmer-Oraiz, 2013; Parker, 2013).

Gugucheva (2010) and Damelio and Sorensen (2008) maintain that US women who work as gestational surrogates are from the lowest socioeconomic backgrounds and do not likely have financial or educational resources, which opens them to exploitation and abuse and thrusts them into the scenario of the rich taking advantage of the poor; despite this assertion, researchers who studied US surrogacy arrangements found that most US surrogates are lower middle-class or middle-class women, many of whom are college educated (Berend, 2012; Stark, 2012). In addition, researchers found that most Western surrogates are in their 20s or 30s and tend to be White, Christian, and married with children (Ciccarelli & Beckman, 2005; Kleinpeter & Hohman, 2000; Stark, 2012; van den Akker, 2003). Women of color appear to be underrepresented among US surrogates (Ciccarelli & Beckman, 2005).

Research on surrogates

Although a plethora of articles has been written on the practice of surrogacy, including discussions and debates related to moral, psychological, legal, policy, economic, and ethical issues, the number of empirical studies on the experiences of surrogates themselves is somewhat limited, and there is certainly a need for additional contemporary research in this area (Ciccarelli & Beckman, 2005; Gugucheva, 2010). The surrogate research that does exist has been greatly influenced by adoption research, particularly studies that focus on birth mothers' feelings after child relinquishment (Teman, 2008) and also liken commissioning parents with intended adoptive parents (Bromfield & Rotabi, 2014; Ciccarelli & Beckman, 2005). Using adoption research to inform surrogacy studies is problematic, as the parallels are limited for all involved, including the surrogates, the commissioning parents, and the children born of the surrogacy arrangements. As Teman (2008, p. 1108) notes:

> The confusion between surrogates and birthmothers is deceiving: surrogates enter into a contracted agreement with the intent to become pregnant and relinquish, while birthmothers make the decision to relinquish under the pressures of an existent confirmed pregnancy…still the conflation of these two roles influences surrogacy studies right down to the questions that researchers ask.

Similarly, children born from surrogacy arrangements are assumed, based on adoption research, to possibly struggle with loss, grief, or issues of abandonment as a result of an established parent–child relationship and then a break in that relationship. However, surrogacy is quite different, most especially in this regard, and in one longitudinal study that examined families created using surrogacy over a ten-year period, the children felt positive about their surrogacy conception and birth origins and the woman who gave birth to them (Jadva, Blake, Casey, & Golombok, 2012). In fact, the parallels between adoption and surrogacy have some real limits (Bromfield & Rotabi, 2014). This conflation between adoption and surrogacy in research may have occurred because as intercountry adoption began to diminish while surrogacy arrangements increased, adoption researchers turned to surrogacy research and conclusions are being extrapolated from one area of inquiry— adoption to the area of surrogacy with a need for more research. The assumptions that are being drawn, bridging from adoption to surrogacy, must be tested before firm assertions can be made about similarities of practice and outcomes in the two different practices. This is especially true in terms of research on children born of commercial global surrogacy arrangements and measuring their perceptions as they age and become adults, particularly when the surrogate is a woman living in poverty in a country like India. Inevitably, this research will emerge in due course.

In Teman's (2008, p. 1109) extensive review of surrogacy studies, she found that in the majority of studies on surrogates' experiences, researchers frame the surrogate's choice as being deviant from "normal" motherhood and view the surrogate's choice as "one of economic desperation, a psychological need for reparation, or as a function of abnormal personality characteristics." The questions that researchers ask are influenced by these negative assumptions, and Teman (2008, p. 1105) argues that "the centrality of motherhood and family as basic touchstones of society make it difficult [for researchers] to accept the repeat finding [in the research] that surrogates are non-psychopathological women." Teman (2008, p. 1108) also found that:

> Whatever reason is proffered for [the surrogate's] choice, the surrogate is constructed as deviant: her altruism ranges beyond normative boundaries; her desire for money is constituted as greed or as a function of extreme poverty; or her reparative motive is indicative of past sins for which she must punish herself.

Despite surrogates being often portrayed as deviant and/or victims in the media, by some organizations, and by some scholars, the empirical studies that exist on Western surrogates suggest that surrogates are not deviant, but challenge traditional notions of family and motherhood and want to help create a family (Markens, 2011; Kessler, 2009; van den Akker, 2003); the sentiment of having a "sense of purpose" has also been prevalent in narratives by surrogates (Ali & Kelley, 2008; Blyth, 1994; Kessler, 2009; Teman, 2008).

Some gestational surrogates report that they enjoy being pregnant, are proud of the accomplishment, and are pleased that they could help another couple build their own family (Stark, 2012). In empirical studies, the most popular motivations for being a surrogate were enjoyment of being pregnant, sympathy for childless couples, financial considerations, and the desire to do something "special" (Blyth, 1994; Teman, 2008).

The majority of Western surrogates report having high satisfaction with the process of being a surrogate (Baslington, 2002; Blyth, 1994; Jadva, Murray, Lycett, Macallum, & Golombok, 2003; Ragone, 1994; Teman, 2008), and surrogates often enter into multiple surrogacy arrangements. The few longitudinal studies that exist on surrogates show that they remain satisfied with their surrogacy experiences over time (Jadva et al., 2003; Teman, 2008). Ali and Kelley (2008) suggest that the surrogates they interviewed for a *Newsweek* article felt a sense of empowerment and self-worth by being surrogates. Jadva et al. (2003, p. 2196) studied 34 UK surrogates' motivations, experiences, and psychological consequences of surrogacy approximately one year after the surrogate delivery and reported that "surrogate mothers do not appear to experience psychological problems as a result of the surrogacy arrangement." Surrogates who were studied also felt that the surrogate experience benefited their own families, and three quarters of surrogates in one study reported that the surrogacy experience affected their own children positively (Ciccarelli & Beckman, 2005). In the United States, surrogates often downplay the financial incentive and focus on altruistic motivations for being a surrogate (Ciccarelli & Beckman, 2005; Hohman & Hagan, 2001; Markens, 2011).

Most of the negative experiences that have been reported by surrogates are related to their relationships with the commissioning parents or that they no longer feel important to the parents after the surrogate pregnancy (Berend, 2012; Blyth, 1994; Ciccarelli & Beckman, 2005; Jadva et al., 2003; Ragone, 1994). In one study that supports this assertion, Berend (2012, p. 913) examined online communication between surrogates on a surrogacy-support online bulletin board and found that surrogates often describe their surrogacy as a "journey of shared love" with the commissioning parents and that surrogates "hope for a long-term friendship with their couple" and often feel betrayed and disappointed when the parents reduce or cease contact after the birth.

Public expressions of surrogate experiences

Despite the paucity of empirical research on surrogates themselves, US surrogates are not an invisible group. They have strong voices in an online presence, both in the form of online forums (Berend, 2012) and through their own blogs, in which bloggers who are surrogates publicly share their journeys. Although it is not generalizable to a wider group of surrogates or even to other surrogate bloggers, to gain insight into US surrogates' public expressions we analyzed 21 publicly available blogs written by US gestational surrogates. For more details regarding this study, a full-length article is available (Bromfield, 2016). This chapter includes a condensed discussion of what is explored in the article.

Regarding the blogs, we were already familiar with the content on a casual basis, and had spent the last several years "following" some of the blogs—we are also familiar with infertility bulletin boards and the common acronyms used in the online infertility/IVF community such as PUPO (pregnant until proven otherwise), 2WW (two-week wait—the time period between an IVF embryo transfer and pregnancy test), and POAS ("pee" on a stick—meaning to take a home pregnancy test). These acronyms were commonly used by the gestational surrogate bloggers as they were undergoing IVF for their surrogacy pregnancies. For the study, after first reading through all of the blogs to get a sense of the overall content, we spent several months reading, coding, and rereading and recoding the blogs in an iterative manner. The blogs were an incredibly rich data source and gave us insight into the public expressions of gestational surrogates in the United States.

After first reading through each blog, we then coded all of the text and photos and grouped them into loose superordinate categories such as "pregnancy photos," "IVF procedure," "birth plan," "birth experience," "doctor's visit," and so forth. Through this process, we found that much of the blog content was similar to other non-surrogacy pregnancy blogs, in which expecting moms blog about their morning sickness, growing bellies, birth plans, birth experiences, and general feelings about pregnancy. This process allowed us to gain an understanding of what generally was included in the blogs in a systematic manner.

After subsequently getting a sense of the blogs and initially coding the paragraphs and photos, we then reread the blogs and began to look closely for expressions of meaning related to surrogacy. We coded the specific passages related to surrogacy such as "relationship with other surrogates," "identification as a surrogate," "surrogate contract issues," "relationship with commissioning parents," and so forth. We eventually identified patterns in these codes across the blogs and identified specific themes and recurring patterns of meaning including expressions of thoughts, feelings, and ideas related to surrogacy.

We analyzed publicly available blogs; no group membership or passwords were required for us to access the blogs; they were not on closed sites and were easily accessible with a Google search. However, we do not include direct quotes from the blogs because of copyright and ethical issues. We encourage our readers to search "gestational surrogacy blogs" on the internet to engage with the bloggers' material and voices directly.

Five thematic expressions were common across blogs written by US gestational surrogates: (a) pride in surrogacy work, (b) identification as a member of a special community,

(c) commitment to surrogacy education and advocacy, (d) emphasis on the child not being the surrogate's baby, and (e) the importance of the relationship with the commissioning parents (also known as intended parents by many of the bloggers), including a sense of loss when the relationship with the commissioning parents diminished. There was also a notable reluctance to discuss the financial transaction involved in surrogacy work, which is interesting considering that there is a significant financial payment involved in commercial surrogacy arrangements.

Pride in surrogacy work

The expression that surrogacy is incredibly important and life-changing work in which the bloggers take a great amount of pride is a common theme throughout the blogs. In fact, after engaging in an email exchange with one surrogacy blogger (this surrogate blogger provided the member check, which is used in qualitative research) she noted that pride was a significant part of the surrogacy experience, and for her the pride continued to grow as people in her community, both online and offline, continued to praise and admire her for being a gestational surrogate for another family. This surrogate also expressed the idea of having a "supernatural" sense of pride in the children that were created from the surrogacy arrangement.

Many of the blogs had slogans on their blog page sidebars that stated "*I make families, what's your super-power? Proud Surrogate.*" This particular slogan included an image of a pregnant Rosie the Riveter, an American cultural icon often used to represent feminism and economic power. This point is interesting to note, because the Indian surrogates who we interviewed (discussed in Chapter 9) mention explicitly the economic power they derive from the surrogacy work, while the US surrogates do not discuss financial aspects of surrogacy in their blogs.

One surrogate blogger expressed her pride in being a surrogate and felt that she would always be defined as both a mother and a surrogate and that the pride will stay with her for years as she looks back on her experience as a surrogate who helped to create families for others. Several surrogates mentioned that they have had surrogacy contracts with gay couples and in addition to the pride that was felt by being a surrogate in general, they also felt additional pride that they were helping gay couples with their family-building options. One surrogate mentioned that she specifically wanted to help gay couples to create families and to show her unequivocal support for gay rights. This same blogger also noted that she feels blessed to have been a surrogate and that it had been one of the most rewarding experiences of her life. The surrogate who provided our member check also noted in an email that she has found that there is advocacy for gay rights on other surrogacy blogs and that she herself felt honored to be able to help a gay couple create a family.

Other bloggers referred to the surrogacy experience as amazing; mentioning that they were grateful and would be a surrogate again, and some noted that they were led to surrogacy by God or a higher power, with some bloggers referring to surrogacy as a calling or destiny. Pande also found that Indian surrogates note the divine in surrogacy (Pande, 2014). Interestingly, the position taken by many critics of surrogacy is that surrogacy should be abolished on the premise that it is dehumanizing to women (Damelio & Sorensen, 2008; Gugucheva, 2010).

Identification and membership as a surrogate

The bloggers we studied strongly identified with being a member of a surrogate community and viewed other surrogates as being part of their support system. This is similar to what Pande

(2014) found in her extensive ethnographic work with surrogates in India. Bloggers discussed their close relationships with other surrogates and shared stories of dinners out and weekends away with other women working as surrogates (or surro-sisters, as a few bloggers call them), as well as secret Facebook groups and forum membership for surrogates to share their experiences and exchange advice. There are also organized social and educational events on surrogacy that surrogates discussed in the blogs.

Some bloggers wrote about meeting other surrogates to share their surrogacy journeys with each other. Other bloggers discussed the special bond that surrogates have with each other that outsiders cannot understand, with some bloggers noting that the surrogate connection would last a lifetime. This connection is especially important for surrogates as they have been portrayed as being socially deviant and participating in a behavior that is unnatural or psychopathological (Teman, 2008). The connection and identification with other surrogates help the surrogates to maintain the shared meaning of surrogacy as being important and selfless work that is done out of love.

Clearly, for US surrogates who blog about their experiences, the relationship with other surrogates is a critical aspect of the surrogacy journey for them, and we can see from reading the blogs that the surrogacy is much more than a financial arrangement, and is a complex network of relationships and support systems that include family, friends, commissioning parents, other surrogates, anonymous people who follow their blogs, and others.

Commitment to surrogacy education and advocacy

Much of the blog content on surrogacy is related to education and advocacy on the surrogacy process. A large part of the surrogate pregnancy, aside from the gestation, is the act of getting pregnant through IVF. The surrogate bloggers inform their readers about different types of surrogacy, the IVF process to get pregnant, details of the surrogacy contract, including what to include and how to negotiate the contract with commissioning parents, and other aspects of the surrogacy process. To calm and encourage prospective surrogates, one blogger included a video of self-administration of a progesterone shot. Another surrogate blogger educated her readers about a legal aspect of surrogacy in an easily understood manner, as she discussed and explained the details of a pre-birth order. Another surrogate confronted a misinformed dominant discourse on surrogacy and expressed anger at the comparison between prostitution and surrogacy that is made in the media, noting that surrogates are real people with children, friends, and spouses (and not fodder for the media).

Several surrogates mentioned that they would serve as educators and advocates of surrogacy in an official capacity. One surrogate shared her plans with her readers to become a writer for surrogacy websites on varying aspects of surrogacy. Other surrogate bloggers now work for surrogacy agencies to support other surrogates as mentors and consultants. Surrogate bloggers noted that they sought out these advocacy opportunities as a way to support surrogacy arrangements and other surrogates.

The surrogates portrayed being empowered, knowledgeable, and in control of their experiences as surrogates, not exploited, uneducated, or deceived women not capable of giving true informed consent, which is the picture of surrogates that is often portrayed in the media and by some bioethics and feminist groups. The lived experience for these surrogates is that not only do they feel knowledgeable about their own surrogacy experiences, including the IVF process, but they feel sufficiently empowered with this knowledge to be able to provide advice and guidance to others either going through IVF procedures or considering becoming surrogates themselves.

Emphasis on the child not being the surrogate's baby

The surrogate bloggers often mention that the surrogate child is not their baby and that they must give him/her away to another family. They frame the baby as not being theirs from the day of conception. When surrogacy researchers ask surrogates about relinquishing the baby after the birth, they often draw on adoption research and frame the questions around loss or grief over child relinquishment (Teman, 2008). The bloggers confront the conflation of these two roles by their insistence that the child is not theirs to feel upset about losing. Surrogate bloggers were adamant that the babies born of the surrogacy arrangements were not their own and they challenged the idea of having to "give up" the babies because the babies are not their children to "give up."

One surrogate did note that she felt sad when the surrogacy contract was completed, but it was not due to handing over the baby; she was sad that the surrogacy arrangement was over after she had longed to be a surrogate for so long.

Perhaps as a result of the significant media coverage of the Baby M case, the bloggers make it a point to express on their blogs that they did not feel as if their surrogate babies are *their* children. The blogger who provided our member check also noted that she is quite clear with people that the baby is not hers and is not genetically related to her, and she noted that bloggers often emphasize this point for the benefit of the commissioning parents and other readers since the surrogates are clear themselves on this point. The bloggers may want to alleviate commissioning parents' potential fears that the surrogate will one day claim the child as her own. The surrogates also want to reassure their readers that they are not giving up their baby, which would be unimaginable to them, but that the meaning in handing over the baby is that they are simply helping another family in creating *that* family's baby and that handing over the baby comes from a place of love and overwhelming joy, not sorrow and loss.

Importance of the relationship with the commissioning parents

The importance of the relationship between the surrogate and the commissioning parents, also commonly called intended parents or IPs, is prevalent throughout the blogs. There is a sense in most blogs that there was more than a contract between the commissioning parents and the surrogates, that there was a relationship. Berend's (2012) study of forum discussions found that a surrogate's relationship with the commissioning parents is extremely important and there are expectations of a friendship.

Surrogate bloggers often expressed strong feelings about their relationship with the commissioning parents. One surrogate saw her relationship with the couple contracting the pregnancy with her as planned by God and that they would be lifelong friends. Another blogger discussed how her commissioning parents are now part of her family, and described the intended mother as a new sister and adopted family. A different surrogate described falling in love with her commissioning parents.

Surrogates also discuss sadness and loss related to the breakdown of the relationship between themselves and the commissioning parents. Another surrogate blogger, whose surrogacy process did not work out because of medical issues, described herself as having a broken heart.

Another surrogate described how she felt that she lost friendships (with the commissioning parents) after completion of the surrogacy contract and felt sadness and loss.

Berend (2012) found in her analysis of an online surrogacy forum that surrogates often use "romantic" language to describe their relationship or desired relationship with commissioning parents, and that surrogates felt "let down" when the relationship didn't continue to meet the expectations that the surrogates had for it or when there was a "falling out" with the couple. The collective meaning that these surrogate bloggers have made of surrogacy is that they are doing an important and selfless service out of love, in order to help another family be created. The relationship with the commissioning parents is viewed by the surrogates as a special, loving, and important relationship, so that they can distance themselves from the notion that the relationship is a financial one in which a service (surrogacy) is purchased and sold. The meaning of the relationship is that they are making a sacrifice out of love or compassion for the commissioning parents. Interestingly, in addition to the financial payment, there is an expectation of a negotiated social exchange between the surrogate and the commissioning parent/s.

Little discussion of payment

Although not a theme, it is also important to note in the findings that the bloggers seldom mention financial incentive in the blogs, with the majority of bloggers avoiding discussion of compensation entirely. This is an interesting finding and a point for further discussion.

It is common for US citizen surrogates to separate themselves from the financial exchange involved in surrogacy, although it is significant and usually a $30,000 or more payment per surrogacy arrangement. Markens (2011) notes that distancing oneself from the financial benefit of working as a surrogate also distances oneself from charges of exploitation, commodification, and questions about baby selling. Perhaps the surrogate bloggers were not purposefully avoiding the discussion of the financial transaction, but we had the sense that this was generally a taboo topic for the bloggers.

One blogger did note that during her mandatory meeting with the surrogacy agency's psychologist, she mentioned money as one of the motivating factors for her pursuing surrogacy; the psychologist told her that most surrogates do not mention money as a motivation for being a surrogate. Another blogger defended the notion that surrogacy is mostly an altruistic endeavor on the part of the surrogates and said that surrogates are not money-hungry people trying to make an "easy" dollar.

This is in contrast to both Teman's (2008) and Pande's (2014) findings in their studies on Israeli and Indian surrogates, where surrogates from both countries mention the financial compensation as being a primary motivation for surrogacy.

Conclusion

At this time, various feminists and bioethics groups dominate the public discourse and debates on surrogacy. Much of this debate is centered on surrogacy in India and other low-resource countries in which surrogacy raises questions regarding human rights violations against vulnerable and impoverished women. Clearly the context for surrogates in low-resource countries and high-resource countries such as the United States and other Western countries are in stark contrast. However, surrogates in the United States are most often left out of the debates and discussions on surrogacy, despite the fact that the United States is a popular global surrogacy destination (Bromfield & Rotabi, 2014; Markens, 2011).

We must reiterate that this analysis of public expressions by US surrogates was not intended to draw any conclusions about US surrogates in general (and certainly not about surrogates in non-Western countries), but to provide a glimpse of some surrogates' expressions of meaning of their own experiences as surrogates. Surrogates who blog are a small group of women and are particularly articulate, introspective, witty, and reflective about their journeys as surrogates. The poor, uneducated, uninformed, and oppressed surrogate who is often portrayed in the media and by some academics does not exist in this group of surrogates.

In some countries, surrogacy has been banned or criminalized, based on feminist and other critiques of the practice (Storrow, 2013; Teman, 2008) that do not include Western surrogates' experiences. By framing all surrogates as being either deviant and/or tricked victims, critics of surrogacy can dismiss the voices and experiences of surrogates as women who are so exceptionally desperate that they are not capable of making sound decisions for themselves and are complicit in their own exploitation as surrogates.

By ignoring the voices, experiences, and meaning making of surrogacy for US surrogates, surrogacy abolitionists can continue to frame surrogacy in this manner, without having to confront the stark contrast of their claims with the experiences of US surrogates. As surrogacy arrangements continue to receive attention and governments continue to regulate or ban them, both commercial and altruistic, all surrogates, including those in the United States, must be included in the debate and discourses on surrogacy. We can no longer claim that surrogates are invisible and marginalized, without voice or agency.

References

Ali, L. & Kelley, R. (2008, April 7). The curious lives of surrogates. Newsweek, 44–51.

Baslington, H. (2002). The social organization of surrogacy: Relinquishing a baby and the role of payment in the psychological detachment process. Journal of Health Psychology, 7(1), 57–71.

Berend, Z. (2012). The romance of surrogacy. Sociological Forum, 27(4), 913–36. doi: 10.1111/j.1573-7861.2012.01362.x

Blyth, E. (1994). "I wanted to be interesting, I wanted to be able to say I've done something interesting with my life": Interviews with surrogate mothers in Britain. Journal of Reproductive and Infant Psychology, 12(3), 189–98.

Bromfield, N. F. (2016). "Surrogacy has been one of the most rewarding experiences in my life": A content analysis of blogs by U.S. commercial gestational surrogates. International Journal of Feminist Approaches to Bioethics, 9(1), 192–217. doi/pdf/10.3138/ijfab.9.1.192

Bromfield, N. & Rotabi, K. (2014). Global surrogacy, exploitation, human rights and international private law: A pragmatic stance and call for meaningful international regulation. Global Social Welfare, 1(2).

Ciccarelli, J. & Beckman, L. (2005). Navigating rough waters: An overview of psychological aspects of surrogacy. Journal of Social Issues, 61(1), 21–43.

Damelio, J. & Sorensen, K. (2008). Enhancing autonomy in paid surrogacy. Bioethics, 22(5), 269–77.

Fixmer-Oraiz, N. (2013). Speaking of solidarity. Frontiers, 34(3), 126–63.

Gugucheva, M. (2010). Surrogacy in America. Council for Responsible Genetics. Retrieved from www.councilforresponsiblegenetics.org/pageDocuments/KAEVEJ0A1M

Hohman, M. & Hagan, C. (2001). Satisfaction with surrogate mothering: A relational model. Journal of Human Behavior in the Social Environment, 4, 61–84.

Jadva, V., Murray, C., Lycett, E., Macallum, F., & Golombok, S. (2003). Surrogacy: The experiences of surrogate mothers. Human Reproduction, 18(10), 2196–204.

Jadva, V., Blake, L., Casey, P., & Golombok, S. (2012). Surrogacy families 10 years on: Relationship with the surrogate, decisions over disclosure and children's understanding of their surrogacy origins. *Human Reproduction*, 27(10), 3008–14.

Kessler, B. (2009). Recruiting wombs: Surrogates as the new security moms. *Women's Studies Quarterly*, 37(1/2), 167–82. doi: 10.1353/wsq.0.0139

Kleinpeter, C. & Hohman, M. (2000). Surrogate motherhood: Personality traits and satisfaction with service providers. *Psychological Reports*, 87, 957–70.

Markens, S. (2007). *Surrogate motherhood and the politics of reproduction*. Berkeley: University of California Press.

Markens, S. (2011). Interrogating narratives: About the global surrogacy market. *Scholar and Feminist Online*, 9(1/2).

Pande, A. (2014). *Wombs in labor: Transnational commercial surrogacy in India*. New York: Columbia University Press.

Parker, K. (2013, May 25). Surrogacy exposed. Washington Post.

Ragone, H. (1994). *Conception in the heart*. Boulder, CO: West View Press.

Stark, B. (2012). Transnational surrogacy and international human rights law. *ILSA Journal of International & Comparative Law*, 18(2). Retrieved from http://scholarlycommons.law.hofstra.edu/cgi/viewcontent.cgi?article=1719&contex

Storrow, R. (2013). New thinking on commercial surrogacy. *Indiana Law Journal*, 88, 1281–8.

Teman, E. (2008). The social construction of surrogacy research: An anthropological critique of the psychosocial scholarship on surrogate motherhood. *Social Science & Medicine*, 67, 1104–12. doi: 10.1016/j.socscimed.2008.05.026

van den Akker, O. (2003). Genetic and gestational surrogate mothers' experience of surrogacy. *Journal of Reproductive and Infant Psychology*, 21, 145–61.

9

PERSPECTIVES OF INDIAN WOMEN WHO HAVE COMPLETED A GLOBAL SURROGACY CONTRACT

With Lopamudra Goswami

FIGURE 9.1   Women working in fields in India
Source: Photo credit Nicole F. Bromfield

In Chapter 8 we explored public expressions of US surrogates that were captured through their publicly available blogs. We now turn to the voices of Indian surrogates. In India, which legalized commercial surrogacy in 2004, the estimates of the overall economic value of surrogacy have been reported to be as low as $445 million annually (Haworth, 2007) while other estimates range beyond that sum. Although official statistics are not available, India is thought to rival the United States in surrogacy arrangements taking place in that country every year, with the numbers growing (Bromfield & Rotabi, 2014; Pande, 2014), and India receives the bulk of the media's attention. While many of the commissioning parents seeking surrogacy arrangements in India have been transnational and citizens of other countries, there may actually be equal numbers of non-resident Indian couples seeking the service "who combine a cheaper treatment with a family visit" (Pande, 2014, p. 13). There were an estimated 1,500 surrogate births in India in 2010 (Magnier, 2011) and that number climbed steadily until controls were put into place in recent years, as we will discuss later. One policy change was made in 2012 when India banned surrogacy for same-sex couples (Pande, 2014), which forced those people to look elsewhere for surrogacy arrangements.

Since the rise of gestational surrogacy in India, a plethora of media attention has focused on surrogacy there, with a *Mother Jones* article (Carney, 2010) highlighting troubling issues in the Indian surrogacy market. One of the disturbing practices described is the routine use of cesarean sections for the benefit of the paying family who can thereby choose a birth date for their child that best suits their desires or needs, and also makes it easier on the clinic as they can schedule deliveries. Furthermore, cesarean-section births are more expensive and thus the medical providers have a higher profit for this particular procedure versus a natural birth. The use of an elective surgical procedure for labor and delivery raises risks related to infection and other issues that arise from an incision; this particular aspect of practice has been called into question because the procedure is carried out largely for the convenience of the adults controlling the transaction, not the baby or the surrogate.

Another cause for concern is the process reportedly used to recruit Indian surrogates. The would-be surrogates are impoverished, often illiterate women who are recruited from rural villages. Surrogacy recruits are brought to the clinics by "head hunters," sometimes calling themselves social workers, where many of the women are required to stay in the clinic's living quarters[1] in a dormitory-like or hostel setting for the entire pregnancy (Carney, 2010). This practice not only allows the clinics to monitor the surrogates' activities, food consumption, environment, and behaviors during the pregnancy, but is also seen as protecting the surrogate from ridicule by family members and neighbors. For many clinics, Indian surrogates not only receive free food and housing during their surrogate pregnancies, they reportedly earn between USD$5,000 and $7,000, which is equivalent to about ten years of work for rural Indian women (Haworth, 2007). With no shortage of available women offering to become surrogates, the practice has been taking place across the country.

Surrogacy is a means for poor Indian women to engage in the global marketplace and provide a service (Pande, 2009a, 2009b, 2014). This sentiment was voiced by Oprah Winfrey in her US-based talk show when she presented surrogacy in India as a family-building strategy that offers economic opportunity to impoverished women (Carney, 2010) and described it as a win–win scenario. Pande (2014) presents surrogacy as social-care work and calls it a "new form of labour" (p. 145), noting that it is stigmatized in India and is thus classified as a form of "dirty work" (Pande, 2009b)—occupations viewed as degrading to the worker, such as the work of a butcher or housemaid.

Pande's (2009a, 2009b, 2014) interviews with surrogate mothers provide insight into the decision to participate in the practice, including some valuable information about consent procedures and the limitations of illiterate women in understanding the surrogacy contract. This issue is a concern that has been raised about surrogates, even for women in industrialized countries who have the benefit of education (Corea, 1986). However, the theme of life improvement—including improving the outcomes of the surrogate's own existing biological children due to the income and material improvement—was clear in Pande's and others' research in India (Markens, 2007; Vora, 2015, 2016). Without question, freedom to participate in a global marketplace is important, especially for poor and marginalized peoples. However, some commercial surrogacy arrangements may challenge notions of free will, informed consent, and ultimately self-determination (National Association of Social Workers, 1999).

Human rights of women involved in commercial global surrogacy

The Universal Declaration of Human Rights, established at the end of World War II, considers motherhood as a vulnerability that must be protected. Developed in the late 1940s, the definition of family was conventional, and the concept of surrogacy was not even an idea in this era. The Convention on the Elimination of Discrimination against Women (CEDAW) provides a framework that refers directly to rights of maternity. Article 4 states that "states are allowed to adopt special measures aimed at protecting maternity." It should be noted that this international human rights instrument was drafted with the intent of protecting rights such as maternity leave from work and other discrimination issues related to motherhood. There is no reference to rights of women engaged in the work that is the "occupation of maternity"—surrogacy as it is practiced today was not even remotely a conception when CEDAW was passed in 1979.[2] Now, at this critical juncture, new dimensions of work and human rights interface with advanced reproduction technologies, leaving critical questions about the exploitation of surrogate mothers and the potential for global regulation (Bromfield & Rotabi, 2014; Cheney, 2014; Hague Conference, 2012; Pande, 2014; Rotabi, 2014).

Surrogacy as "work"

We recognize that there is a great deal of controversy about surrogacy being framed as *work*, and there are moral arguments against such a conception (Cheney, 2014; Darnovsky & Beeson, 2014). However, research evidence is clear that many surrogate mothers in India view themselves to be engaged in an occupation or the *work* of global gestational surrogacy (Pande, 2009b, 2014).

Pande (2014) carried out seminal research in Gujarat, India, and found that surrogate mothers are required to view themselves as "both a worker-producer and a mother-reproducer" (p. 64). In addition, with the linkage of a surrogacy arrangement to the idea of work, the women in Pande's study talked of both "sweat" and "blood" as a part of their surrogacy experience (Pande, 2009a). In their own personal narratives about their surrogate motherhood, the women clearly viewed their work as legitimate, albeit work with obvious emotional burdens in the short and long term (Pande, 2014). We will consider the emotional issues and related rights later in this chapter. We now turn to the human rights of surrogate mothers.

Evidence: Indian surrogate mothers and their views on "work"

In our own study in Gujarat, India, like Pande (2009b, 2014) we also found that women reported their choice to participate in surrogacy as *work* to be the result of limited employment opportunities in the context of extreme poverty. Moving from the work premise to rights includes the right to a safe workplace and also the consent to engage in the workplace. In the case of a high-quality fertility (surrogacy provider) clinic in India, the issue of workplace safety is relatively low risk as the surrogate mothers receive good-quality healthcare and other amenities, including adequate nutrition, in order to ensure that a healthy infant is the result of the transaction. In fact, some women have reported being relieved to be in the maternity hostel removed from the ordinary work of housekeeping and other labor that was necessary in their daily routines prior to the surrogacy experience—some saw the hostels as a welcome break from daily obligations (Pande, 2014). As Pande found, many of the surrogates recognized the importance of minimizing daily stress for the well-being of the child and also reported that one of the benefits of the hostel was an opportunity to learn new skills (e.g. computer and/or craft skills) as a result of classes offered in that setting.

Issues of safety of medical procedures (including hormone injections for IVF processes), labor and delivery, and other risks are of concern as problems related to cesarean-section births are not insignificant considerations (Bromfield & Rotabi, 2014). However, the reality is that this work is not more dangerous than many forms of labor that are available to these particular women living in poverty in India.

Poor women working in India often deal with the reality of long transportation times to workplaces where there are limited or no safe passageways; rape is a serious risk in a country with endemic rates of violence against women. Also, there are long work hours (10–12-hour shifts) in factories such as textile settings where women's health is compromised (e.g. lung and other health issues due to chemical exposures, etc.). Additionally, women may be in a situation where they must leave their village or even country to seek work such as a housemaid, which may prevent them from seeing their husbands and/or children for years at a time. Furthermore, the women engaged in such work do not have any medical benefits, and most women do not have the resources to pay for childcare so they often end up bringing their children to the unsafe environments of their work sites. Accidents in these cases are common and usually go unreported. Women also work in places with very minimal or no sanitation, leading them to either choose between skipping work or contracting diseases related to these unsafe environments. Finally, the unfortunate reality of most Indian communities is chronic unemployment, which has been a push factor for exploitation, including human trafficking, and specifically women and girls being coerced into a range of activities related to the sex industry.

In their own voices: interviews with Indian surrogates

To capture the voices of Indian surrogates ourselves, instead of relying on media reports or others' research findings, for this book we interviewed 25 surrogates in Gujarat, India, where Pande (2014) conducted her seminal work. We interviewed Indian women who had followed through with at least one contract pregnancy, which had taken place at least six months before the interview. We required this timeframe because we wanted them to have time to reflect on the experience in hindsight. Furthermore, we interviewed the women in the community rather than in the clinic setting. In these extensive interviews with Indian surrogates, we found several topics of discussion around their surrogacy experiences that were common across all of the interviews. The themes that we explore here are the economic status of surrogates and their decision making in the context of poverty, medical issues, and emotional connections, including a desire to remain in touch with the family, and a cost–benefit analysis that underlies the decision to participate in commercial global surrogacy.

Economic status of Indian surrogates and motivation for surrogacy

The 25 women who were interviewed for our study were all from impoverished backgrounds, the majority of them housewives or working as maids prior to their surrogacy arrangement. A number of women in our study mentioned how engaging in surrogacy has been a better way to earn money in a short period of time. Some reported earning an average of US$30 a month in their jobs and have earned US$5,000–$7,000 in one pregnancy, an exponential growth in income for them, unavailable in any other venture. The resulting ability to participate in a cash economy with the power of lump-sum payments was clearly seen by those interviewed as a source of economic empowerment. This new sense of *power* was obvious during interviews. The women were very clear that they did not feel used or exploited. Rather, they saw themselves as exercising their autonomy to engage in a well-paid enterprise.

Women stated that instead of working in the fields under extreme weather conditions, their surrogacy earnings gave them an opportunity to start their own entrepreneurial ventures such as a sewing business, buying an auto rickshaw for their husbands to drive, or opening a beauty salon. Some mentioned that it gave them a sense of confidence after being trained in various skills during their stay in the surrogacy hostel. Their status in their family seemed to rise with them, bringing in the financial resources and thus economic stability. Some women mentioned that they would like to engage in future surrogacy contracts, as they saw surrogacy as the only avenue through which they could augment their financial conditions significantly (Pande, 2014).

When asked how the women planned to spend their earnings from surrogacy, most frequently purchasing a house and educating their children was the response. One surrogate said:

> I didn't have a house before. To build a house I told my husband that I wanted to be a surrogate. Our salaries were less so couldn't have built a house with that. My husband didn't agree with this, but I told him that I will definitely go for it. I said only if I become a surrogate will the house be built, otherwise it wouldn't. And if anything is remaining I will keep some for my child for his education. That is how I decided. Later my husband and I were on the same page.

Another surrogate said:

> I needed to get my daughter married, educate my sons, fix the house. In nine months, forget that. Even if I worked for five years, I wouldn't have been able to make this amount of money. And it's a good job. Money is good but then to give happiness to someone is a big thing.

The above quote further underscores gender inequality in India as a marriage dowry is one of the powerful social forces that impinge on family economic decision making and issues of gender and power. This quote also captures the win–win idea that is often promoted by the proponents of commercial global surrogacy. Finally, the idea of bringing happiness to others was another theme found in surrogate interviews as a number of the women reported the ability to give of themselves in this way to couples in need. These findings were echoed in other studies, and this conception of a gift—almost a selfless giving, albeit financially compensated—was mentioned by a number of women, and their sentiments are consistent with the idea of a "gift child" (Pande, 2011; Vora, 2016). Part of that gift is the sharing of blood—the blood connection being tremendously powerful in traditional and collectivist societies such as India (Pande, 2009a, 2014).

Medical issues

As Carney (2010) found in his investigative report on surrogacy in India, all of the Indian surrogates we interviewed had cesarean deliveries for their surrogate pregnancies. This is a notable difference between the Indian surrogates and the US surrogates who blog about their surrogacy experiences. For the US surrogates who blog, the birth of the child is a major event that involves the commissioning parents and often includes elements of a "natural" or unmediated birth experience, which is most often documented on their blogs.

All of the women we interviewed reported cesarean births. A handful of the Indian surrogates we interviewed reported minor discomfort related to IVF and pregnancy, such as nausea. One surrogate (quoted below) reported having a complication during the cesarean section.

Healthcare during and after surrogacy is an important concern. Because the health and safety of the surrogate mother is of utmost concern for the clinic healthcare providers during pregnancy, there is little evidence of consistent problems during this phase of the surrogacy arrangement. Fundamentally, clinics facilitating the surrogacy process have a vested interest in providing the finest care during pregnancy in order to produce a healthy infant. However, concerns have been raised about post-delivery healthcare, especially since cesarean-section delivery is a common practice in surrogacy arrangements.

One surrogate mentioned:

> I thought every C-section was quite regular and they [medical staff] would have the delivery and go away. But during my time [of C-section birth], it got quite complicated and they told me that I might have to have my uterus removed. I really got surprised by this. I was wondering what I will do, so I prayed. The bleeding stopped and they didn't have to take my uterus out and I got fine.

Emotional connections

Like Pande's (2014) findings, we found that most of the surrogates, and even one respondent's children, identified some emotional turmoil that resulted from their experience, and this is one of the greatest costs of surrogacy arrangements for these women. As children are often removed from the surrogate mother immediately after labor and delivery, this critical moment can be quite difficult for obvious reasons. When asked about how it felt to hand over the infant, one mother who gave birth to twins said:

> I didn't feel good because I kept them in my belly for 9 months. When they took them away, I cried a lot. I felt like I was giving away my own children and I regretted it a lot. I went back home and couldn't eat anything, I was crying a lot. Then my husband

explained that those were their babies and of course they will take them away. Madam also told me that they were not my kids. So like that slowly I forgot about it.

Another surrogate said:

When you have a baby, you feel good. Of course, when you have to give them away you feel sad, but keeping a stone in our hearts, we do give them away. The baby is theirs after all. When my children found out that we had to give the baby away, they told me that let's not take the money but take the baby home instead. But then I explained to them that we have come here for the money and this child belongs to the commissioning parents.

A different surrogate stated:

After I gave birth I was thinking I have given birth to such a beautiful child. Then I thought that I have to give the child away…keeping this in mind, I stopped thinking of her. Because if I kept thinking of her, she'll feel some discomfort. Hence, I stopped thinking of her.

This particular quote indicates coping mechanisms that are similar to those used in cognitive behavioral therapies. It appears that some cognitive restructuring is taking place, in the case of the above surrogate, to avoid further emotions related to the pain of separation.

Just as Pande (2014) and others have identified, we found that surrogate women most often expressed a desire for further connection with the intended family and at least know about the well-being of the child. Vora (2015, 2016) identifies that some surrogate mothers reported a wish that the relationship continue and that the foreign family may be willing to help in educating the surrogate's own biological children or help out financially in some other way. An ongoing relationship is entirely outside of the surrogate's control, because fundamentally the decision to actually meet the surrogate mother in the first place[3] (Deomampo, 2014) and then participate in an ongoing relationship hinges on the commissioning parents' desire and willingness to do so and then ensure that communication is maintained. It appears that some commissioning parents viewed the surrogate as having a kind of familial relationship and engaged with her in a manner that honored her contribution to the family, while others simply saw the surrogate mother as a worker, and any further relationship was quickly terminated upon labor and delivery (Pande, 2014). One surrogate mentioned:

Now I have no connection with them [commissioning family] anymore, but when they left with the babies, they used to stay in touch for about three years. They used to send stuff for me. They used to mail me and send pictures of the kids. They were very nice.

This particular quote indicates a fading out of a relationship over time. Sadness about this particular aspect of some women's experience was not an area for probing in our study. However, quite obviously the expectations that are set—sometimes the commissioning family makes promises for further support and sending gifts—are important (Vora, 2015, 2016). How long such relationships last, the satisfaction in the relationship for both the surrogate and commissioning parents, and a deeper sense of reciprocity in the relationship are topics for future research. As we noted in Chapter 8, US surrogates also invest a great deal into the relationship with commissioning parents.

Cost–benefit analysis

Surrogate mothers in our study spoke of their difficulties as related to the decision to participate in surrogacy. One woman actually spoke of her cupboards being empty and the practical need to feed her own children. Another woman spoke of selling her blood to make ends meet. This is not unlike Karandikar et al.'s (2014) study that identified that one woman and her husband considered the idea of his sale of a kidney—in the end she chose surrogacy as the better option of the two pathways for earning money. Even if a woman is not considering such a drastic way to earn a living, she is often comparing surrogacy to other far less attractive work options with pay that will never enable her to save and get ahead. These facts, combined with long work hours that take the surrogate away from daily family life and other issues that we have already presented related to health and safety. Also, while our study did not probe broadly into problems in the surrogate's personal life, Deomampo (2013b) found in her study that a number of surrogates in Mumbai were making the decision to participate with a history of divorce and marital separation in their backgrounds; serious problems like physical abuse and partner/husband substance abuse were reported by some of the women she interviewed. All of this considered, there is clearly a cost–benefit analysis equation operating in which perceived threat and perceived benefit are factored into the decision-making process. The social exchanges in this process are complex and the context for each woman is different in terms of personal problems, personal opportunities, and one constant for the surrogates of India—poverty.

In sum, when the women in our study were asked if they felt taken advantage of, or felt used, they *all* said no. One woman even brought up the idea of "benefit," when she responded to this question by saying:

> No. Why will they take advantage? They haven't asked me to become a surrogate. It was my situation which pushed me into becoming a surrogate. I went there myself. I thought if someone else benefits only then will I benefit. They have no advantage here. It's a good work as someone got a child and our poverty also got erased.

Another woman stated:

> No, nothing like that. We come here at our own will. No one pulls us here. We also have some problems, so we come on our own. No one is taking any advantage. We go on our own to the hospital, tell Madam that we want to be surrogate and if she feels that we can be taken in, only then she will agree. We have to be married, should have had our own kids, have to show her pictures etc and only then she will take us in. If there is any problem, she then refuses.

And, finally another woman responded to this question while highlighting the consent procedure saying, "No. Nothing like that. They give us counseling, make us sign an agreement so it's all taken care of."

Research generalizability

When drawing conclusions about commercial global surrogacy in India, it is important to point out that this particular study was carried out in a community that arguably is home to one of the best fertility and surrogacy clinics in the country. This particular medical center, the Akanksha Fertility Clinic, has the leadership of Dr. Nayna Patel, who has appeared on Oprah Winfrey's TV show and other documentaries as a proponent of the practice. Her clinic is a model of what is possible, and the women we interviewed clearly view the fertility services provided there positively. None of those women interviewed reported any dissatisfaction with the medical process or any abuse of their human rights. In fact, the women were quite clear that they viewed the experience to be positive on the whole, even with the emotional burdens, and most were interested in future contract pregnancies as they were typically allowed two surrogacy arrangements at this particular clinic.[4]

We do assert that these findings, along with Pande's (2014) and others' (e.g. Deomampo, 2013a, 2013b; SAMA, 2012; Vora, 2015), are important in the consideration of commercial global surrogacy in India. We also recognize that there are potentially hundreds of clinics operating in India,[5] and inevitably there are poor practices and problems, because commercial surrogacy has increased in a relatively unregulated manner in India. Even though there have been changes in policies, the reality is that the services provided are only as good as the clinics and the integrity of the people managing the business of surrogacy. This is particularly true because the clinics operate without oversight, even though accreditation standards have been developed. However, apparently there is no will to institutionalize and enforce standards of care in India (Saxena, Mishra, & Malik, 2012). Without a doubt there are unscrupulous entrepreneurs, but we cannot speak to the related unethical and illicit practices from an empirical perspective as our study did not extend into this area of human rights concerns.

New policy changes in India

At this juncture, India has begun to change some policies that curb (and even halt) the practices rather than truly regulate the industry. As of late 2015, the Indian government instituted a policy that global surrogacy could be carried out only by couples in which one person is an Indian passport holder (Najar, 2015). Because this is not a binding legal change—rather a change of policy regulated through "surrogacy visas" for travel related to medical tourism—the long-term future of this policy is unknown. However, in March 2016, India went a step further and banned the shipment of embryos into India by non-Indians (personal communication, Kavita Panjabi, May 7, 2016). Again, these policy changes are not legally codified as was attempted in the past in 2010 draft legislation (Saxena et al., 2012). These policies have resulted in the current ban of surrogacy services for non-Indians and are now being considered by the Supreme Court of India with legal challenges being lodged. Ultimately the legal officials must make some critical decisions about the future of commercial global surrogacy in India.

The question of *why* such policy changes have taken place without an actual change in the law has only speculative answers at this point. One issue was the fact that the 2010 draft bill was weak in addressing the rights of women, as the bill was written with a great deal of influence from the surrogacy service providers (doctors, clinics, etc.) and thus it has been called "weak" by experts in Indian law (Malhotra & Malhotra, 2013). Consequently, protection of the clinics and the contracting process (contract law) were emphasized over women's rights in the draft bill (SAMA, 2012; Vora, 2016).

We will note here that as this book was going to press, the Indian government unveiled a draft law to ban commercial surrogacy (BBC News, 2016). The result may be an altruistic-only surrogacy policy with the allowable surrogate being a close family member of a married, Indian citizen couple. At the time of the final version of this book, such a step limiting the practice to altruistic surrogacy is uncertain. To date, no such law has passed through the legislative process of India and entered into force.

When these policy changes occurred, the media reported that prominent officials in India said that they found the practice of commercial global surrogacy to be a source of embarrassment (Najar, 2015). Of course, there has been a plethora of documentaries interrogating the practices and the vulnerabilities of all involved, particularly the surrogates (see "Made in India" and "Google Baby" documentaries). Fundamentally, the practice has been highly criticized by outsiders as morally deficient and riddled with human rights issues, given the vulnerabilities of poverty and inequality in India. This fact collided with an Indian government that has been pushing a highly nationalistic approach and growth in "Made in India" products. Being known for gestational surrogacies may have actually been contrary to "Brand India" (Rajan, 2016), in which a whole range of medical tourism extending far beyond surrogacy—a multi-billion dollar industry—was compromised by the ethical dilemmas in this small niche of medical tourism.

In the end, India is invested in promoting their medical industrial complex as high quality and highly organized in terms of medical ethics and congruent procedures for a wide range of services including organ transplants and heart bypass surgeries. The bad press of commercial global surrogacy may well have threatened the reputation of the entire medical tourism model to the point that the current government instituted policy changes that create a de facto moratorium for non-Indian consumers. Only time will tell in terms of the legal outcome as there are already challenges being lodged in courts, including a challenge to the ban on importing foreign embryos. Public policy and contractual law are challenged, and some defining moments inevitably lie ahead. Regardless of the court findings, surrogacy continues for Indian citizen–consumers (including non-resident Indians) in significant numbers and *if* regulations emerge from this current legal reflection on the practice, *then* will the voices of surrogates be considered, including their clear desire for fair and consistent wages (e.g. set compensation by regulation) and other conditions related to what they clearly see as work (Deomampo, 2014; Pande, 2014; Vora, 2015).

Conclusion

The rapidly growing commercial global surrogacy industry raises multiple ethical concerns that strike deep at our sensibilities about human need, economics, and human vulnerability, including a power imbalance between the consumer and surrogate, especially when that woman is living in poverty. This is complicated, because protective regulations aimed primarily at securing the rights of vulnerable women and their children are lacking or non-existent in developing countries, where the highly profitable fertility industry has taken root to serve the global surrogacy marketplace. The conception of *marketplace* is important to consider, including the inherent issues of regulation, as many of the women who are participating in global surrogacy arrangements are some of the poorest, most vulnerable, and most oppressed women in the world. The power divide between these women, the sophisticated organizations developing the services, and the consumers (relatively wealthy customers) is such that human protections are an absolute imperative (Elster, 2010; Hague Conference on Private International Law, 2012).

Because of an undeniable demand for healthy babies (Goodwin, 2010), policies need to be developed on an international level above and beyond standards created by actors in the private sector. This means that when global surrogacy is practiced, it must be done in a safe, honest, and ethical manner for surrogates and egg/sperm donors, as well as the individuals and couples purchasing the surrogate's services. An important consideration is the environment in which such an ethical approach can be guaranteed.

In all likelihood, the forces against regulation will be such that it will not take place unless an international body becomes involved and develops new human rights protections (e.g. international private law) related to fertility technology integrated with an expanded definition of human trafficking, to include coerced surrogacy arrangements.

Inevitably, a charged debate has emerged, those benefiting from incomes related to surrogacy businesses versus those who stand to benefit from purchasing surrogate services, interfacing with human rights defenders. A power imbalance is inevitable, and policy makers and human rights defenders must be aware of the global surrogacy market and the risks that may accompany it for all involved—most especially to the surrogate mothers and the children who are born from these arrangements. Not only are there social justice implications for the surrogate mothers, there can be lasting repercussions for the children as well. It is possible now for a child that was born out of global surrogacy to have a genetic mother, a gestational (or biological) mother, and a legal mother all from completely different cultures (and legal jurisdictions). Such complexity requires sensitivity to the rights and needs of children, which we will consider in our conclusion.

Globalization and technology are rapidly changing the world (Singer, 2002), resulting in consequences that we could not have fathomed when IVF was first introduced in the late 1970s (Goodwin, 2010). Debates will unfold, and ultimately what prevails will be significant as we enter a new frontier of fertility and family building (Deomampo, 2013a). Wants versus needs will become pushes and pulls, and women in developing countries stand to be exploited (Singer, 2002). Nonetheless, when the activity occurs in developing or low-resource settings, it will be discussed and marketed as an "opportunity" for women. The surrogates living in poverty, too, will often talk of the opportunity to improve their material circumstances as the macro-structural conditions continue to constrain their choices for fairly paid work. And, opportunities to "get ahead" and improve their lives, in terms of work in which savings can be achieved, will inevitably be elusive for most women in India.

Given these realities, many challenges lie ahead. Nussbaum (2000), in her discourse on sex and social justice, points out that the sale of a woman's body for sex and other activities are common phenomena. This is consistent with the idea of "the oldest profession" in the world (sex work/prostitution) and women's bodies have been sold at the hands of many different actors. Those orchestrating the transactions are not only formed by organized criminal networks, but women's family members may also be a part of the transaction. Self-determination of women involved in the sex industry is never a simple conversation; the underlying decision making, or inability to make a free decision to participate, varies depending on circumstances. And poverty, too, is not a simple consideration when making an analysis of the situation at hand, including ideas of free and informed consent (Green, 2010). The case of commercial global surrogacy—the sale of one's capacity to reproduce—is undoubtedly complex. As a result, global surrogacy practices require immediate attention to address the inherent and emerging problems (Cheney, 2014; Deomampo, 2014; Darnovsky & Beeson, 2014; Karandikar et al., 2014; Pande, 2014; Rotabi, 2014; Vora, 2016).

Notes

1   The use of hostels vary on a clinic-by-clinic basis. Hostels are commonly found in clinics that market services to foreign consumers.

2   Gena Corea wrote *The mother machine: Reproductive technologies from artificial insemination to artificial wombs* in 1985. In this seminal work, she presented a very detailed discussion including ideas like surrogates as "breeders" and the issue of women of color and living in poverty being exploited. Corea did not anticipate globalization and the neoliberal environment that has fueled commercial global

surrogacy today. One may argue that it was essentially impossible, in the mid-1980s and at the time of the Baby M case, to anticipate the growth and opportunity related to commercial global surrogacy and the inherent dilemmas across global space and place.

3   Many clinics advise the commissioning couples against meeting the surrogate. However, the clinic related to the women that we interviewed does allow for such interchange.

4   While this clinic has a limit of two surrogate pregnancies, some other clinics do not have such rules. Some women will complete two pregnancies with this clinic and then seek a different clinic to continue with more surrogacy arrangements.

5   The number is not known due to the unregulated nature of the business, but there are estimates that there may be 300 or more clinics. With India being a large country with a booming medical tourism model, this number of clinics is entirely possible.

References

BBC News. (2016, August 25). India unveils plans to ban surrogacy. Retrieved from www.bbc.com/news/world-asia-india-37182197

Bromfield, N. F. & Rotabi, K. S. (2014). Global surrogacy, exploitation, human rights and international private law: A pragmatic stance and policy recommendations. *Global Social Welfare: Research, Policy and Practice*, 1, 123–5. doi: 0.1007/s40609-014-0019-4

Carney, S. (2010, March/April). Cash on delivery: Gestational dormitories, routine C-sections, quintuple embryo implants. Brave new world? Nope, surrogacy tourism. Mother Jones, 69–73.

Cheney, K. E. (2014). Executive summary of the International Forum on Intercountry Adoption and Global Surrogacy. ISS Working Paper Series/General Series, 596, 1–40. Retrieved from http://hdl.handle.net/1765/7740

Corea, G. (1986). *The mother machine: Reproductive technologies from artificial insemination to artificial wombs.* New York: Harper and Row.

Darnovsky, M. & Beeson, D. (2014). Global surrogacy practices. ISS Working Paper Series/General Series, 601, 1–54. Retrieved from http://hdl.handle.net/1765/77402

Deomampo, D. (2013a). Gendered geographies of reproductive tourism. *Gender & Society*, 27(4), 514–47.

Deomampo, D. (2013b). Transnational surrogacy in India: Interrogating power and women's agency. *Frontiers: A Journal of Women's Studies*, 34(3), 167–88.

Deomampo, D. (2014). Beyond wombs for rent: Indian surrogates and the need for evidence-based policy. Somatosphere. Retrieved from http://somatosphere.net/2014/06/beyond-wombs-for-rent-indian-surrogates-and-the-need-for-evidence-based-policy.html

Elster, N. R. (2010). Egg donation for research and reproduction: The compensation conundrum. In M. B. Goodwin (Ed.), *Baby markets: Money and the new politics of creating families* (pp. 226–36). New York: Cambridge University Press.

Goodwin, M. B. (2010). *Baby markets: Money and the new politics of creating families.* New York: Cambridge University Press.

Green, D. M. (2010). The paradox of self-determination for marginalized individuals. *Social Work and Society*, 8(1). Retrieved from www.socwork.net/2010/1/green

Hague Conference on Private International Law. (2012). A preliminary report on the issues arising from international surrogacy arrangements. Retrieved from www.hcch.net/upload/wop/gap2012pd10en.pdf

Haworth, A. (2007, July 29). Surrogate mother: Wombs for rent. Marie Claire. Retrieved from www.marieclaire.com/world-reports/news/surrogate-mothers-india

Karandikar, S., Gezinski, L. B., Carter, J. R., & Kaloga, M. (2014). Economic necessity or a noble cause? Exploring motivations for gestational surrogacy in Gujarat, India. *Affilia*, 29(2), 224–36.

Magnier, M. (2011, April 18). A bundle of joy with baggage: India surrogacy is successful, but new parents feel duped. Los Angeles Times.

Malhotra, A. & Malhotra, R. (2013, August). Surrogacy: Imported from India—the need for a regulatory law. In International Social Services/International Reference Center Team (Eds), *ISS monthly review (special issue): The international resort to surrogacy: A new challenge to be addressed urgently* (pp. 8–9). Geneva: International Social Services.

Markens, S. (2007). *Surrogate motherhood and the politics of reproduction.* Berkeley: University of California Press.

Najar, N. (2015, October 28). India wants to ban birth surrogacy to foreigners. New York Times. Retrieved from www.nytimes.com/2015/10/29/world/asia/india-wants-to-ban-birth-surrogacy-for-foreigners.html?_r=0

National Association of Social Workers. (1999). Code of ethics. Revised by the 2008 NASW Delegate Assembly. Washington, DC: Author. Retrieved from www.socialworkers.org/pubs/Code/code.asp

Nussbaum, M. C. (2000). *Sex and social justice.* New York: Oxford University Press.

Pande, A. (2009a). "It might be her eggs, but it's my blood": Surrogates and everyday forms of kinship in India. *Qualitative Sociology*, 32(4), 379–97.

Pande, A. (2009b). Not "an angel," not "a whore": Surrogates as "dirty" workers in India. *Indian Journal of Gender Studies*, 16, 141–73.

Pande, A. (2011). Transnational commercial surrogacy in India: Gifts for global sisters? *Reproduction Biomedicine Online*, 23, 618–25.

Pande, A. (2014). *Wombs in labour: Transnational commercial surrogacy in India.* New York: Columbia University Press.

Rajan, K. S. (2016, May). *Speculations on the constitution of the experimental subject. Gujarat/Guatemala: Marketing care and speculating life.* Ithaca, NY: Cornell University.

Rotabi, K. S. (2014). Force, fraud, and coercion: Bridging from knowledge of intercountry adoption to global surrogacy. ISS Working Paper Series/General Series, 600, 1–30. Retrieved from http://hdl.handle.net/1765/77403

SAMA. (2012). Birthing a market: A study on commercial surrogacy. Retrieved from www.samawomenshealth.org/publication/birthing-market-%E2%80%98commercial-surrogacy-india

Saxena, P., Mishra, A., & Malik, S. (2012). Surrogacy: Ethical and legal issues. *Indian Journal of Community Medicine*, 37(4), 211–13.

Singer, P. (2002). *One world: The ethics of globalization.* New Haven, CT: Yale University Press.

Vora, K. (2015). *Life support: Biocapital and the new history of outsourced labor.* Minneapolis: University of Minnesota Press.

Vora, K. (2016, May). *Contracting care: Indian commercial surrogacy as life support. Gujarat/Guatemala: Marketing care and speculating life.* Ithaca, NY: Cornell University.

10

THE FUTURE OF INTERCOUNTRY ADOPTION, GLOBAL SURROGACY, AND NEW FRONTIERS

FIGURE 10.1 Women walking in India
Source: Photo credit Nicole F. Bromfield

Global intercountry adoption rose significantly during the mid- to late 1990s, and by the year 2000 the Millennium adoption boom was well under way. Then the bust came, with a dramatic decline after a 2004 global peak of 45,000 adoptions. As a result, adoption scholars and experts have considered the future of the practice, from varying perspectives (Ballard, Goodno, Cochran, & Milbrandt, 2015; Briggs & Marre, 2009; Gibbons & Rotabi, 2012). On the whole, scholars are not promoters of intercountry adoption, rather they tend to be pragmatic in their perspective, calling for reform and strengthening of the practice for long-term sustainability (Rotabi & Bunkers, 2011; Rotabi & Gibbons, 2009). Rarely do you hear a call from them to abolish intercountry adoption outright.

Speculation about the long-term viability of intercountry adoption today is not a new discussion. As early as 1991, Altstein and Simon questioned the future of the practice, predicting major changes as a result of an array of ethical and policy concerns that had already emerged by the early 1990s. Even earlier, Altstein (1984) pointedly posed the following, "one overriding question exists in relation to intercountry adoption. Is it moral and humane to remove a child from his native society to be reared in a culture other than his own?" (p. 202, as cited by Selman, 2015). This dilemma continues to be considered today, with scholars such as Hübinette (2012) now offering stunning evidence of increased rates of suicide among intercountry adoptees in Sweden as he interrogates issues such as racism and belongingness. Ethnographic research further highlights the issues, documenting the intersection of identity and the longing to know one's background, including the complexities of race and racism (Yngvesson, 2010).

In addition, there is always the ethical question of spending more than US$20,000 on a single adoption when impoverished families in countries like Ethiopia and elsewhere could simply be helped out of a crisis situation and meet their child's needs with several hundred dollars of cash transfer. As we have outlined, the problems are vast and there is a myriad of questions pondering the ethical dilemmas (Ballard et al., 2015), most of which boil down to the intersections of poverty, privilege, and the resulting pushes and pulls into intercountry adoption (Fronek, Cuthbert, & Willing, 2015).

Nonetheless, it should be said that there have been adoption scandals in Western European countries whose social-democratic government structures have a welfare system to provide basic needs. Problems of adoption fraud have occurred there too in recent times, including the Baby J case in the Netherlands. This particular young child was sold via internet communication for 15,000 euros. The child was transferred from the Netherlands (the child's country of birth) to Belgium, crossing state lines. Both the biological mother (selling the child) and the adoptive family (buying the child) were prosecuted. In Belgium, it was determined that the child sale was a crime and a violation of human dignity. That finding was repeated in the Netherlands court. The use of the concept *human dignity* is indicative of a human rights lens in the case analysis and prosecution; human dignity is a core human rights principle that dates back to the 1948 Declaration of Human Rights.

The high cost of an ethical adoption

Unethical adoption and the extraordinary sums that prospective families are willing to pay is obviously a violation of human dignity, without a doubt. However, a lesser told discussion point is the high sum of an ethical adoption in the regulatory environment that is prevailing today. There are now actually new worries about rising fees due to increased bureaucracy in the post-Hague Convention environment; new layers of paperwork and red tape have been lamented as an unintended consequence of the HCIA (Bailey, 2009; Wardle, 2015).

The removal of money from the intercountry adoption equation inevitably arises as part of the discourse, and the idea of a "global gift" (Triseliotis, 2000) has been raised as a critical underlying value, given the humanitarian imperative to intervene without financial incentives.

The language around the child as a gift decommodifies the transaction (Vora, 2016), just as we touched upon when considering the narratives of surrogates in India (Pande, 2011). The "gift-child" idea buffers the reality that the exchange of money for children is uncomfortable for most people; many people view the value of children and family life to be far above a simple price or sum of money. Most people who adopt internationally will admit that the discussion of the amount paid for adoption is inevitably an uncomfortable subject.

When pondering the future of ICA, one might rightfully ask: How do we carry on with the practice while removing the financial pressures from the process? Some ideas have been put forth for controls to limit fraud. For example, Maskew (2010) suggested the engagement of a well-established foundation to manage donations from adoptive families and adoption agencies. As an impartial organization, donations could be distributed based on evidence-based practices for family support and care of orphaned and vulnerable children in the countries of concern (Gibbons & Rotabi, 2012). Funding could be distributed with an orientation towards the strengthening of systems of care and generally promoting empowerment of families in poverty (e.g. livelihood/poverty-reduction programs). That way, charitable donations would not be connected to one specific adoption/child or adoption agency, thus preventing problems that emerge when donations and adoption processes mingle.

However, even with the best of ideas and intentions, there has been no real and meaningful change in actually extracting the money from the intercountry adoption equation. On the positive side, it must be said that in the post-HCIA environment there is greater transparency, with safeguards and regulation to prevent fraud. These controls, while not preventing force, fraud, and coercion in all cases, have been important steps forward in the management of funds for adoption and general improvement in practices.

One may rightfully argue that it is impractical to develop a system that truly extracts the money from the process, as a high-quality adoption process carried out by a highly trained adoption social service sector requires salaries that compensate for long hours, foreign travel, and hands-on supervision and risk management. The argument may also be that there simply has been no real will to actually change the finances of the process in such a manner that truly removes the influence of money. Others may assert that there is simply no way to proceed with an ethical adoption system when the privilege of resources/money and the desperation of poverty come together, especially when there are deep corruption problems in many countries of origin where the judiciary is weak and impunity is common.

This latter point of corruption is one of the most critical of persistent issues; much of the corruption is based on macro-structural problems of the country of origin, and thus the exercise of control by prospective adoptive parents, adoption agencies, and even central adoption authorities is limited by contextual issues, including rule of law and civil society. As a result, problems persist, with the resulting debate (Ballard et al., 2015; Bartholet & Smolin, 2012). Those of us involved in that conversation as scholars, activists, and families affected by adoption have invested a great deal in the discourse with the satisfaction of some real and meaningful changes. However, there is still much more to achieve moving forward in developing ethical systems of child welfare, emphasizing family support first rather than resorting to intercountry adoption as a primary solution.

A compelling argument and the flaw

All of this considered, a truly compelling argument is what Bartholet (2010) considers the child's right to a "permanent family." She takes a firm stance when considering other reform perspectives in her position on human rights in the debate on intercountry adoption (Bartholet & Smolin, 2012). As Bartholet (2010, p. 94) points out:

> Human rights issues are at the core of the current debate over international adoption. Many of us who support international adoption see it as serving the most fundamental of human rights of the most helpless of humans—the rights of children to the kind of family love and care that will enable them to grow up with a decent chance of living a healthy and fulfilling life.

Without a doubt, Bartholet is well intentioned, and she makes valid points that cannot be dismissed. As a legal scholar and adoptive mother herself, she is clearly positioned as a proponent of the practice. However, Bartholet has too often ignored or been blind to the scale of the problems and realities on the ground (Briggs, 2012; Oreskovic & Maskew, 2008). As she stated herself, she sees kidnapping or child buying as a "tiny part of the larger picture [and] very unfortunate" (Bartholet, 2005, p. 1). Fundamentally, Bartholet sees the problems (unethical and illicit acts) in intercountry adoption to be a distraction from the larger picture and greater good for thousands of children in legitimate need. On the whole, in her promotion of a permanent family as a human rights imperative, she fails to acknowledge the sheer scale of the problems and the profound nature of the resulting human rights abuses.

This became clear when Bartholet was making comments at an adoption conference in Guatemala City in 2005; she criticized reformists—many who were Guatemalan human rights defenders—saying that they are "condemning thousands on thousands of kids to life and death in the intolerable conditions typical of the world's orphanages" (p. 8). She went on to say that Guatemala, at that point, was one of the best places in the world for intercountry adoption. History has proven otherwise and the illicit and unethical practices in Guatemala have left a deep scar, especially for those families who experienced child abduction into adoption.

Nonetheless, one fact is certain in regards to Guatemalan and other intercountry adoptions; without a doubt some children's lives were truly saved by the intervention. One cannot underestimate that fact, especially when looking at intercountry adoption on a case-by-case basis and factoring in the perfectly legitimate adoptions that have occurred in Guatemala and globally.

As we move forward today, in Guatemala and elsewhere, even with the strengthening of child-protection systems around the world and improvements in adoption processes specifically, there will always be children who are truly appropriate for intercountry adoption. This is particularly true for special-needs children who have conditions that can be easily treated in a high-resource country (Pinderhughes, Matthews, Pertman, & Deoudes, 2015). However, even with the hope of special-needs children being matched with ready and willing families, some critics will say that it is also cruel to require a parent in poverty to relinquish a child so that the child can receive life-saving (or disability-ameliorating) treatment in another country. That parent may rightfully ask: Why do I have to give *my* child to someone else for medical care? Why can they not just help me financially cover the care and allow me to carry on parenting *my* child? There again poses yet another ethical dilemma, and the answers are not easy when one truly considers the issues at hand. Regardless of this unfortunate scenario, there are many children in institutions who were abandoned because of the combination of disability and poverty, and sometimes because of the shame of a child's disfigurement and/or other issues of stigma, shame, misunderstanding of disability, and lack of adequate care systems in that child's community.

Ultimately, intercountry adoption is not a "fix" for the vast majority of children and their families or the social problems that underlie the practice. To suggest otherwise is a flaw in the argument and is a distraction from the realities and needs of most children and families globally. Thus, to invest heavily (with vast sums) in intercountry adoption as an intervention without a concerted effort in developing child welfare systems globally, is simply unethical and is a reminder of the term "baby scoop" as we explored in our earliest discussion about the history of child adoption in Chapter 1.

Globally: how do we intervene ethically?

One cannot look at the facts without asking the obvious question: How can one ethically intervene? To answer that question briefly in terms of social service interventions is impossible. However, there are some key points that we will consider, specifically focusing on family preservation and the deinstitutionalization of children.

We begin with the important conception, related to prevention—most families will find solutions and resolve problems of caring for children within their own group through informal care practices, especially if provided support to do so (Roby, 2011). This is particularly true for communities where there is a strong sense of communal living. For those families who need help and assistance, family-preservation services within the child-protection and welfare services model is essential, and building such systems of care is an obligation as identified in the Convention on the Rights of the Child (Art. 19 as discussed in Chapter 5).

Essential for meeting the obligations of Article 19 is programming in family preservation to assist families during crisis (e.g. death of a parent or loss of employment) in caring for their children and ultimately prevent long-term child–family separation or any separation at all (Hague Conference on Private International Law, 2008). This orientation honors the fact that most children have family as a basic resource system (at least one living parent and extended family) and a civil society has an obligation to support the family in caring for the child (Roby, 2011; Roby & Maskew, 2012). A continuum of social care, with an orientation to prevention strategies and especially avoidance of residential childcare institutions while supporting families, is essential in ethical adoption practice with a child–rights orientation (Fronek & Cuthbert, 2011; Roby, 2007).

To meet this end, a range of programs and services can be implemented, including foster care for crisis situations, cash transfers and economic empowerment programs to help families through difficult economic times, support for grandparents and others who provide relative/ kinship guardianship of children, and other social supports that can be applied to each case based on the best interests of the child in question (International Reference Centre for the Rights of Children Deprived of Their Family, 2015; Roby, 2007). These approaches to family support reject the notion of "orphan" in most cases and recognize that for many children their social-support systems—family and kinship networks—can be engaged to respond to the child's needs, given appropriate social services and family support/assistance (Williamson & Greenberg, 2010).

Obviously, for success in these areas, adequate funding must be put into place. The social-service workforce must be effectively trained. Furthermore, laws, policies, and procedures must honor the conception of family preservation and ultimately support the Hague Convention on Intercountry Adoption principle of subsidiarity (Harris & DiFilipo, 2015). However, in all fairness it is important to note that in many countries, gradual development of social service systems is not progressing fast enough to meet the needs of children and their families in crisis today. To suggest that intercountry adoption is the panacea is unrealistic, and for some countries the practice has actually been a diversion from a critical task at hand: the development of systems of care that broadly serve children and their families in a holistic manner.

The answer to the question of *how* we intervene ethically is not easy. Outsiders to the process of development in low-resource countries must look for ways to contribute logical aid to meet these ends, provide technical assistance as appropriate—not assistance motivated by adoption as the primary goal—allowing low-resource countries to move forward with their own self-determination while encouraging progress in the development of child-rights legislation and social service systems development. This means, in many cases, stepping back and ceasing to interfere (with the adoption agenda) as local systems develop and align to protect children and support families across the continuum of care.

We do acknowledge that critics will call this position unrealistic as children suffer. However, it is essential to acknowledge that less than 1 percent of all children in need of social services globally were served by intercountry adoption when it was at its peak in practice in 2004. To simply remove children from their families and local communities without concerted efforts to improve and build systems of care is ultimately inhumane. Furthermore, building residential childcare facilities—a common response of those making contributions to the "cause" of "orphans"—is an approach that is counterproductive at this time, given the need to dedicate resources that focus on family preservation.

Preventing institutionalization and the movement towards deinstitutionalization of children

Can a country absolutely guarantee that a child will stay with their biological family? No. In fact, sometimes children are removed by authorities from their family system for their care and protection, especially in cases of gross abuse of the child. Those children will often land in out-of-family care and impersonal residential childcare facilities. While not all facilities are poorly managed and deeply harmful to children, globally there are far too many large-scale residential childcare institutions that are damaging to the child's health and development.

One of the answers to this problem is that a country can build programs and social services that promote the right for children to grow and develop in a family setting (Preamble of the CRC), including extended family members who may be willing to step in to protect a child. Many of these strategies of engaging the family and kinship system to respond, when carried out effectively and systematically, will prevent the institutionalization of children in the first place. This preventive strategy reinforces a social justice approach to intercountry adoption by building upon family strengths and capacities to care for their own children (Fronek & Cuthbert, 2011; Fronek et al., 2015; Roby, Rotabi, & Bunkers, 2013; Rotabi, Pennell, Roby, & Bunkers, 2012; Roby, Pennell, Rotabi, Bunkers, & Ucles, 2014). When a child is already institutionalized, reconnecting with those family and kinship group members who are able to care for the child increasingly becomes a priority within innovative deinstitutionalization initiatives (see Riley, 2015). Greater emphasis is now being placed on family and community reintegration of children, including development monies being dedicated to initiatives to include social service workforce training as well as testing family support and other related innovations in the field. Rwanda is one such example of a country that has taken on the deinstitutionalization of children with a concerted community and family reintegration plan as national policy and the closure of residential childcare institutions; the initiative has been globally applauded as a model of what is possible (Broadhead, 2012) with all of the residential childcare institutions, opened since the genocide in 1994, now being shut down in the year 2016 (Ssuuna, 2016).

Poverty and intercountry adoption

Much of what we have considered thus far pivots on issues of poverty. When looking at poverty and the miserable and coercive conditions that arise from poverty, it is important to look at Article 25 of the Universal Declaration of Human Rights, which states that:

> Everyone has the right to a standard of living adequate for the health and well-being of himself and of his family, including food, clothing, housing, and medical care and necessary social services, and the right to security in the event of unemployment, sickness, disability, widowhood, old age or other lack of livelihood in circumstances beyond his control. Motherhood and childhood are entitled to special care and assistance. All children, whether born in or out of wedlock, shall enjoy the same social protection.
>
> *(United Nations, 1948)*

Nonetheless, poverty is clearly one of the most powerful social forces in intercountry adoption that cannot be denied, and the question is: What is the ethical response to the human right to live with "a standard of living adequate for the health and well-being of himself and his family" in the context of coercive and disabling conditions of poverty?

Smolin (2015), an adoptive father himself and a legal scholar with a pragmatic stance, points out that some of those who promote intercountry adoption view the practice as an ethical response to poverty. "The argument is that since anti-poverty programs at current scales will not reach all of the poor, and since ICA is an additional intervention that may assist those who otherwise might not be assisted, ICA thereby has a positive impact as a response to poverty" (p. 254). In other words, proponents do not see intercountry adoption diverting resources away from anti-poverty programming. In fact, proponents take the view that intercountry adoption "brings large numbers of persons, as adoptive parents, into the effort against global poverty who otherwise would not be involved" (Smolin, 2015, p. 254). Smolin goes on say that:

> In a world in which perhaps one billion people live under the international standard for extreme poverty of $1.25 a day, and in which another two billion living under $2 a day are quite economically vulnerable, it is exploitative and absurd to label the children of the poor as eligible for intercountry adoption.
>
> *(p. 257)*

Consequently, the United Nations and International Social Services, along with the African Child Policy Forum, are clear in their position that poverty should never be the single reason for intercountry adoption (Fifth International Policy Conference on the African Child, 2012;

International Reference Centre for the Rights of Children Deprived of Their Family, 2015). Specifically, the United Nations Alternative Care of Children Guidelines of 2009 state that:

> Financial and material poverty, or conditions directly and uniquely imputable to such poverty, should never be the only justification for the removal of a child from parental care, for receiving a child into alternative care, or for preventing his/her reintegration, but should be seen as a signal for the need to provide appropriate support to the family.
>
> *(Guideline 14)*

The development priorities of UNICEF and other UN development organizations are oriented to systematic changes across the broad spectrum of societal need with both social and economic planning for social development. Successful systems transformation ultimately translates into a more responsive civil society that meets the welfare needs of the entire population with a commitment to those who are most vulnerable, especially children.

Poverty: turning to commercial global surrogacy in India

We undertook research in India with the primary goal of asking women about their perspectives on commercial global surrogacy and their roles as surrogate mothers. It was critically important for us to seek the voices of these women living in poverty rather than draw generalizations about their rights and needs. We have seen too many generalizations based on moral positioning that have failed to recognize the views and opinions of the women themselves (Bromfield, 2016; Bromfield & Rotabi, 2014; Rotabi, 2014)—women who often live under extreme stress of poverty and related conditions that regularly create circumstances of significant vulnerability, including exploitative labor.

Without a doubt, poverty was the driving force in the decision-making process related to surrogacy in India, and the desperate conditions of poverty have been illustrated in their voices. Their perspective and the importance of meeting these basic needs of housing and children's education should not be ignored. It is shortsighted to dismiss the fact that with poverty often come desperation and the willingness to consider all of the options for survival. Many of the alternatives to surrogacy for the women we interviewed were not only less desirable, but were those in which the women and their families would only survive rather than get ahead and save and invest in their future.

The big or macro picture that drives this reality for women in poverty requires us to consider the structural conditions that lead to poverty and vulnerability. The reality is that children in these circumstances are often unhealthy as a result of malnutrition and other preventable conditions. Women, as mothers in poverty responding to this reality, face decisions that are unthinkable for most people reading this book. An example that builds upon malnutrition is removing children from school and involving them in child labor from necessity to meet the most basic of household expenses—sometimes families find it necessary to remove an older child (often a girl) so that younger (frequently male) siblings may eat and attend school. These realities and how families in poverty speculate on their future should not be underestimated. This is particularly true when we consider poverty and desperation as part of the cost–benefit equation that underlies many decisions of women in poverty, including commercial global surrogacy, in the case of Indian women.

We submit that the real answer to the concerns of the critics of commercial global surrogacy is the right for women to engage in work that is compensated fairly. This is in contrast to exploitative conditions that women in India and other impoverished countries face on a daily basis. Sadly, right now, even with concerted poverty-alleviation efforts emphasizing gender equity, the foreseeable future holds extreme poverty for millions of women and their families. With that comes a myriad of human rights abuses (Khan, 2009).

Child rights in commercial global surrogacy

The area of child rights has received far less consideration in the literature thus far. Just as in the case of intercountry adoption, there are articles of the Convention on the Rights of the Child that may be applied directly to commercial global surrogacy, for example, the rights to citizenship in the case of children who become stateless as discussed in Chapter 7 as well as child rights of origin and identity. The application of these child-rights articles is essential as the whole equation of surrogate mother and child are considered. Expanded conceptions are necessary in the consideration, including the right to knowledge of one's origin. Limited knowledge of one's background has already been a problem for adoptees who must mark their medical records as "unknown" for their family history of problems such as cancer. Then, of course, there is the discussion about preserving records so that the offspring of commercial global surrogacy arrangements may go back and search for information about the process (contract, etc.) and potentially seek to meet their gestational surrogate.

Turning to the issue of money, the Convention on the Rights of the Child Optional Protocol for the Sale of Children, Child Prostitution and Child Pornography defines the "sale of children" as "any act or transaction whereby a child is transferred by any person or group of persons to another for remuneration or any other consideration" (Art. 2. A). This particular definition, without a doubt, is grounds for human rights defenders to call for abolishment of the practice of commercial global surrogacy. Others will respond that a service is being sold rather than a child being sold. Which argument will prevail in the long term is unknown at this point. Even if those who argue that commercial global surrogacy is child sales win the debate on an intellectual level, such an outcome does not mean that the practice will cease. In fact, we think it is abundantly clear that stopping the purchase of surrogacy as a service is not practical as the marketplace is a powerful force. Furthermore, considering the surrogates in our study and other studies (e.g. Pande, 2014) and their views on the practice as well as the needs of commissioning parents, clearly both of these parties benefit from the practice of commercial global surrogacy.

Like us, many pragmatists will agree with the reality that stopping the practice is not only unlikely but is impossible when one considers the demand for healthy infants (Bromfield & Rotabi, 2014; Goodwin, 2010). We also have fears that abolishing the practice—if that is even possible—would just push activities underground and create the vulnerabilities of practices that take place in the shadows. With that comes the question of how to engage in the practice ethically and in a socially just manner, protective of all parties (Rotabi, Bromfield, & Fronek, 2015).

There currently is a movement to develop guidelines for commercial global surrogacy practices from the perspective of rights and the need for regulation. One such effort is under way by the International Social Services of Australia (2015, p. 1), presumably as a result of the Baby Gammy case (Chapter 7). The organization has developed recommendations for the government of Australia focused on both domestic and international concerns, including recommendations that there be:

- Cross-jurisdictional recognition of birth certificates and parentage orders
- Provisions to ensure the informed consent of surrogates

- Processes for counselling, education, and legal advice for all parties relating to psychosocial, legal, and medical issues
- Measures for the screening and assessment of suitability of intending parents and surrogates, including criminal and child protection history
- Measures to collect and preserve information to facilitate the surrogate-born child's future access to information regarding origin and identity
- Operational standards for surrogacy service providers
- Medical standards for the care of the surrogate-born child and surrogate
- Measures in the event of the breakdown of the surrogacy arrangement, the intending parents' relationship, multiple births, or child disability
- Regulation of financial transactions so as not to constitute sale of a child
- Measures to guard against child trafficking
- Measures to prevent trafficking of women for surrogacy.

These recommendations, reported above verbatim, come as the General Secretariat of the International Social Services is convening experts to prepare guidelines for commercial global surrogacy from a child-rights perspective (personal communication, Mia Dambach of International Social Services, January 2016). Approaching the problems of commercial global surrogacy from a child-rights orientation is needed, as this particular aspect has received considerably less attention than the rights of surrogates (see Darnovsky & Beeson, 2014; Karandikar, Gezinski, Carter, & Kaloga, 2014; Pande, 2014; Vora, 2015). However, some of these recommendations may have unintended consequences, as have the strict regulations related to advanced reproductive technologies in the UK and many Western European countries.

Our recommendations for protecting surrogates

In our own work, we have given social protections of surrogates considerable thought, especially protections for women and children living in poverty (see Bromfield & Rotabi, 2014; Rotabi et al., 2015). In reality there are a range of issues and needs in regulation of commercial global surrogacy, and here we will address three critical social protections, mainly for surrogates with implications for everyone involved in the transaction: (1) informed consent, (2) rights to health insurance for follow-up care, and (3) accreditation of fertility clinics, including a regulatory tie to medical licensure.

1. Issues of informed consent are considerable, as it is imperative that a potential surrogate mother understand the risks of IVF and other related procedures that result from commercial global surrogacy. The manner in which that consent is gained, especially the need for an impartial counselor who is *not* employed by the entity that is financially gaining from surrogacy (fertility doctors/clinics) is a critical element to setting an ethical framework of practice. Consent documentation must be both written and verbal, especially in the surrogate mother's native language. Furthermore, it must be both thorough as well as stated as simply as possible for understanding. Lastly, as we have discussed, context is critical for ethical work, and when a country is characterized by corruption and impunity along with endemic levels of violence against women, it may actually be impossible to guarantee a fair and free informed consent process. This is particularly true when there is a lack of confidence that authorities will intervene as necessary to enforce social protections.

2. Health of the surrogate after labor and delivery (or after a failed surrogacy) is often an overlooked area of concern. Follow-up care for physical and mental health is essential such that the surrogate can seek appropriate services as she requests. Health insurance is an important developmental area that needs attention. Furthermore, life insurance should be considered in regulatory control in the unusual case of a surrogacy-related death.

3. Accreditation of fertility clinics/healthcare facilities that carry out the necessary procedures for surrogacy is essential. Although standards have already been drafted in India, they have not been enacted (Saxena, Mishra, & Malik, 2012), and an accreditation system there must be established. Further, we recommend that medical doctor licensure be tied to ethical practices in commercial surrogacy. Such an approach to regulation is already true in India in its ban on sex-selective abortion. A replication of this credential-based control is critical to true and professional accountability in both social and medical ethics.

These are three of the more pressing issues that we have looked at in more expansive and previous work. Other scholars have also contributed considerably to the conversation, including the importance of labor issues like setting standards for pay to include minimum payments and protections for workers. Some of those areas were captured in the draft 2010 law in India (Saxena et al., 2012). Pande (2014) has documented the surrogate mother's opinions on the matter of payment and other related labor issues (including rights of payment when there is a miscarriage or stillbirth, etc.). We encourage the reader to look to broader discourse than we can offer in this brief discussion, including the work of human rights defenders such as the SAMA Resource Group for Women and Health (see SAMA, 2012) and others in India and elsewhere engaged in advocacy work.

Responding to the human rights issues: a convention on global surrogacy or parentage?

A 1990 Hague Permanent Bureau report on intercountry adoption was a watershed moment in defining illicit activities and the array of problems in adoption practice globally; *trafficking* was used as a term, and the report made the point that the concept is relevant even if there is no child exploitation at the end point (van Loon, 1990). In this early report, surrogacy was also briefly mentioned as an area of concern without elaboration.

As commercial global surrogacy arrangements have become more common, so too have problems related to statelessness and other issues in which parentage has been contested (Hague Conference on Private International Law, 2012). Most of the cases of statelessness thus far have involved India, which has ostensibly solved this issue through newly enacted visa requirements that require commissioning parents to provide a letter of support of the surrogacy from their citizen countries.

The Hague Conference on Private International Law considered some of the pressing issues when the question was raised as to whether the Hague Convention on Intercountry Adoption was applicable to the practice of global surrogacy. Ultimately, it was decided that the HCIA is not applicable and that new international agreements would be necessary— and a new international private law should be considered to address the cross-border problems of commercial global surrogacy. The work undertaken by the Hague Conference on Private International Law, considering the identified problems, resulted in a 2012 report in which the major concerns and legal issues at hand received considerable elaboration (Hague Conference on Private International Law, 2012). To address the issues and consider future legal applications, an Experts' Group on Parentage/Surrogacy was constituted with the mandate to "explore the feasibility of advancing work on the private international law issue surrounding the status of children, including issues arising from international surrogacy agreements" (Hague Conference on Private International Law, 2016, p. 2). In 2016:

> The group noted that surrogacy arrangements are prohibited in some States, permitted in other States and unregulated in others. The group recognized concerns at the international level regarding public policy considerations of all those involved with surrogacy arrangements, including, for example, the uncertain legal status of children and the potential for exploitation of women, including surrogate mothers.
>
> *(Hague Conference on Private International Law, 2016, p. 3)*

As this group of experts continues to deliberate the future of regulating surrogacy practice, it is predicted that any future international private law will focus more broadly on parentage, with issues of commercial global surrogacy being included in this umbrella of "parentage." Any such international private law would require a lengthy drafting and deliberation process, and such work will require a number of years of concerted effort both legally and intellectually as well as politically.

Protections and the limits of regulating practices

Dillon (2003) points out that the Hague Convention on Intercountry Adoption focuses on unethical and illicit adoptions "over the damage of no adoption at all, and fails to provide proper balance between the two poles of this human rights dilemma" (p. 214). Furthermore, there is a time paradox when the obligations of the principle of subsidiarity results in a child further languishing in residential care facilities to ensure all steps are taken in an ethical adoption (International Reference Centre for the Rights of Children Deprived of Their Family, 2015). The process, when one considers one child at a time, is considerable, often protracted, and far from perfect.

The future of commercial global surrogacy, within a global regulatory framework similar to the Hague Convention on Intercountry Adoption, is uncertain. In all likelihood any such agreement will result in unintended consequences, as have the regulations around surrogacy in much of Western Europe and Australia that have pushed people to seek surrogacy arrangements in other countries. Some of the potential problems or consequences may ultimately fail to protect *all* of those involved in a surrogacy arrangement, including commissioning parents (Bromfield & Rotabi, 2014; Rotabi et al., 2015). It is too early to tell, but the reality of regulating practices for the human endeavor of supporting and building families—whether by adoption or surrogacy—is frequently imperfect. And, when one must apply laws to family and family life, the greater good sometimes comes at a cost to others. The question is, at what cost and to whom?

Embedded in the answer is the fact that no human rights instrument entitles one to the absolute right to build a family through alternative means. Rather, the Universal Declaration of Human Rights (United Nations, 1948) generally states that "Men and women of full age, without any limitation due to race, nationality or religion, have the right to marry and to found a family…[and] The family is the natural and fundamental group unit of society and is entitled to protection by society and the State" (Art. 16).

Infertility is a known harm for individuals and couples wishing to build a family. Those seeking fertility services have themselves been vulnerable and have faced exploitation by unscrupulous agencies and individuals who prey on their desperation to build a family.

The argument could be made that those suffering from infertility also should be entitled to some level of social protection and/or access to state-funded infertility-treatment options.

The future of intercountry adoption and commercial global surrogacy

Intercountry adoption, as practiced in recent history, is over as we have known it in terms of a significant flow of children from low-resource countries to high-resource countries. The practice will continue, but we predict that the trend of countries sending relatively few children will prevail even if a country has a rise in practice—a fall in that country will most likely occur once clear and persistent problems set in. There may be exceptions, especially if a country of origin develops a system with the safeguards needed to support families and prevent fraud. In the meantime, as countries slow down or shut down, there will be many missed opportunities for children who are truly appropriate for intercountry adoption as a result of the continuum of poor and illicit practices that we have illustrated extensively.

We predict that like intercountry adoption, there will continue to be country closures or significant limitations on the practice of global surrogacy (e.g. the 2015 policy changes in India). There will also be shifts to new countries as we saw in Nepal, which now has a closure (Chapter 7). While we cannot confirm it, there are reports that some Indian surrogates are being transported to countries in Africa so that the global surrogacy contracts with Indian women can continue (Vora, 2016). Even if Indian surrogates are not transported to other countries as happened in the case of Nepal (Chapter 7), it is certain that the marketplace will shift to other low-resource countries with limited social protections and an absence of laws related to surrogacy. Ghana is showing some signs as a potential location for surrogacy with African women being encouraged to take on surrogacy contracts. One advertisement seeking women to participate as surrogates in Ghana promises "insurance, good meals and good accommodation to ensure the safety of the unborn child" (Boakye, 2016, p. 1). Also, this same advertisement includes the following emotive appeal:

> Many marriages in Ghana break down due to childlessness. If you accept to be a surrogate mother, you save a marriage and grow a family which Pope John Paul sees as the sanctuary of love, a place where life is nurtured and protected…In some tribes in Ghana, a woman who has difficulty getting children may be given a child by a sibling or close relative. Surrogacy could be a better option. You will look back and be proud of what you have done.
>
> *(Boakye, 2016, p. 1)*

It should be noted that there is no clear evidence at this time of a commercial global surrogacy model emerging with Ghana being the next destination country. Furthermore, there has been little discussion of Ghana as a potential surrogacy destination on the online infertility bulletin boards frequented by those interested in commissioning surrogacy at this time. However, it is certain that new commercial global surrogacy locations are being forged, and agencies in various countries will be interested in getting involved in this lucrative business. Cambodia, neighbouring Thailand, was one of the next surrogacy locations. Given the serious fraud there during the ICA boom, such an industry emergence in the post-conflict country is not an insignificant concern for human rights defenders (Maza, 2016). However, in early November 2016, Cambodia banned commercial surrogacy in a surprise to some and a relief to those concerned about the rights of Cambodian women living in desperate poverty.

With the increased global surrogacy pressure falling on countries other than India, Mexico was one country that was anticipated to have an increase in surrogacy activity. However, in December 2015 gay men and foreigners were barred from surrogacy in the state of Tabasco, the only state in Mexico engaged in commercial global surrogacy (Associated Press, 2015). Another previously somewhat attractive global surrogacy destination that has now become problematic is the Ukraine. However, conflict with Russia and the uncertainty that comes with unrest and potential for all-out war are likely curtailing the practice of commercial global surrogacy there, although the Ukraine had never taken off as a desirable global surrogacy destination, as had the US, India, and Thailand.

As the momentum continues, the question becomes: Where next? We have already mentioned African countries, and while that is not yet a clear phenomenon, we are certain that countries with poverty, weak social protections/legal frameworks, and the medical infrastructure that can support IVF (or at least embryo transfers) will be attractive and potential locations for migration of surrogacy. At one time, it appeared that Guatemala might be an emerging location based on a website advertising services that the agency was planning on providing surrogacy in Guatemala (Rotabi & Bromfield, 2012); the website material has since been taken offline. Whether Central America becomes the next commercial global surrogacy destination remains to be seen. We do not rule out such a possibility.

Emerging technologies to address infertility and family building

As artificial reproductive technologies evolve, new technology will emerge that will address infertility problems more effectively, including the possibility that uterus transplants, artificial wombs, and artificial fallopian tubes, among other advances, will eventually be possible. While this may sound like science fiction, one can say that was once true with regards to IVF and the "test tube baby" (Goodwin, 2010). As the future unfolds, these technologies and other advances in capacity to reproduce will be explored, tested, and promoted. This is inevitable as the marketplace for providing services to aid in building family continues with untold billions of dollars at stake. Investors are speculating on these futures, and the resulting problems and consumer demands, along with other technological advances, will continue to test our social ethics. The industry will respond to needs and desires; some entrepreneurs will become greatly enriched in the process while we grapple with the ethical dilemmas (Goodwin, 2010).

Regulatory frameworks are essential for social protections (Cheney, 2014), and the question becomes: Who will decide? Will medical ethics and the health industry prevail as the dominant voice? Will international labor law enter into the equation (Pande, 2014)? In addition, there are women's rights groups who are locked into a debate on the issues of abolish versus regulate surrogacy. Whose feminist perspective will prevail, if any?

Constructing life with technology

When considering the creation of a human being in a contractual arrangement, the ability to select for characteristics such as hair and eye color, height, and intelligence also raises bioethical questions and lends itself to a moral debate. The debate surrounding the ethical issues related to sperm and egg donorship is not new and has evoked strong emotional reactions, especially from critics of advanced reproductive technologies. These dynamics combined with emerging technologies such as gene editing (Achenbach, 2016) and other opportunities to control human genetic characteristics (e.g. embryo screening) will result in some arguing that new forms of eugenics are playing out. Others, especially commissioning parents in the case of surrogacy arrangements with a donor gamete, will see themselves building their family and their choices as a private matter that have nothing to do with genetic superiority; rather, they are seeking a child that is similar to themselves (physically and also potentially in intelligence). Regardless of the arguments put forth, what once was the fantasy of science fiction and the quest for the perfect or "designed" human may be here upon us in this age of advanced fertility technologies and relatively new techniques of characteristics selection (Vint, 2016). A detailed discussion of gamete donorship in the case of surrogacy arrangements is beyond the scope of this book, but it should be noted that this issue has received political, policy, and media attention and is expected to continue to do so, as fears of designer babies continue to captivate the public's imagination.

Conclusion

Building families through alternative means, including the use of technology to meet the end goal of family life, is a compelling story in which the ethical dilemmas continue to play out. We have presented a historical narrative as a way of exploring *how* and *why* adoption fraud plays out in intercountry adoption. Then we bridge to commercial global surrogacy contracts, again considering the ethical dilemmas and vulnerabilities of everyone involved in the transaction. We have presented part of the conversation about human rights, responsibilities, regulation, and human dignity, all of which are embedded with the concept of *exploitation*.

While we have been clear about exploitation in intercountry adoption, our position is far more flexible in commercial global surrogacy, especially as it relates to women in the United States and India. Our analysis indicates that US surrogates do not view themselves as exploited. This is also true about the women we interviewed in India. This latter group was quite practical about their day-to-day lives and the need for a solution for which they indicated commercial global surrogacy was satisfactory for them.

When considering these results, a basic definition of exploitation is useful in interrogating the inherent issues. Wertheimer and Zwolinski (2013) offer a definition of exploitation as *the act of taking unfair advantage of another for one's benefit*. The critical term in that definition is "unfair advantage." That said, it is important to note that a verdict of exploitation does not rest entirely with the women/surrogates themselves. Those who stand to be exploited do not have to personally define or voice a sense of exploitation—or unfair advantage at the hands of another—in order for the arrival at the conclusion of exploitation in a broad or global sense. There is also the question of the children created. How will they ultimately define their perspective on exploitation as they age, become adults, and form opinions about the practice? Research on the children born of surrogate arrangements thus far indicates that these children have not suffered from issues faced by some adoptees, and those studied were well adjusted (Jadva, Blake, Casey, & Golombok, 2012). It should be said, however, that every person's perception and experience of lived events is unique, and this is clearly an area of future and expanded research as related to commercial global surrogacy.

In reality, exploitation is a tricky area to define, as perspectives vary. How we as people of privilege (most people with access to this book) define exploitation may well be quite different from people living in extreme poverty, in many cases. Honoring the latter view while adhering to human rights doctrines leads to the real and persistent question: Does commercial global surrogacy cross the line into child sales and a violation of human dignity for the surrogate and/or the child? That question remains unanswered in terms of United Nations weighing in on the subject. In due course, there may be some movement in this area and perhaps even an attempt to install some global regulatory standards with international private law.

We close this chapter with a final thought on the feminist debate on sex work and the parallel critiques involved in commercial gestational surrogacy. Christian conservatives and radical and other groups of feminists continue to speak out against surrogacy and liken surrogacy to prostitution, sex slavery, and/or human trafficking, while some radical feminists denounce the use of all reproductive technologies, citing patriarchal dominance of women by men (Kessler, 2009). Women's bodies are continually regulated and politicized.

Third-wave and other pragmatic feminists cite women's reproductive freedom (Markens, 2011; Matson, 2014) and right to self-determination and maintain that women should be able to have control over their own bodies (Matson, 2014), and we agree with this position. While the best interests and rights of women should be protected through pragmatic surrogacy regulation (Bromfield & Rotabi, 2014; Rotabi et al., 2015), we ultimately believe in women's right to choose how to use their own bodies. As authors, we don't agree on every aspect of surrogacy arrangements and surrogacy regulation, but we do strongly agree on these points and especially on protecting vulnerable women, today and in the new fertility frontiers.

References

Achenbach, J. (2016, May 4). Pondering the consequences of gene editing. Washington Post. Retrieved from www.pressreader.com/usa/the-washington-post/20160504/281809988099323

Altstein, H. (1984). Transracial and inter-country adoptions: A comparison. In P. Sachdev (Ed.), *Adoption: Current issues and trends* (pp. 1995–2003). London: Butterworth.

Altstein, H. & Simon, R. J. (1991). *Intercountry adoption: A multiple perspective*. New York: Praeger.

Associated Press. (2015, December 15). Mexican state votes to ban surrogacy for gay men and foreign people. Retrieved from www.theguardian.com/world/2015/dec/15/mexico-tabasco-state-surrogacy-gay-men-foreign-couples

Bailey, J. D. (2009). Expectations of the consequences of new international adoption policy in the US. *Journal of Sociology & Social Welfare*, 36, 169–83.

Ballard, R. L., Goodno, N., Cochran, R., & Milbrandt, J. (Eds). (2015). *The intercountry adoption debate: Dialogues across disciplines*. Newcastle upon Tyne: Cambridge Scholars Publishing.

Bartholet, E. (2005, January 20). In the best interests of children: A permanent family. Keynote address presented at the Focus on Adoption Conference, Guatemala City, Guatemala. Retrieved from www.law.harvard.edu/faculty/bartholet/FOCUSONADOPTION.pdf

Bartholet, E. (2010). International adoption: The human rights issues. In M. B. Goodwin (Ed.), *Baby markets: Money and the new politics of creating families* (pp. 94–117). New York: Cambridge University Press.

Bartholet, E. & Smolin, D. (2012). The debate. In J. L. Gibbons & K. S. Rotabi (Eds), *Intercountry adoption: Policies, practices, and outcomes* (pp. 233–54). Farnham: Ashgate Press.

Boakye, J. (2016, April 23). Will you be a surrogate mother? Retrieved from www.graphic.com.gh/lifestyle/relationships/62643-will-you-be-a-surrogate-mother.html?template=testkphp7&is_preview=on

Briggs, L. (2012). *Somebody's children: The politics of transracial and transnational adoption*. Durham, NC: Duke University Press.

Briggs, L. & Marre, D. (2009). *International adoption: Global inequalities and the circulation of children*. New York: New York University Press.

Broadhead, I. (2012, March 13). Rwanda child policy spells possible end of orphanages. *Voice of America*. Retrieved from www.voanews.com/content/rwanda-child-policy-spells-possible-end-of-orphanages-142619126/179890.html

Bromfield, N. F. (2016). "Surrogacy has been one of the most rewarding experiences in my life": A content analysis of blogs by U.S. commercial gestational surrogates. *International Journal of Feminist Approaches to Bioethics*, 9(1), 192–217.

Bromfield, N. F. & Rotabi, K. S. (2014). Global surrogacy, exploitation, human rights and international private law: A pragmatic stance and policy recommendations. *Global Social Welfare*, 1(3), 123–35. doi:10.1007/s40609-014-0019-4

Cheney, K. E. (2014). Executive summary of the International Forum on Intercountry Adoption and Global Surrogacy. ISS Working Paper Series/General Series, 596, 1–40. Retrieved from http://hdl.handle.net/1765/77408

Darnovsky, M. & Beeson, D. (2014). Global surrogacy practices. ISS Working Paper Series/General Series, 601, 1–54. Retrieved from http://hdl.handle.net/1765/77402

Dillon, S. (2003). Making legal regimes for intercountry adoption reflect human rights principles: Transforming the United Nations Convention on the Rights of the Child with the Hague Convention on Intercountry Adoption. *Boston University International Law Journal*, 21, 179.

Fifth International Policy Conference on the African Child. (2012, May 29–30). Guidelines for action on intercountry adoption of children in Africa. Retrieved from www.wereldkinderen.nl/websites/implementatie/mediadepot/8559606e8da.pdf

Fronek, P. & Cuthbert, D. (2011). The future of inter-country adoption: A paradigm shift for this century. *International Journal of Social Welfare*, 21(12), 215–24.

Fronek, P., Cuthbert, D., & Willing, I. (2015). Intercountry adoption: Privilege, rights and social justice. In R. L. Ballard, N. Goodno, R. Cochran, & J. Milbrandt (Eds), *The intercountry adoption debate: Dialogues across disciplines* (pp. 348–65). Newcastle upon Tyne: Cambridge Scholars Publishing.

Gibbons, J. L. & Rotabi, K. S. (Eds). (2012). *Intercountry adoption: Policies, practices, and outcomes*. Farnham: Ashgate Press.

Goodwin, M. B. (Ed.). (2010). *Baby markets: Money and the new politics of creating families*. New York: Cambridge University Press.

Hague Conference on Private International Law. (2008). The implementation and operation of the 1993 Hague Intercountry Adoption Convention: Guide to good practice. Retrieved from www.hcch.net/upload/wop/ado_pd02e.pdf

Hague Conference on Private International Law. (2012). A preliminary report on the issues arising from international surrogacy arrangements. Retrieved from www.hcch.net/upload/wop/gap2012pd10en.pdf

Hague Conference on Private International Law. (2016). Report of the February 2016 experts group meeting on parentage/surrogacy. Retrieved from https://assets.hcch.net/docs/f92c95b5-4364-4461-bb04-2382e3c0d50d.pdf

Harris, R. & DiFilipo. T. (2015). Creating systems that protect children: Elements of success. In R. L. Ballard, N. Goodno, R. Cochran, & J. Milbrandt (Eds), *The intercountry adoption debate: Dialogues across disciplines* (pp. 708–29). Newcastle upon Tyne: Cambridge Scholars Publishing.

Hübinette, T. (2012). Post-racial utopianism: White color-blindness and "the elephant in the room": Racial issues for transnational adoptees of color. In J. L. Gibbons & K. S. Rotabi (Eds), *Intercountry adoption: Policies, practices, and outcomes* (pp. 221–32). Farnham: Ashgate Press.

International Reference Centre for the Rights of Children Deprived of Their Family. (2015). *Manifesto for ethical intercountry adoption*. Geneva: International Social Service.

International Social Services of Australia. (2015). Submission to the Senate inquiry into regulatory and legislative aspects of international and domestic surrogacy arrangements. Retrieved from www.iss.org.au/our-publications/major-reports/

Jadva, V., Blake, L., Casey, P., & Golombok, S. (2012). Surrogacy families 10 years on: Relationship with the surrogate, decisions over disclosure and children's understanding of their surrogacy origins. *Human Reproduction*, 27(10), 3008–14.

Karandikar, S., Gezinski, L. B., Carter, J. R., & Kaloga, M. (2014). Economic necessity or a noble cause? Exploring motivations for gestational surrogacy in Gujarat, India. *Affilia*, 29(2), 224–36.

Kessler, B. (2009). Recruiting wombs: Surrogates as the new security moms. *Women's Studies Quarterly,* 37(1/2), 167–82. doi: 10.1353/wsq.0.0139

Khan, I. (2009). *The unheard truth: Poverty and human rights.* New York: Norton & Company.

Markens, S. (2011). Interrogating narratives: About the global surrogacy market. *Scholar and Feminist Online,* 9(1/2).

Maskew, T. (2010). Implementing your recommendations: Best practices for maximum impact. Presented at the Intercountry Adoption Summit, Waterloo, Canada.

Matson, E. (2014, April 11). Is preventing surrogacy feminist? No, it's anti-choice. RH Reality Check. Retrieved from http://rhrealitycheck.org/article/2014/04/11/preventing-surrogacy-feminist-anti-choice/

Maza, C. (2016, October 14). Surrogacy industry blossoms amidst a shroud of secrecy. Phnom Penh Post. Retrieved from http://www.phnompenhpost.com/post-weekend/surrogacy-industry-blossoms-amidst-shroud-secrecy

Oreskovic, J. & Maskew, T. (2008). Red thread or slender reed: Deconstructing Prof. Bartholet's mythology of international adoption. *Buffalo Human Rights Law Review,* 147, 71–128.

Pande, A. (2011). Transnational commercial surrogacy in India: Gifts for global sisters? *Reproductive Biomedicine Online,* 23, 618–25.

Pande, A. (2014). *Wombs in labor: Transnational commercial surrogacy in India.* New York: Columbia University Press.

Pinderhughes, E. E., Matthews, J. A. K., Pertman, A., & Deoudes, G. (2015). Voices from the field of intercountry adoption: Children with special needs, openness, and perspectives on the role of the Hague Convention. In R. L. Ballard, N. Goodno, R. Cochran, & J. Milbrandt (Eds), *The intercountry adoption debate: Dialogues across disciplines* (pp. 680–706). Newcastle upon Tyne: Cambridge Scholars Publishing.

Riley, M. (2015). An imbalance of justice: Birth mothers in Uganda. In R. L. Ballard, N. Goodno, R. Cochran, & J. Milbrandt (Eds), *The intercountry adoption debate: Dialogues across disciplines* (pp. 618–25). Newcastle upon Tyne: Cambridge Scholars Publishing.

Roby, J. L. (2007). From rhetoric to best practice: Children's rights in intercountry adoption. *Children's Legal Rights Journal,* 27(3), 48–71.

Roby, J. L. (2011). Children in informal alternative care. UNICEF. Retrieved from www.unicef.org/protection/Informal_care_discussion_paper_final.pdf

Roby, J. L. & Maskew, T. (2012). Human rights considerations in intercountry adoption: The children and families of Cambodia and Marshall Islands. In J. L. Gibbons & K. S. Rotabi (Eds), *Intercountry adoption: Policies, practices, and outcomes* (pp. 55–66). Farnham: Ashgate Press.

Roby, J. L., Rotabi, K. S., & Bunkers, K. M. (2013). Social justice and intercountry adoptions: The role of the U.S. social work community. *Social Work,* 58(4), 295–303.

Roby, J. L., Pennell, J., Rotabi, K. S., Bunkers, K. M., & Ucles, S. (2014). Pilot training and contextual adaptation of the family group conferencing model: Early evidence from Guatemala. *British Journal of Social Work,* 45(8), 228–40.

Rotabi, K. S. (2014, December). Force, fraud, and coercion: Bridging from knowledge of intercountry adoption to global surrogacy. ISS Working Paper Series/General Series, 600, 1–30. Retrieved from http://hdl.handle.net/1765/77403

Rotabi, K. S. & Bromfield, N. F. (2012). Intercountry adoption declines lead to new practices of global surrogacy in Guatemala: Global human rights concerns in the context of violence and the era of advanced fertility technology. *Affilia,* 27(2), 129–41. doi: 10.1177/0886109912444102

Rotabi, K. S. & Bunkers, K. M. (2011). In the era of reform: A review of social work literature on intercountry adoption. *Sage Open.* doi: 0.1177/2158244011428160. Retrieved from http://sgo.sagepub.com/content/early/2011/11/14/2158244011428160.full#aff-1

Rotabi, K. S. & Gibbons, J. L. (2009). Editorial. *International Social Work,* 52(5), 571–74.

Rotabi, K. S., Pennell, J., Roby, J. L., & Bunkers, K. M. (2012). Family group conferencing as a culturally adaptable intervention: Reforming intercountry adoption in Guatemala. *International Social Work,* 55(3), 402–16.

Rotabi, K. S., Bromfield, N. F., & Fronek, P. (2015). International private law to regulate commercial global surrogacy practices: Just what are social work's practical policy recommendations? *International Social Work*, 58(4), 575–81.

SAMA. (2012). Birthing a market: A study on commercial surrogacy. Retrieved from www.samawomenshealth.org/publication/birthing-market-%E2%80%98commercial-surrogacy-india

Saxena, P., Mishra, A., & Malik, S. (2012). Surrogacy: Ethical and legal issues. *Indian Journal of Community Medicine*, 37(4), 211–13.

Selman, P. F. (2015). Global trends in intercountry adoption: 2003–2012. In R. L. Ballard, N. Goodno, R. Cochran, & J. Milbrandt (Eds), *The intercountry adoption debate: Dialogues across disciplines* (pp. 9–48). Newcastle upon Tyne: Cambridge Scholars Publishing.

Smolin, D. M. (2015). Can the center hold? The vulnerabilities of the official legal regimen for intercountry adoption. In R. L. Ballard, N. Goodno, R. Cochran, & J. Milbrandt (Eds), *The intercountry adoption debate: Dialogues across disciplines* (pp. 245–76). Newcastle upon Tyne: Cambridge Scholars Publishing.

Ssuuna, I. (2016, April 16). Rwanda closes orphanages created after genocide. All Africa. Retrieved from http://allafrica.com/stories/201604160317.html

Triseliotis, J. (2000). Intercountry adoption: Global trade or global gift? *Adoption and Fostering*, 24(2), 45–54.

United Nations. (1948). Universal Declaration of Human Rights. Retrieved from www.un.org/en/universal-declaration-human-rights/

van Loon, H. (1990, April). *Report on intercountry adoption*. The Hague: Hague Permanent Bureau.

Vint, S. (2016, May). *Post-vital speculative fictions of life and death. Gujarat/Guatemala: Marketing care and speculating life*. Ithaca, NY: Cornell University.

Vora, K. (2015). *Life support: Biocapital and the new history of outsourced labor*. Minneapolis: University of Minnesota Press.

Vora, K. (2016, May). *Contracting care: Indian commercial surrogacy as life support. Gujarat/Guatemala: Marketing care and speculating life*. Ithaca, NY: Cornell University.

Wardle, L. D. (2015). Legal perspectives on some causes of and remedies for declining international adoptions. In R. L. Ballard, N. Goodno, R. Cochran, & J. Milbrandt (Eds), *The intercountry adoption debate: Dialogues across disciplines* (pp. 278–302). Newcastle upon Tyne: Cambridge Scholars Publishing.

Wertheimer, A. & Zwolinski, M. (2013). Exploitation. In E. N. Zalta (Ed.), *The Stanford Encyclopedia of Philosophy*. Stanford, CA: Stanford University Press.

Williamson, J. & Greenberg, A. (2010). Families, not orphanages: Better Care Network working paper. Retrieved from http://bettercarenetwork.org/IAI/details.asp?id=23328&themeID=1003&topicID=1023

Yngvesson, B. (2010). *Belonging in an adopted world: Race and identity in transnational adoption*. Chicago, IL: University of Chicago Press.

INDEX

Page entries in **bold** refer to tables and those in *italics* refer to figures.

adoption 2–4, 5, 36, 133
adoption agencies 2, 4, 15, 94, 99–100, 106–7,
  112, 115; United States 44–5, 80–1, 94, 95–6,
  97–8, 99, 105, 106
adoption fraud 12–13, 20, 21, 27, 47, 77, 156, 157;
  Africa 111, 113, 114; Cambodia 17–19, 20;
  Guatemala 69–70, 99; India 91, 93; Romania
  39, 40; Russia 45–6
adoption professionals 4, 20, 45, 76, 80, 83, 94,
  96, 99–100
adoptive families 2, 3, 4, 24, 113, 114, 115;
  Guatemalan children 65, 73, 78, 79; Liberia
  111, 115; Romanian children 38, 40
Africa 28, 53, 56–7, 103–4, 105–14, 115–16,
  167, 168
African Child Policy Forum 103–4, 116, 161
African children 103–4, 105–14, 115, 116
Altstein, H. 156
Argentina 14
Armistead, Lucy 22
artificial reproductive technologies 126, 127, 135,
  137–8, 152, 168–9
Astakhov, P. 41, 45
Australia 5, 25, 107, 163–4

Baby Cotton case 122
Baby Gammy case 125
Baby J case 156
Baby M case 122
baby selling 122, 123–4, 139
Balaz case 127
Banks, Scott and Karen 24
Bartholet, E. 157–8

Belgium 94, 156
Berend, Z. 134, 138, 139
best interests, of child 57, 58, 59, 60, 79, 90, 158
Bhargava, V. 91
birth families 18, 24, 52–3, 55, 58–9, 108
birth mothers 12, 25, 52–3, 57; Guatemala
  66–7, 68–9, 70, 71, 74, 75–7, 83; Marshall
  Islands 54–5; South Africa 53, 56–7; Tamil
  region 55–6, 91; United States 53–4
Black children 4
Bos, P. 55–6, 91
Brazil 12–13
Buck, Pearl 4

Calcetas-Santos, O. 67, 70
Cambodia 17–19, 20, 23–4
Canada 5, 14, 94
Casa Alianza, Guatemala 67–8
Ceauşescu, Nikolae 37
CEDAW *see* Convention on the Elimination of
  Discrimination against Women
Celebrate Children International 81, 106–7
Chadian children 23
child abduction 12–14, 21, 66, 74, 79, 91;
  Guatemala 14, 72–3, 75–7, 79–80
child development 3, 27, 37, 38, 46–7
child laundering 13, 20, 99, 108
child protection 8, 57, 60, 91, 158, 159; Africa
  108–9, 116; India 91, 92–3, 99
child relinquishment 21, 53, 54, 55, 56, 76, 77
child removal 4, 5, 8–9, 22, 23, 25, 90, 160
child rescue 2, 5, 15, 36, 104–5; Haitian children
  21, 22–3; Vietnam Babylift 8–10

child rights 13, 20, 27, 163
child sales 12, 67–8, 77, 163
child trafficking 60, 73–4, 92, 107–8
China 14–17
Chinese children 14–17, 65
CICIG *see* International Commission against
    Impunity in Guatemala
CNA *see* Consejo Nacional
coercion *see* child abduction
commercial surrogacy 122–4, 125–6, 127, 152,
    163–4, 165–6, 169–70; India 124, 150, 151
commissioning parents 123, 124, 128, 133, 134–5,
    136, 138–9, 143, 148, 169
compensation 25, 94, 96, 139
Congo, Democratic Republic of (DRC) 114
Consejo Nacional (CNA) 81–2, 83
continuum of care *see* subsidiarity, principle of
Convention on the Elimination of
    Discrimination against Women
    (CEDAW) 144
Convention on the Rights of the Child (CRC)
    6, 20, 27, **60**, 60, 89, 163
Cruz, Norma 77–8

Devin, Lynn 17, 19, 20
domestic adoptions 7–8, 15, 40, 81–2, 93
donations 15, 157
DRC *see* Congo, Democratic Republic of
Duncan, W. 58

El Salvador 13–14
Erickson, Theresa 123
Escobar, Ana 75
ethical adoptions 27, 90, 159–60, 166
Ethiopia 105–8
Ethiopian children 105, 106–7
Evangelical groups 110–11
exploitation 20, 74, 140, 145, 169

family preservation 8, 59, 159
family support 8, 47, 89–90, 93, 159
femicide 66–7
Fessler, A. 53, 54
Fonseca, C. 12
force *see* child abduction
France 23

Galindo, Lauryn 17–18, 19, 20
gestational surrogacy 121–2, 128, 134, 170;
    United States 132–3, 135–6
Ghana 167
GHRC *see* Guatemalan Human Rights
    Commission
gift child 14–15, 55, 146–7, 156–7
global surrogacy 121, 127, 128, 151–2, 162–3,
    165–6, 167–8

Guatemala 14, 64–70, 71–3, 77–8, 81–5, 98–9,
    158, 168; adoption fraud 69–70, 99; birth
    mothers 66–7, 68–9, 70, 71, 74, 75–7, 83; child
    abduction 14, 72–3, 75–7, 79–80; intercountry
    adoption 64–6, 67, 70–1, **82**, 84, 99
Guatemalan children 14, 64–6, 67–9, 71–3, 75–7,
    78, 92; United States 64, 68, 78, 79–81, 84
Guatemalan Human Rights Commission
    (GHRC) 69

Hague Conference on International Private
    Law 165–6
Hague Convention on Intercountry Adoption
    (HCIA, 1993) 57–9, 60, 83, 89, 99, 100, 156,
    165, 166
Haiti 20–3
Haitian children 21, 22–3, 105
HCIA *see* Hague Convention on Intercountry
    Adoption
Högbacka, R. 56
Holt International Children's Services 7, 9
human dignity 156, 169
humanitarian intervention 2, 5, 6, 36, 40, 116
human rights 6, 68, 144, 158, 166
human trafficking 19, 21, 44, 67–8, 69–70, 74, 75

ICA *see* intercountry adoption
illegal child adoptions 13–14, 15, 23, 75–7
illicit adoptions 3, 14, 20, 28, 59; Cambodia
    17–19, 20, 23–4; China 15, 16; Guatemala 14,
    67–8, 71, 81; Samoan Islands 24
immigration law 5, 6
impoverished families 2–3, 4, 81, 139, 143, 156
India 90, 91–3, 99; child protection 91, 92–3, 99;
    commercial surrogacy 124, 150, 151; global
    surrogacy 127–8, 150–1; poverty 145, 149, 151,
    152, 162–3; surrogacy 142–3, 146–7, 149–50,
    162–3; surrogate mothers 125–6, 136, 143–9,
    150, 162–3, 165, 167, 169; Tamil region 53,
    55–6, 91; women 145, 150, 152
Indian chldren 91–2, 93
infertility 2, 167
informed consent 76, 77, 108, 164
institutionalization 27–8, 37, 46–7 *see also*
    residential care institutions
intercountry adoption (ICA) 2–4, 5–6, 7–11,
    27–8, 36, 40, 47–8, 79, 90, 96, 128, 155–60,
    167; Africa 103–4, 109, 110, 111–12, 113,
    115–16; Guatemala 64–6, 67, 70–1, **82**, 84,
    99; India 90, 99; United States 90–1, 94, 95,
    96, **97–8**
International Commission against Impunity in
    Guatemala (CICIG) 71, 74
International Social Services 22, 89, 161, 163–4
Ireland 24–5
Israel 42, 125, 126, 139
IVF procedures 126, 127, 135, 137–8, 168

John, Elton 121–2
Johnson, K.A. 15, 16
Jolie, Angelina 104, 105

Kenya 115–16
Korean War 7

Latin America 11–14
Liberia 110, 111–12, 115
low-resource countries 126, 152, 160

Madonna 109–10
Magdalene Laundries, Ireland 24–5
Malawi 108–10
Markens, S. 132, 139
Marshall Islands 53, 54–5
Masha A. 44
Matsumura, S. 54, 55
McGinnis, H. 7–8
medical treatment 84, 158
Mexico 168
Mezmur, B.N. 107–8
money 19, 23–5, 77, 94, 96, 139, 156–7, 163
Mónico, C. 74
multi-fetal pregnancies 126–7

National Association of Black Social Workers 4
Nepal 27, 125–6
Netherlands 94, 156
New Life Children's Refuge (NLCR) 21

one-child policy, China 14–15, 16
orphanages 2, 10, 53 *see also* residential care
    institutions
orphaned children 5, 27, 128
"orphans of Tenegru" 5
Osborn, Shyrel 78

Pande, A. 136, 139, 143, 144, 145
paper orphans 27, 108
Par Socop, Raquel 75–6
poverty 4, 55, 71, 76, 77, 128, 152, 161–2; India
    145, 149, 151, 152, 162–3
Pro-Búsqueda, El Salvador 13, 14
prospective parents 2, 15, 21, 22 *see also*
    commissioning parents
Putin, Vladimir 41–2

race 4–5
radical attachment disorder 47
refugees 6, 13
rehoming 45, 111, 114–15
residential care institutions 3, 27–8, *36*, 37–8, 40,
    46–7, 90, *103*, 112–13, 159, 160–1
restitution 19, 23–5
Roby, J.L. 24, 54, 55
Rodriguez, Loyda 79–80
Romania 28, 36, 37–40

Romanian children 37–40
Roosevelt, Eleanor 5, 6
Russia 28, 36, 37, 40–2, 45–6
Russian children 40–6, *65*
Rwanda 161

same-sex couples 42, 81, 121, 124, 136, 143
Samoan Islands 24
Saveliev, Artyom "Justin" 42–3
Scheper- Hughes, N. 12
Seattle Adoptions International 17–19, 20, 105
Smolin, D.M. 20, 91, 161
social protections 20, 57, 58, 164, 167, 168
social support 57, 90, 159
South Africa 53, 56–7
South Korea 7–8
South Korean children 7–8
Soviet Union 28, 36–42
Spain 25–7, 42, 114
statelessness 124, 127–8, 165
subsidiarity, principle of 58, 59, 89, 160, 166
surrogacy 121–3, 128, 132, 133–4, 136, 137, 139–
    40, 144, 166, 169
surrogacy contracts 122, 126, 127, 128, 137, 138
surrogate bloggers 134–9, 140, 147
surrogate mothers 121–2, 123, 124, 125–6, 128–9,
    133, 134–9, 144, 152, 164–5; India 125–6,
    136, 143–9, 150, 162–3, 165, 167, 169; United
    States 126–7, 132–3, 134, 135–8, 139–40, 147,
    148, 169
Survivors Foundation 77–8

Tamil region, India 53, 55–6, 91
Taylor, L. 5 '
Teman, E. 133, 134, 139
Thailand 125
transracial adoptions 4

Uganda 112–13
Ukraine 121, 168
United Kingdom 5, 14, 122, 134
United Nations 161, 162
United Nations Declaration of Human Rights
    (UNDHR) 6, 144, 161, 166
United States 4, 7, 10, 28, 91, 92, 99, 114, 124,
    127; adoption agencies 44–5, 80–1, 94,
    95–6, **97–8**, 99, 105, 106; birth mothers
    53–4; Cambodia 17–19, 20; Chinese children
    14, 15, 16, *65*; domestic adoptions 53, 54;
    Ethiopian children 105, 106–7; gestational
    surrogacy 132–3, 135–6; Guatemalan chil-
    dren 64, 68, 78, 79–81, 84; Haitian children
    21, 22; immigration law 5, 6; intercountry
    adoption 90–1, 94, 95, 96, **97–8**; Romanian
    children 38, 39–40; Russian children 40–1,
    42–6, *65*; surrogate mothers 126–7, 132–3,
    134, 135–8, 139–40, 147, 148, 169; Vietnam
    9, 10, 11

Universal Declaration of Human Rights
   see United Nations Declaration of
   Human Rights

Vietnam 8–11
Vietnam Babylift 8–10
vulnerable children 5, 27

Waiting Angels 80–1
war orphans 5–6, 7, 9

Welcome House 4, 9
White families 4, 7, 104
White, J. 68–9
women 144, 145, 150, 151, 152, 170 *see also* birth
   mothers; surrogate mothers
World War II 3, 4–6

Yakovlev, Dmitri 43–4

Zoe's Ark 23